WHERE TO GO IN TURKEY

THOMSON HOLIDAYS

COLOUR EDITION

Reg Butler

SETTLE PRESS

HIPPOCRENE BOOKS INC.

© 1988 R. A. Butler
All rights reserved. No part of this publication may be reproduced or transmitted in any form or by any means without permission.
First published by Settle Press (1988)
This edition 1989
32 Savile Row
London W1X 1AG

Maps and City Plans by Mary Butler

ISBN 0907070 57 4

Published in USA by Hippocrene Books Inc
171 Madison Avenue,
New York N.Y. 10016

ISBN 0-87052-717-7

Printed by Villiers Publications Ltd
26a Shepherds Hill, London N6 5AH

Contents

Foreword

We are particularly pleased to be able to be associated with Reg Butler's "Where to Go in Turkey" at the same time as we launch our new "Discover Turkey" brochure. Together we are sure that they will enable you to discover the true spirit of this unique country.

"Where to Go in Turkey" is full of the kind of practical and personal observations which are so useful whether you are visiting Turkey for the first time or returning to discover yet more of its magnificent scenery and culture.

This Thomson Colour Edition provides a refreshingly lively and individual view of this country which is obviously so well loved by the author and will be an invaluable guide in helping you to plan your next holiday to Turkey.

Thomson Holidays

Chapter One
Turkey The Splendid

Introduction

Turkey offers all the important raw materials of tourism: areas of outstanding natural beauty, rich historical remains of past civilizations, colourful folklore, 300 days a year of blue skies, warm bathing from sandy beaches, and a different way of life.

Compared with other European countries like Italy, Spain and Greece which have fully developed - or over-developed - their holiday industry, Turkey has been a late starter.

Turkey's tourism potential is enormous, mainly concentrated around the edges. With three times the land area of the United Kingdom, and 5000 miles of Black Sea and Mediterranean coastline, Turkey offers wide scenic variety - from tiny beaches around the rocky coast, through fertile agricultural regions, to mountains that offer the greatest challenge to climbers this side of the Himalayas.

There is scope for beach holidays, cultural and religious tourism, water-sports, mountaineering, winter skiing and bird-watching, while Istanbul is a complete destination in itself.

Formerly Istanbul and Izmir were the only centres with good facilities. Outside those cities, only determined travellers were willing to endure the one-star hotels and rugged highways.

Over the past decade, however, highways have been vastly improved, giving easier access to hundreds of miles of unpolluted Mediterranean shores, hot-spring resorts, and the cultural treasures from 7000 years of history. New resorts, holiday villages, hotels and camp-site complexes have been constructed, especially on the Aegean and southern coasts, often with foreign management.

Most of the new beach developments are located in the southwest corner of Turkey: a rugged coastal area of greatest possible beauty. Imagine the Norwegian fjords relocated in a Californian climate with no smog. The waters are clear as gin, so totally unpolluted that even a single discarded cigarette end is immediately visible and looks totally out of place. Conditions are ideal for all forms of swimming, diving and snorkelling.

There is great variety along this coastline. You can go to a different beach, or different site, every day of a fortnight's holiday. Each location has its own charm. But virtually every beach and cove offers superb warm-water bathing.

By night the Turkish coastal villages take on an air of almost unearthly beauty. You can linger for a few leisured hours over evening meal at an open-air restaurant. Coloured electric lights are strung across from tree to tree; above is only the blackness of the velvet sky, pierced by a myriad stars.

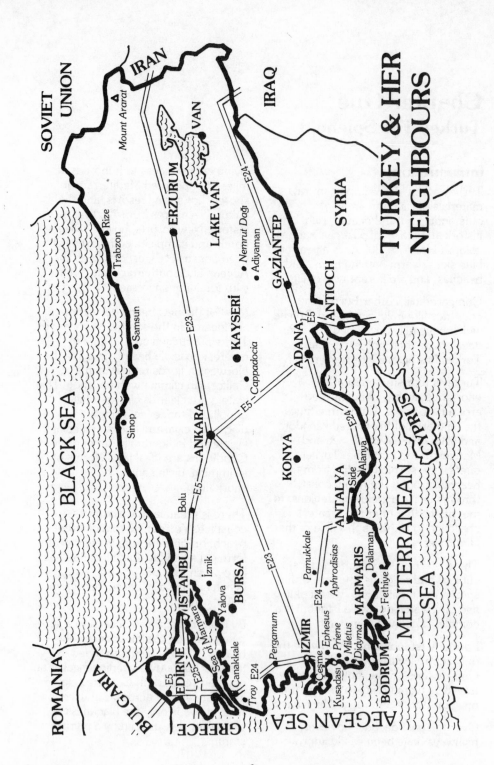

TURKEY & HER NEIGHBOURS

6

In the harbour alongside, gaily-painted fishing-boats swing slowly at anchor, while the deep daytime blue of the sea has changed to inky black. Over it all comes the insinuating wail of Turkish radio music. The local people sit peacefully at their tables - drinking coffee, talking, playing backgammon or cards, or just sitting. Then, gradually, as the evening wears on, they drift away home; till finally you are left with just your few companions, sitting there under the calm trees. Such moments can never be forgotten.

The great wealth of archaeological sites provides ample scope for motor-coach and mini-bus excursions. Several operators have organised complete coach tours, sometimes led by archaeology lecturers. Cruise-ship itineraries likewise include shore excursions to major sites like Side, Perge, Aspendos, Ephesus, Pergamum and Troy, in addition to an Istanbul stopover.

Certainly Turkey can offer rich archaeological variety, rivalling that of neighbouring East Mediterranean countries. Over 4,000 years of recorded history reach from the Hittites to the Persians, Greeks, Romans, Byzantines, Crusaders and Turks.

Many travellers have come to Turkey since Noah. Two of the Seven Wonders of the ancient world - the Mausoleum at Halicarnassus (today's Bodrum) and the Temple of Diana at Ephesus - could attract an estimated 700,000 visitors in a single season, two thousand years ago. But those locations today would find it impossible to accommodate such numbers.

Faced with escalating demand, the largest single problem now is a shortage of tourist beds. Despite a building boom, with many resorts echoing to the tune of hammers and bulldozers, hotel capacity is barely at the level that Greece attained 20 years ago. But Turkey is now catching up fast, though firmly resolved to avoid becoming another Spanish Costa lined with multi-storeyed glass and concrete shoe-boxes.

Many summer holiday arrangements split a fortnight between a beach resort and Istanbul, which is also a popular destination for 'winter-break' packages, October until May. Istanbul, the Bosphorus and the Princes Islands in the neighbouring Sea of Marmara together comprise one of Europe's great tourist 'naturals' - so packed with sightseeing interest that sore feet and swollen ankles are inevitable.

Steep pie-dish hillsides overlook the Golden Horn - a four-mile inlet which has sheltered shipping ever since the 7th century B.C., when Greek colonists first established a settlement.

Capital of the Byzantine Empire for 1,100 years, Istanbul has a variety of archaeology, ancient monuments and historic sites that can rival the tourist wealth of Rome. Mile upon mile of massive city walls are a reminder that ancient Constantinople was the last major stronghold to resist the all-conquering Turks.

Golden mosaics cover the walls of St.Sophia and the Kaariye Mosque - now both preserved as museums. The serenity of the tile-hung mosques is a fitting memorial to the best period of the Ottoman Empire, when immense wealth was poured into public buildings. Topkapı Palace is packed with treasures. Elegant Turkish fountains, crowded bazaars and lattice-screened balconies on wooden houses give a touch of the Orient.

Is Turkey oriental or western? Geographically, the answer is simple: 97% of the land area comprises the mountainous plateau of Asia Minor, with only a relatively small bridgehead on the European continent.

Historically, the Turks come from the steppes of Central Asia; but politically and economically they face west. Forty centuries of inter-marriage of Europe with Asia have given Turkey its unique enchantment: in architecture, cuisine, folklore and way of life.

Travelling to the Greco-Roman sites of the southern coastal regions, there is vivid contrast between the bustling go-getting life of Istanbul, and the serenity of the countryside. In local market centres, peasant women are dressed in brightly-printed baggy trousers and cotton scarves. With faces bronzed by exposure to sun and wind, they squat beside their eggs, fruit, goat-cheese and cans of yoghurt. In sophisticated Istanbul, T-shirts and blue jeans are the standard unisex dress of the younger generation.

Turkey is full of these contrasts of ancient and modern, Oriental and Western. In villages and small towns you can enjoy the traditional Middle Eastern way of life, sitting for an hour or two in the tree-shaded tranquility of a coffee or tea house.

Men drowse away the time with a hubble-bubble pipe; cloth-capped farmers go by with a sheep or two on a string; an occasional elderly horse-carriage clatters past over the cobble-stones; in a mosque courtyard, old men and children feed pigeons. In the background are the characteristic Turkish sounds: the cries of street vendors, the tinkle of horse-bells, the wailing of Turkish music from the tea-house radio, the constant rattle of backgammon dice, and the periodic call of the muezzin from mosque minaret loudspeakers.

However, let's forget any misconceptions about mysteriously-veiled women, harems, red fezzes and camels. Turkey has undergone a major western face-lift over the past 50 years. That doesn't mean Turkey has become an up-to-date industrial nation overnight. But the old Ottoman glamour - so beloved by film makers - has gone, along with such oriental accessories as backwardness, illiteracy, lethargy and low living-standards. Typically, wearing of the fez was banned in 1926, as part of a drive to underline that Turkey had changed from a religious state to a secular republic. Virtually overnight, peasants and labourers took to wearing cloth caps, just like in Wigan. Over 60 years later, cloth caps are still the working-class norm. Even so, remnants of old-fashioned Turkey still remain. That is a key part of Turkey's charm for the holidaymaker.

Of Turkey's 52-million population, 66% live off the land. Peasant farmers are cautious folk. They believe in clinging to the tried-and-trusted methods of the past, until finally convinced of the value of change. The process is slow.

Unlike other countries which have to cosset traditional crafts, folklore and costume specially for tourists' benefit, Turkey is rich in living relics from the immediate medieval past. You will no longer see a bronze-age plough drawn by oxen, working alongside a Caterpillar tractor. Today, the tractors have almost entirely won out. Even so, an occasional pair of oxen can still be seen, working the fields. Maybe once in a two-week tour you'll see a working camel, apart from those who earn a living at posing for tourists on sandy beaches.

With a floating exchange-rate that fully compensates the holidaymaker for Turkey's domestic inflation, tourist out-of-pocket expenses are downright cheap, whether for transport, drinks, meals or local entertainment. That basic generalisation applies at all levels of tourism, from de luxe grade down to simple back-packing. The first-time visitor, paying for his restaurant meal, initially finds it hard to believe the low cost - barely one half of an equivalent meal in USA or western Europe.

For the lover of unusual food, the Turkish cuisine is among the world's most varied, with innumerable kebabs, stuffed-vegetable dolmas, and great choice of fish, good fruit and pastries. Restaurant food is fresh rather than processed, and the difference is instantly recognized by the taste-buds.

Even modest restaurants offer a menu choice of one or two hundred dishes. Aubergine or eggplant alone can be prepared in forty different ways. Yogurt can appear quite literally at every course: with soup, with fish, with roast meat, with dessert. The best is made from buffaloes' milk, rich as thick cream.

People who have already discovered Turkey say it's like Greece used to be, before mass tourism took off. Here you can get away from the highly commercialised type of holiday. A friendly welcome awaits travellers who enjoy venturing to new resorts which are not yet "spoiled" because everyone else goes there.

Of course, Turkey is not everybody's choice. If you want your tourism well-scrubbed and sterile, try Scandinavia instead. But if you want a whiff of the Orient, and a mild taste of off-beat travel adventure, then Turkey is worth a visit. Better go now, before the big rush starts.

Which Resort Guide

The recipe for a perfect Turkish holiday is spiced with different ingredients. The principal cities and resorts are given star ratings for ease of access, beaches, sightseeing and night-life. The overall Butler rating is a personal assessment on how these ingredients combine into a good mixture for an interesting holiday. But everyone to his own taste. Some folk may feel that total absence of night-life should be a plus point, deserving five stars!

Key

Flights
★★★★ airport with direct or connecting flight from Britain
★★★ an easy drive, between 1 and 2 hours from airport
★★ between 2 and 3 hours from airport
★ a long haul from the airport, at least 3 hours

Beaches
★★★★ excellent, with easy access
★★★ good, in the area
★★ scattered in coves
★ limited

Water sport - Yes, or No

Sites
★★★★ spectacular
★★★ several interesting sites to see
★★ one or two sites
★ within range, on day trips

Scenery
★★★★ superb
★★★ special
★★ good
★ average

Eating out
★★★★ excellent variety of food and restaurants
★★★ above-average choice of restaurants
★★ average
★ limited choice

Nightlife
★★★★ pulsating
★★★ plentiful
★★ average
★ sleepy

Butler's Rating Tables

	Flights	Beaches	Water sport Y/N	Sites	Scenery	Eating out	Night life	Rating
Istanbul	★★★★	★	N	★★★★	★★★★	★★★★	★★★	9
Izmir	★★★★	★	N	★★★	★★	★★★	★★	5
Çeşme	★★★	★★★★	Y	★★	★	★★	★★	6
Kuşadası	★★★	★★	Y	★★★★	★★	★★	★★	8
Altinkum	★★	★★★★	Y	★★	★	★	★	4
Bodrum	★	★★	Y	★	★★★	★★★	★★★★	9
Datça	★	★★	Y	★	★★	★	★	3
Marmaris	★★	★★	Y	★	★★★★	★★★	★★★	8
Fethiye	★★★	★★★	Y	★★	★★★★	★★	★	6
Kalkan	★★	★★	Y	★	★★★★	★	★	5
Kaş	★★	★★	Y	★★	★★★★	★	★	6
Kemer	★★★	★★	Y	★★	★★★★	★	★	5
Antalya	★★★★	★★★	Y	★★★★	★★★★	★★★	★★	8
Side	★★★	★★★★	Y	★★★	★★	★★	★★	7
Alanya	★★	★★★★	Y	★★	★★★	★★	★	6
Ankara	★★★★		N	★	★	★★★	★★	2

Personal Recommendations

Families - Çeşme, Alanya, Side, Marmaris, Ölü Deniz, Altınkum, Gümbet
Windsurfers - Bodrum, Marmaris, Güvercinlik
Walkers - Cappadocia
Campers - Datça peninsula
Naturalists - Dalyan
Painters - Istanbul, Cappadocia
Culture vultures (Classical) - Izmir, Kuşadası, Antalya, Side, British Museum
Culture vultures (Byzantine) - Istanbul, Cappadocia
Culture vultures (Seljuk and Ottoman) - Istanbul, Bursa, Konya, Kayseri, Sivas
Students - Istanbul, Bodrum
Ravers - Bodrum
Hermits - Cappadocia
Beach bums - Gümbet, Side
Gays - Bodrum, Istanbul
Trend-setters - Marmaris
Plutocrats - Marmaris
Spa-curers - Yalova, Bursa, Pamukkale, Ilica (Çeşme)
Honeymooners - Side
Speleologists - Kaş, Kalkan
Sport-lovers - Club Med
Seasoned travellers - Eastern Turkey
Masochists - Ankara
Bird-watchers - Bursa, Cappadocia
The rest of us - Istanbul, Kuşadası, Bodrum, Marmaris

Which Site Guide?

	Build-ings	Set-ting
Classical		
Troy	5	8
Pergamum	7	7
Sardis	3	3
Ephesus	10	6
Priene	6	8
Miletus	5	4
Didyma	8	4
Aphodisias	8	5
Knidos	4	8
Halicarnassus	1	5
Caunus	3	6
Telmessos (Fethiye)	5	6
Xanthos	6	4
Antiphellos (Kaş)	3	8
Myra (Demre)	5	5
Phaselis	4	8
Antalya	3	4
Termessus	5	8
Perge	7	4
Aspendos	7	4
Side	7	6
Ankara	3	3
Byzantine		
Istanbul	10	10
Selçuk	5	6
Cappadocia	8	10
Seljuk and Ottoman		
Istanbul	10	10
Bursa	8	7
Konya	8	4
Antalya	5	6
Alanya	6	8
Natural Wonders		
Pamukkale	5	8
Cappadocia	8	10

13

Temperatures - midday averages (°F)

Region/centre	JAN	FEB	MAR	APR	MAY	JUN	JUL	AUG	SEP	OCT	NOV	DEC
Med Coast/Antalya	52	54	56	63	70	77	84	84	77	70	61	54
Aegean/Izmir	48	50	54	61	70	77	82	82	75	66	59	52
Marmara/Istanbul	43	43	45	54	63	70	75	75	68	61	54	47
Black Sea/Trabzon	47	47	48	54	61	68	73	75	68	63	57	50
Central/Ankara	34	34	41	54	63	68	75	75	66	56	47	37
Eastern/Van	26	26	34	45	56	65	72	72	63	52	41	30

Hours of Daily Sunshine

Centre	JAN	FEB	MAR	APR	MAY	JUN	JUL	AUG	SEP	OCT	NOV	DEC
Antalya	5	6	7	9	11	12	13	12	10	8	7	5
Izmir	4	6	6	6	10	12	13	12	10	8	6	4
Istanbul	3	4	5	7	9	11	12	11	9	6	4	3
Trabzon	3	4	4	5	6	8	7	7	5	5	4	3
Ankara	3	4	6	7	9	11	13	12	10	7	5	3

Bright Days Per Month

Centre	JAN	FEB	MAR	APR	MAY	JUN	JUL	AUG	SEP	OCT	NOV	DEC
Antalya	18	18	23	24	26	28	31	30	26	26	23	18
Izmir	17	18	23	23	25	28	30	30	26	26	22	18
Istanbul	14	15	17	21	24	25	28	28	25	21	18	14
Trabzon	18	16	18	19	20	21	23	24	20	20	19	20
Ankara	19	17	21	20	20	22	28	29	24	24	22	18

Average Sea Temperatures (°F)

Centre	JAN	FEB	MAR	APR	MAY	JUN	JUL	AUG	SEP	OCT	NOV	DEC
Alanya	64	62	62	66	70	77	82	84	82	77	71	66
Antalya	64	62	62	64	70	75	81	82	82	77	71	66
Bodrum	62	61	61	62	68	71	73	75	75	71	68	64
Kusadasi	61	59	59	61	68	73	73	75	73	68	62	61
Izmir	52	52	54	61	68	75	79	79	77	70	62	57
Istanbul	47	45	47	52	61	68	73	75	70	62	57	50
Trabzon	52	49	49	50	57	68	75	77	75	68	61	55

Chapter Two
Choosing A Holiday

When To Go

When you go to Turkey is just as important as *where*. For Turkey is a land of widely different climatic zones. What other country can simultaneously be harvesting bananas and cherries? So let's consider each area separately.

On the southern coast - favourite setting for a beach or watersport holiday - you can expect bright, sunny and totally cloudless days from June through September. Rain during that period is virtually unknown. The average sea temperature is 65°F in spring, 75° in summer, 68° in autumn. Unless you plan to spend most of your time cooling off in the water, most British holidaymakers find the July-August temperatures overpowering. Regularly the shade temperature can stay in the nineties for days on end.

Hence a warning: be cautious of the sun! Many people arrive tired at their resort after a long journey by air, followed by perhaps several hours of transfer by coach from the arrival airport. They catch up lost sleep on the beach, and wake up severely burned. Virtually everyone knows the basic rules about exposure to the sun. But, judging by the number of holidaymakers with peeling skins on the return aircraft, the advice is often forgotten.

July and August, most resorts cannot fully cope with the tourist numbers, boosted by Turkish city-dwellers who likewise take family-beach holidays at that period. The popularity of Turkey has grown faster than the available accommodation. The centres of popular resorts like Bodrum and Marmaris will be extremely lively and crowded. But, with Turkey's 5000 miles of coastline, it is still easy to avoid the crowds, if you prefer.

May, June, September and October are ideal months for sunshine which can easily rival other Mediterranean destinations. Those are the best recommended months for the southern coast, both for beaches and watersports. Temperatures are also more favourable for sightseeing.

Finally, November till April is a peaceful time for comfortable sightseeing of the classic sites: quite warm, with a light overcoat needed only in the evenings, though a brolly is necessary. You can find accommodation anywhere, at minimal rates, with owners ready and willing to talk discounts.

Along the Aegean coast, the pattern is very similar - except that temperatures are a little cooler year-round, the further north you go; and there is much more rain during winter.

Istanbul is another story. During summer, the city is hot and dry, with perhaps an occasional thunderstorm. June till September are the peak tourist months, both from Europe and from the Gulf States. In fact, Arab tourists can outnumber the

Europeans. They stay longer, often renting apartments for three months along the Bosphorus.

April and May, mid-September and October are ideal months for Istanbul sightseeing, which can be too hot and crowded in peak summer. The major five-star luxury hotels are often completely filled, either with regular business visitors or with delegates to the numerous Conferences held in Istanbul. But go down a hotel grade or two, and there will be few accommodation problems.

Finally, a winter break in Istanbul can be a gamble. The weather changes course about every three days: cold, and bright skies when the winds blow from the north, via Russia; mild, wet and foggy when the winds come from the Aegean. Cold and bright can be delightful, with a sparkle to the air; but the wet days can be miserable. Winter weather in Istanbul is little different from London, and one should dress accordingly.

Climate of the Black Sea coast is different again. Expect plentiful rainfall any month of the year; and much cooler weather than along the Aegean coast. As yet, the Black Sea coast is not ready for tourism, despite the beauty of the shoreline.

Coach tourism takes holidaymakers into the Anatolian plain, mainly to visit highlights such as Konya or the weird landscape of Cappadocia. With the plateau mostly at around 3,000-feet altitude, summers are hot and parched; winters are icy cold. Ankara's winter climate has the added misery of smog. So inland Turkey is best avoided in winter and high summer, but spring and autumn are very pleasant.

Travel further east, into the high mountains, is strenuous. It should be considered only by the hardier types who can cheerfully accept rugged transportation and ungraded hotels. Most of the eastern provinces are completely snowed in during winter; and the remaining seasons are squeezed into April through September.

Accommodation

As a relative newcomer to industry-scale tourism, Turkey is now rapidly expanding its bed capacity.

In the coastal resorts, the Turks are fighting shy of the high-rise shoebox style of hotel architecture. They say: "We have learnt our lesson from Spain." Everywhere, national and local tourism policy coincides on the basic strategy of keeping hotel development low profile. Generally, resort hotels are small to medium-size. The international five-star palaces will surely come - in fact, some are now under construction as big money moves into the industry. But most hotels are still more like family businesses, with friendly and personalized reception.

Bedrooms are simply furnished, kept spotlessly clean by chambermaids who are not afraid of a scrubbing brush. Generally, meals are straight Turkish, with a few concessions to the taste-buds of northwest Europeans, like eggs for breakfast but not bacon. Young waiters - first generation out of the villages - may not yet have qualifications for the London Ritz, but they are cheerful and willing.

Especially popular are "holiday villages" of bungalows, villas or duplexes nestling among pine trees and spread around a bay or into a hillside. In greater or less degree, these developments are linked with a range of sport and entertainment facilities. At one end of the scale, the villages are self-catering, with much of the accommodation taken by Turkish families.

At the luxury end are the famous international management groups like the French-oriented Club Méditerranée, the more international Club Salima, or the Club Robinson where German is the dominant language. Every imaginable sport and entertainment is included in the tariff, with international rather than purely Turkish cuisine, and unlimited wine at meals. There is gated entrance to these communities, with Turkey left outside the fence. Most of these holiday villages use the famous Club Med system of paying for drinks, snacks and laundry with plastic beads. You might just as well be in Tahiti.

Closer to the Turkish life-style are villas and pensions, which are very popular with UK holidaymakers. If you are looking for a room in a pansiyon, the key words to spot are "boş oda var" - meaning room vacant. You can expect a friendly welcome. Even if the owners cannot speak much English, they'll smile a lot.

The normal arrangement is bed and breakfast: usually tea, bread, olives, butter, honey or jam, and white cheese. If it's a room-only deal, you can always get a 75p-breakfast at neighbouring restaurants any time till noon or later.

In recent years, credits from the Tourism Bank have sparked the great conversion of houses into pensions. Villagers have been able to install a good standard of furnishing, with bathrooms. Very often, water is heated by solar panels. This means you can usually get a hot shower at 6

p.m., but the water temperature plunges as other guests use the hot tap. By morning, the water runs cold. Owing to the cost of fuel, owners are usually reluctant to boost with an immersion heater.

Local tourist authorities keep an eye on standards, but obviously some marginal accommodation gets onto the market, with an ultra-low tariff to compensate. Tourism to Turkey is currently being promoted as a successor to Spain for those who just want the cheapest possible combination of sun and sand. On some of the cheapie tours, if anything has four walls and a door, they'll put you in it.

Certainly it's true that Turkey is a very low-cost country. You can enjoy some of that price structure by choosing a higher-grade package which still costs much less than any equivalent grade of holiday elsewhere in the Mediterranean. Those who buy an ultra-low-cost Turkish package will get what they paid for.

Finally, avoid accommodation which is next to a building site, or located on a busy unmade road. The dust can be choking as a simple fishing village is converted into a full-blown tourist resort. Elderly houses are gutted, to give them new life as pensions, restaurants or shops. Several resorts ban major construction during the summer season, and valiant attempts are made to beef up the infrastructure first - highways, water, sewage, telephone lines. But these services can show the strain in high season. Numerous hotel bathrooms ask guests to be economical with water.

Most of the better hotels are classified by the Ministry of Tourism, using the categories of Luxury, and 1st class down to 4th. Non-classified hotels and pensions are always handily located near to bus stations, ferry landing-stages, and in town centres. You can easily find them, just by keeping your eyes open. The sub-basic grades charge extremely low rates, like £2 per bed, with washing and toilet facilities along the corridor. When in doubt concerning where to stay, ask advice from the local Tourist Information Office.

Self-Catering

For maximum independence, many holidaymakers prefer self-catering. Most of the accommodation on offer is newly built or refurbished to good standards. Furnishings are usually ethnic but comfortable. Often the apartments have patios or balconies for dining or relaxing in the shaded open air, with massed bougainvilia growing around the doorstep. Frequently the owner lives on the premises, or around the corner; so any problems can quickly be settled.

Cost of the average food basket is about half that of Britain, right across the board: fruit, vegetables, bread, meat, drinks. Shopping for victuals is no problem, whether in colourful markets for fruit, vegetables and fish, or in the usual international style of supermarket.

For motorists and backpackers, Turkey is now well equipped with camp-sites, some with chalets to let. In July and August they are heavily used by Turkish families who are priced out of the resort hotels and pensions. The sites are often beautifully located in pinewoods that border the shoreline. Outside the high season, they look idyllic. Many of the camps are operated by well-established companies that offer an international standard of facilities.

British Petroleum, for instance, has a long-standing Turkish subsidiary called BP-Kervansaray which administers a chain of Mocamps along the main routes of Turkey, and outside the principal sites and cities of tourist interest.

Typical is a camp at Kuşadası, handily placed for visiting Ephesus. The site has hot and cold water, butane-gas cooking equipment, electric points, ice, shower compartments, Western-style WC's, a tiled laundry section, and a self-service restaurant with very reasonable prices.

Beaches

Most of the summertime holiday traffic between Britain and Turkey consists of beach packages that link a chartered or scheduled-service flight with resort accommodation. The bulk of the traffic is routed either through Izmir for the Aegean coastal resorts; to Dalaman for the western end of the Mediterranean coast; to Antalya (either direct or via Istanbul) for the Turquoise Coast each side of Antalya.

With some 5000 miles of coastline, Turkey offers a rich choice of beaches. However, as a late starter in holiday business, only a relatively small percentage of that total has been developed. For most practical purposes, you can reckon that Turkey has no more than twenty seaside resorts on offer.

In making your selection, decide what else you want besides sun and beach.

If you want to hit the nightlife, remember that many of the resorts spread themselves to a scattering of satellite bays and fishing villages, maybe a dozen miles from the centre. During daytime these satellite beaches are linked by shuttle services of very low-cost mini-buses and jeeps. But after dark you'll probably find that only taxis will be operating. Night owls can save money by choosing central accommodation.

Conversely, if you like to be asleep before midnight, bear in mind that accommodation in the centre of lively resorts such as Bodrum and Marmaris can be swamped with the sound of music and wassail till 3 a.m.

Maybe you want to visit some of the major classic sites? In that case, choose resorts like Kuşadası, Antalya or Side which are better placed for easy access to Greco-Roman remains. Distances in Turkey are considerable. If you want to visit Istanbul, most of the southern resorts are at least 16 hours' away by bus. Instead, choose a two-centre package with domestic air travel included.

Regrettably, the Istanbul area has relatively little beach resources. Instead, Turkey's finest and best-developed beach resorts are located much further south, along the Aegean and Mediterranean coastlines.

With rapid access from Izmir, several beaches have been developed along the road towards Çeşme, skirting the Gulf of Izmir and facing the Greek island of Chios. Further south, Kuşadası is 2 hours from Izmir, but Bodrum is a four-hour slog.

In recent years, one of Turkey's most important tourism developments has been the opening of Dalaman Airport, to serve the resorts of the south-west corner of Anatolia. The airport, specially planned to cater for international charter flights, is 32 miles from Fethiye, 16 miles from Köyceğiz, 55 miles from Marmaris, and 103 miles from Bodrum. Dalaman Airport has brought one of the most beautiful regions of the Mediterranean into easy reach: a yachtsmen's paradise.

The Turkish government is very conservation conscious. They do not want an overcrowded seaboard walled with concrete and glass, as in so many other Mediterranean countries. Hopefully this glorious coastline will remain unscarred into the foreseeable future.

The coast between Fethiye and Antalya is the most recent entrant on the tourism map, with all the K's - Kalkan, Kaş and Kemer - set in locations of great beauty. The South Antalya project area covers almost 50 miles of coastline, all within the Olympus-Bey Dağları Coastal National Park.

The Antalya region is another major area designated for tourism expansion. Developments are in full swing from southwest of Antalya and eastwards to Side and Alanya along the so-called Turquoise coast. The magnificent pine-forested Taurus Mountains plunge down to the Mediterranean, leaving a fertile coastal belt of citrus fruits, and banana and date plantations. Golden sandy beaches stretch for mile after mile, with hotels, holiday villages and camp sites scattered like plastic beads on a necklace.

Still further east from Alanya, via Anamur and Silifke to Mersin and thence further round in a semi-circle to the Syrian border, are several hundred miles of coastline with virtually 'nil' development of the beaches. That applies equally to beaches along almost the entire Black Sea coast. Their time will come. Meanwhile, in the holiday brochures, they don't exist.

Istanbul

On the motor-coach in from Istanbul airport to the city centre, the tour

19

guide said: "Don't think of this as a holiday. By the end of your stay you'll be footsore and weary. You'll be on the go every day and most nights. But, by the time you leave Turkey, I'll guarantee that you'll all qualify for your belly-dancing certificates."

The basic list of Istanbul's five-star monuments keeps the tour buses rolling year-round. Even throughout winter there is regular influx of sightseeing groups from western Europe on long weekend packages. Annually the Topkapı Palace Museum - former home of the Ottoman Emperors - attracts over 1.5m visitors, mostly foreigners.

All the tourist highlights have been renovated and restored, cleaning off the dust and grime of centuries, uncovering more mosaics, and flood-lighting the monuments. Istanbul rates high among the great tourist cities of Europe.

Most tour operators feature Istanbul breaks in their programmes, particularly for spring and autumn. It's best to choose the bed and breakfast arrangements, leaving you totally free to enjoy the wide range of Istanbul restaurants, rather than being tied to a half-board deal.

During spring, summer and autumn, many holidaymakers link a few days' sightseeing of Istanbul either with a beach resort package or with a coach tour. The two-centre or three-centre permutations are endless, building on the base of an Istanbul stopover. A four-night Istanbul interlude is enough for the main sights; a full week is better for the more dedicated culture-vulture.

Water Sports

According to a T-shirt slogan, "On the

eighth day, God went windsurfing." He probably chose the Turkish coast, which is near enough to Paradise. The deeply indented bays offer calm waters with light morning breeze for learners at sailboarding, freshening in the afternoon to give the experts a fast run, and then dying down in the evening for the beginners again.

Many sport holidays are based on Turkey's superb coastal waters, with wind surfing easily the most popular activity. At a typical centre, all watersports are included in the price: wind-surfing, water-skiing, sailing, snorkelling. It's a great chance for beginners to learn some of these skills, with friendly instruction at no extra charge.

Around the southwest corner of Turkey, conditions are ideal for all forms of diving, in waters clear as gin. This superb clarity encourages many swimmers to try snorkelling. Gear can be borrowed or hired, but anyway the local price of around £8 is cheap enough.

Scuba diving is rated among the best in the Mediterranean - unexplored reefs with spectacular drop-offs, caves and magnificent rock formations covered in multicoloured sponges. Divers can enjoy meeting octopus, moray eels, tuna, groupers and playful dolphins. It is illegal to disturb any underwater archaeological site or historical wreck. No treasure hunting!

Blue Voyage

Specially popular in recent years is the Blue Voyage. This means sailing for a week or two anywhere between Bodrum and Antalya: an idyllic way of exploring the natural beauty of Turkey's southern coast. Many of the coves and beaches are still inaccessible by road. Using on-board snorkelling or windsurfing equipment, you can have a calm and peaceful bay entirely to yourself.

There is plentiful choice of bareboat hire, flotilla sailing, or cruising aboard a Turkish 'gulet' with a three-man crew to look after about eight or ten passengers. Yachting is a major growth area, with an increasing number of international yachting and yacht-broking companies now shifting to Turkish waters - especially based on the marinas of Kuşadası, Bodrum and Marmaris. Whether located in Britain or in Turkey itself, the specialist yacht brokers offer a high standard of personal service. They are warm and friendly folk, who always have time to discuss the type of boat, the yacht's inventory, the necessary travel arrangements, and even what winds to expect. From personal experience, they can also suggest suitable cruise itineraries.

For keen sailors, bareboat charter is the answer, providing a holiday rich in challenge and freedom. For those of middling skill, uncertain about local conditions along the Turkish coast, flotilla sailing is well developed. If sailing your own yacht is too much like hard work, or you lack experience, then a skipper can be supplied. For a larger party, a Turkish 'gulet' is crewed with a captain, deckhand and cook.

The 'gulet' is a beautiful pine-wood vessel built to traditional design in the Bodrum area. Typical gulets are from 17 to 20 metres in length. The new generation of gulets include toilet and shower facilities to each cabin, whereas older boats normally have shared facilities. Throughout, the craftsmanship is superb. Cabins look charming with varnished planked ceilings and colourful Turkish materials.

Gulets are spacious, in comparison with narrower-beam yachts. The sails are more for decoration than use, with the engine as the prime mover. One tour operator insists that the sails should be set for at least five hours a week, if only for the benefit of the photographers.

One of the functions of a local yacht broker is to check out a gulet to ensure everything is completely ship-shape before the charter party arrives. Sometimes a boat owner neglects small details. A broker can bring him sharply back into line. Likewise, the local agent, collaborating with a British operator, can form a team which ensures good standards.

Essentially, gulets are not for "real" sailors, who choose other types of craft. Gulets are built for comfort with a friendly crew to serve drinks, cook meals, bring the craft expertly into harbour or anchor in a cove, while passengers just sit back and enjoy themselves. But it's still theirs to command - where to go, how long to stay, what the programme is - worked out with the captain.

As an approximate guide-line to prices, reckon £30 a day per person in a double cabin, with meals and table wine included. Extras are few. You can arrange your own party, or join a tour operator's package deal with flight, cabin and meals included. Meals are normally taken on the aft deck beneath an awning. Sunbathing is for'ard, or on the saloon roof. Stops are frequent, for fishing or swimming, or to go exploring ashore - a tiny village, perhaps, quite unchanged over the centuries; or some ancient ruins, which have not been fully picked over by the archaeologists. Culture stops

21

are not obligatory, but there's fun in making your own discoveries.

Then, after visiting a site, you can stay on the beach while cook prepares a barbecue. Evening-time, maybe they will tie up to a rickety jetty, rustle up some musicians and have a sing-song and dance around a beachside camp fire. Over-nighting in a marina or fishing harbour, yachtsmen can go rollicking ashore to dine and hit the night-spots, sleeping it off next day on the sun deck.

Another option: landlubbers can do much of the Blue Voyage in penny numbers. At each of the coastal resorts, there is wide choice of half-day and whole-day trips to the surrounding bays, beaches, caves and classical sites. Most day-trip boats are equipped with sound systems and Kaptans who enjoy playing their cassettes at top volume. If you want to save your ear-drums for future use, position yourself at the sharp end of the vessel, where the sound-waves are lessened.

Cruising in Turkish Waters

Turkey can claim to have been the world's first cruise-ship destination. For Noah's Ark is reputed to have landed on 17,000-ft Mount Ararat in Asia Minor, whence the Old Testament tribes spread through the Bible lands. Today's cruise-ship captains prefer to anchor off-shore or tie up in harbour, with a fleet of sightseeing coaches awaiting at each port-of-call. Because of the wealth of classic sites, all within easy reach of the coast, Turkey is featured on virtually every luxury cruise in the Eastern Mediterranean, combined with Greece, Israel or Egypt.

The majority of Med cruises are geared mainly to the relaxation and entertainment market, with shore excursions as an optional extra. The most popular ports-of-call are Kuşadası, Izmir and Istanbul, where the joys of shopping compete with sightseeing. But if you'd like a deeper understanding of the ancient world, it's worth considering a more specialised package that includes the southern ports of Alanya, Antalya, Fethiye, Marmaris and Bodrum.

The classic pioneer is Swan Hellenic Cruises. The idea is unique: to use the ship - comfortable, but not luxurious - as a floating hotel, cruising from site to site with well-known guest lecturers to set the background whenever there is spare time at sea.

It may sound heavy going. In fact, the talks are at Radio 3 or 4 level, designed for the layman with an average non-technical interest in the subject. Attendance is quite voluntary, and nobody need feel ashamed at ducking a lecture in favour of sun-bathing on deck! Some of the afternoon audience doze off in the comfortable armchairs of the lecture lounge, but that is probably due to an over-hearty lunch.

Even then, all is not lost. For every passenger is given a massive one-kilo handbook with descriptions and site plans for all the several hundred locations visited during the year's programme. Before going ashore, passengers can bone up on the day's ruins. In addition, single-sheet site plans and background notes are available for each shore excursion - a handy pocket reminder for what had been forgotten or slept-through. Often the cruise lecturers give an additional on-site briefing, to supplement the patter of the local guides.

For cruising in Turkish waters alone, Turkish Maritime Lines operate regular 11-day circuits aboard the MS Akdeniz from Istanbul to Alanya and back, with shore excursions included. This gives ample opportunity to visit major sites such as Pergamum, Ephesus, Perge, Aspendos and Side, with time for leisured sightseeing at Izmir, Bodrum, Marmaris and Fethiye. Sunquest Holidays are the sole UK passenger agents.

Coach Tours

Coach tours through Turkey split into two main groups: low-cost trekking holidays based on camping or economy-hotel accommodation, mainly designed for the young and adventure-minded; and the standard "luxury" coach tour for those who like their travel and overnight comforts.

On the treks, everyone helps around the camp-site with tent erection and meal preparation. The vehicle may be a somewhat elderly coach which has seen better days; or, with smaller groups, it could even be a converted truck or mini-bus. Often meals are not included in the price, but everyone contributes to a food kitty.

On the "luxury" tours you can expect a modern and comfortable coach, probably a Mercedes-Benz, with a properly working P.A. system and sometimes air conditioning (worth checking first, if you plan to travel during the July-August heat). For smaller groups, a Volkswagen mini-bus is the most likely vehicle. Accommodation is usually in good 3-star or 4-star hotels, but rarely in 5-star palaces, which are thin on the ground outside the main cities. Lunches en route are ethnic, usually taken at delightful open-air restaurants, full of Turkish character. Breakfast is normally self-service buffet; evening meal likewise is frequently a buffet, to give plentiful choice.

Even in two weeks, you cannot expect to see all Turkey. Most itineraries start with a few days in Istanbul, with city sightseeings either included or offered as an optional extra. From there, a popular routing takes in Gallipoli and the Dardanelles, Troy, Pergamum, Izmir and Kuşadası (for Ephesus, Priene, Miletus and Didyma); and thence either via Pamukkale to Konya and Cappadocia, or on a southward swing to the Mediterranean coast.

Obviously there are numerous variations on these routings. Very popular is to make Izmir the starting point, and to circle round Pamukkale, Antalya, the southwest coast via Marmaris and Bodrum, and thence back to Ephesus and Izmir. On a longer tour, somewhat more strenuous, the dramatic mountain scenery of the eastern provinces can be explored in relative comfort, staying in the best available hotels.

Some tours are wrapped around a special interest. Thus, complete coach tours are available that include one or two classical or religious-interest sites each day; or there are specialist coach tours for bird-watchers.

Shorter-period coach tours can easily be linked with a static week at a resort; or even with a one-week Blue Voyage. One-day coach excursions are operated from all the main tourist centres to regional points of sightseeing interest. The permutations are endless.

Guides are mostly university educated, with good knowledge of their routes. Particularly they always know where carpet shops are located.

Special Interest Holidays

Biblical Interest

Like other Middle Eastern countries, Turkey is rich in sites of Christian and Biblical tradition.

Specialist tour operators like Inter-Church Travel offer a variety of coach tours that focus on Old and New Testament locations. A particular favourite is to follow in the steps of St. Paul, whose missionary adventures around the coast of Turkey and inland to Konya are well chronicled. Born in Tarsus, Paul preached at many of the classical sites which are central to modern-day tourism: Ephesus, Miletus, Perge.

An alternative theme is to follow the itinerary outlined in Revelation 1:11 ". . . unto the seven churches which are in Asia: Ephesus, Smyrna, Pergamos, Thyatira, Sardis, Philadelphia and Laodicea." All seven locations can be easily visited from Izmir (ancient Smyrna), though 'churches' probably meant congregations rather than physical buildings.

Other tours can include centres of early Christianity such as Antioch, the troglodyte churches and monasteries of Cappadocia, and cities of Byzantine interest including Istanbul.

Spa Holidays

Hot water springs eternal from the hillsides of Yalova, Bursa and Pamukkale, which double as spa resorts. Hope wells up for all kinds of cures, thanks to the high mineral content of the waters. True believers are probably halfway towards easing their nervous tension, rheumatism or whatever. Maybe the other half comes from the pleasant relaxation in blood-temperature water for an hour each day of the cure.

Few people travel to Turkey just to take the waters, though Turks themselves are fervent devotees. However, a visit to these hot springs can yield an added sightseeing interest, with bath remains that date back to the Romans, Byzantines and Ottomans. Hotels can offer mineral baths within their premises - even, in Bursa, through your own bathroom tap.

The beach resort of Ilıca, adjoining Çeşme, offers similar hot-water solutions to a variety of ailments. A damp cave called Damlataş at Alanya is promoted for asthma.

Bird-Watching

Turkey, as the land bridge between Europe and Asia, offers large and varied habitats ideal for bird-life. During a Turkish holiday, even the untrained layman can expect to spot numerous storks and their nests, usually perched high on ruined castle walls or on classical columns at Greek or Roman sites. Every Istanbul mosque on the tourist circuit is packed with pigeons, eager for bird-seed; and most mornings you awaken to the dawn squawking of rooftop gulls, limbering up for their breakfast of Bosphorus fish.

For the more dedicated bird-watcher, the principal migration flights are in March/April and September/October: eagles, storks and varied birds of prey, for instance, are then streaming across the Bosphorus - best seen from the Çamlıca hills on the Asian shore. The charm of Turkish birding is that viewing is in areas of magnificent landscape or against a theatrical backdrop of historic remains. Bird-watching can be combined with top-flight sightseeing. Here is a check-list on where to go - as suggested by leading specialist tour operators - and what your binoculars can hope to see.

Bursa can be a useful base for a few days. From within the city you can take the cable-car up Mount Uludağ with the chance of spotting Krüper's Nuthatch and the Red-fronted Serin among the pine trees; or go still higher to the snow line for Water Pipit, Crag Martin, Shore Lark, Pallid Swift, Alpine Accentor and Rock Thrush. Also watch out for Lammergeir and Golden Eagle.

In greatest possible contrast, from Bursa you can easily reach the shallow Marmara Lakes - Manyas and Apolyont - which offer good variety of wetland birds: herons, egrets, marsh terns, Dalmatian Pelican, Spoonbill, Pygmy Cormorant, Blackwinged Stilt, Penduline Tit and Glossy Ibis. Twenty kms southwest of Bandırma along the road to Gönen, a bird sanctuary called Kuş Cenneti (Bird Paradise) National Park on Lake Manyas has recorded 200 varieties.

Another favoured destination is the Cappadocia region of central Turkey, where villagers keep pigeons in the ancient rock dwellings and where Black Redstart, Rock Thrush, Rock Nuthatch, Bimaculated Lark, Crag Martin and Alpine Swift likewise find plentiful nesting places. In the surrounding hills and cultivated areas are Black-eared and Finsch's Wheatears, White-throated Robin, Scops Owl, Nightjar and Penduline Tit. Higher up on the slopes of the local extinct volcano - Erciyes Dağı near Kayseri - the meadows are home to the Alpine Chough and Snowfinch.

En route between Cappadocia and Ankara is the salt Tuz Gölü and a smaller freshwater lake which are good for marsh birds and wildfowl. Birdwatchers can expect Greater Flamingoes, Ruddy Shelduck, Ruffs, Avocets and Black Winged Stilts. Passing birds of prey include varieties of Buzzards, Eagles, Egyptian Vultures, Red Footed Falcons and Lesser Kestrel.

One of the world's rarest birds, the Bald Ibis, returns each year to Birecik township on the Euphrates River between Gaziantep and Urfa near the Syrian border. The World Wildlife Fund helps protect this breeding ground for some 40 remaining birds.

And so the list continues . . . A typical group of enthusiasts led by Cygnus Wildlife Tours reported a bird list of 229 species and a butterfly list of 39.

D.I.Y. Travel

While most holidaymakers to Turkey buy a tour operator's package, some travellers prefer the D.I.Y. path. Outside the obvious peak months, it's possible to buy a low-cost flight-only deal, particularly on charters to Izmir or Dalaman. Somewhat more expensive, but more flexible on travel dates, are excursion fares by British Airways or Turkish Airlines to Istanbul.

Turkey's domestic transport system is far, far cheaper than anywhere in Europe or the Mediterranean. Services are frequent, usually crowded, but unbelievably cheap. A bus-ride any distance across Istanbul, or a ferry across the Bosphorus from Europe to Asia, costs around 12p. A long-distance 500-mile bus journey, 15 hours from Istanbul to the southern coast, costs £5 and a saddle-sore bottom. Let's look closer at how an individual traveller can explore Turkey on his own.

Istanbul City Buses

You need a ticket before boarding a bus, as the driver (no conductor) does not accept money. Tickets are bought individually or in bundles of ten from kiosks at major bus-stops. It's worth carrying a small stock. Otherwise time is wasted queuing for a ticket, or wandering in circles to find where to buy one. Shoeshine boys often sell tickets at a modest mark-up.

At the bus entrance, everyone drops a ticket into a transparent box beside the driver. He just watches to see that everyone contributes, apart from travellers with a seasonal pass. Never board without a ticket! Otherwise some kindly Turk will donate a ticket and you'll feel embarrassed because he'll refuse all payment.

Avoid the morning and evening rush hours, when buses are not worth the hassle and sweat.

Bosphorus Ferries

Buy metal tokens (jeton) at the landing-stage; use them for passing through the turnstile.

Dolmuş

Most visitors soon learn the Turkish word 'dolmuş', which means a 'stuffed taxi'. It's a shared vehicle which follows set routes at a low fare fixed by City Hall, with a destination board on the windscreen. The dolmuş has been phased out from shorter journeys in Istanbul and Ankara (in favour of individual taxis) but still flourishes in other cities and resorts, and also for longer journeys to Istanbul suburbs.

At the main dolmuş ranks, barkers stand calling out the destination: "One seat left, Beyazit!" When the vehicle is full, off it goes, dropping off passengers along the chosen route, just like a bus. The driver collects payment and makes change while he's weaving through the traffic, one hand on the steering wheel, another on the gear lever. It's very exciting. On the dolmuş dashboard you often see the word Maşallah, which roughly translates as "May God protect you".

On the dolmuş system, anywhere is a request stop. You just stand at the roadside looking hopeful; and every passing dolmuş that can stuff in another passenger will slow down. In central town areas, however, the municipality tries to reduce traffic chaos by designating fixed stops. These are marked by a rectangular sign with a blue D in a white square, and the word Dolmuş beneath.

There are several breeds of dolmuş. In Istanbul, routes across to Asia and to the Bosphorus villages are served mainly by ancient Dodges and Chevrolets, De Soto and Bel Air, from the Great Tailfin Age, AD 1950-1957. Old, rusty and battered, in most countries they would long since have been reincarnated through the scrap heap. But in Istanbul they still lead a useful life, on the daily relentless grind up and down the cobbled hillsides that occasionally shake off the odd bumper or exhaust.

In coastal resorts, dolmuş vehicles are more often jeeps or mini-buses. At the departure point, when a 12-seater minibus has collected 15 passengers, the driver moves off. This leaves sufficient room for him to pick up another two or three clients en route.

Sometimes the passenger flow is one-way - morning-time to a beach, for instance. In that case, each dolmuş waits until another has arrived, and then takes off, even half-empty. Generally, the system works well. The services are very flexible, and even operate medium-distance from town to town at little more than bus fares.

Taxi

Regular taxis are easily recognised by a TAKSI sign on the roof, and - in the principal cities - are painted yellow, with a black and yellow chequered band. One of the great reforms of recent years is that taximeters are fitted, and no haggling is necessary. You just pay what's on the meter, and tipping is not expected, though the drivers appreciate when you wave aside the odd few coins to the nearest 100 liras. It works both ways: if the meter reads 520 liras, most cabbies are content with 500 to save the trouble of making change. For tourists, taxi prices seem extremely cheap. Taxis are extremely prolific in Istanbul. In central locations they swarm like bees with their yellow and black decor.

For brief journeys in central Istanbul, it's preferable to take a taxi, rather than jostle onto a crowded bus. A five-minute cab-ride costs about what you'd pay for a minimum bus or tube journey in central London.

However, on longer journeys, end to end of Istanbul, check on bus or dolmuş routes that charge one price however far you go. Otherwise, the taxi may run to several pounds.

Inter-City Buses

For longer journeys, Turkey is very well served by fiercely competitive private-sector bus lines, with fares that average £1 per hundred miles. The number of destinations offered is quite remarkable. There is not the slightest difficulty in travelling at good speed to virtually any city or resort in Turkey. Leading companies include Varan and Pamukkale. You can buy a 'Turkey Trotter' coach rover ticket through Sunquest Holidays in UK, giving go-as-you-please travel mainly on the west and south coasts, using the Varan network. In larger cities they operate downtown reservation offices. Otherwise just go to the bus station - otogar - and check who's going where, at what time.

There is a standard layout to all Turkish bus stations. In the central area are the ticket offices for the competing companies. Barkers call out the destinations of buses in the loading bays - peron - or accost likely-looking travellers.

Your ticket gives you a reserved seat. Bus departures are 100% punctual. Meanwhile you can take refreshment or a meal at the various cafés and bars within the bus-station complex.

Some long-distance buses are air conditioned. When several companies are serving the same destination, check whether the bus company is offering a direct express service (which can carve a quarter off the journey time), and whether the vehicle is air conditioned. It can make a great difference on a long journey, like 15 hours from Istanbul to the southern coast.

A window seat is not necessarily worth fighting for, unless you enjoy the Turkish sun beating down until you feel like a greenhouse tomato. It's often more comfortable to reserve an aisle seat - called koridor - to enjoy the cooler slipstream of the slightly open roof. On a long journey during summer, consider taking a night bus.

Inter-city buses always travel with a conductor who passes out bottles of ice-cold mineral water at frequent intervals. He also dowses passengers with toilet water - 80 degree lemon-perfumed cologne. It's all part of the service.

A brief halt is made at a wayside restaurant or a bus station about every two or three hours. Lavatories are smelly, and the attendant expects a donation of 3p. If you want a quick meal, you normally have only 20 minutes to locate a restaurant, order, eat, pay, and be back in your seat before the bus departs. Pinpoint your target restaurant as the coach is making its final slow approach to the landing-bay. That saves another precious minute in the scramble to eat in the 20 minutes allowed. Otherwise you can easily buy snacks or fruit for eating en route.

Motoring

Self-Drive

Several tour operators offer fly-drive arrangements, with delivery in Izmir and the main coastal resorts. Car hire is costly in Turkey, reflecting the high price level of both local and imported vehicles. But there are compensations. Petrol is cheap - 22p a litre for super, say £1 an imperial gallon. The self-drive motorist can stay in lower-cost accommodation outside the resort centres. Rooms are easy to find, except during July-August.

Road signs are standard European. Main highways are well indicated, with turn-offs to archaeological and historic sites marked by yellow signposts. Avoid driving in Istanbul, which can be nerve-wracking for anyone who doesn't know the city layout.

Unsurfaced off-trail mountain roads

should also be avoided. They can be quite hideous, unless you hire a jeep. Otherwise, the main road links along tourist itineraries present no difficulties.

When planning your route, remember that Turkey is a very large country - more than Britain and France added together. Distances are considerable. You cannot do all Turkey in two weeks! Pick your area, and take it slowly.

Touring With Your Own Car

The quick route to Turkey is about 2,000 miles on highway E5, mostly motorway across Belgium, Germany, Austria, Yugoslavia and Bulgaria. The border town of Edirne gives the first taste of Turkey, with one of Turkey's greatest mosques to inspect.

Thence E5 continues to Istanbul. A better scheme is to turn your itinerary around, and leave Istanbul for the final days of a Turkish interlude. Frankly, the closer E5 gets to Istanbul, the more murderous becomes the traffic: an unending stream of juggernauts from all across Europe, trundling along with supplies for Iran, Iraq and the rest of the Middle East. It is not a road to enjoy.

Instead, turn south after Edirne on highway 550, crossing E25 (which comes in from Greece) and stay with E24 which crosses the Dardanelles at Çanakkale. This is a much more pleasant and scenic route past enormous fields of sunflowers, and with plentiful views of the stately procession of vessels that ply across the Sea of Marmara and through the historic Straits.

After the low-cost ferry crossing, E24 then continues parallel with the Aegean coast. It offers very pleasant driving, with easy access to small seaside resorts and the sightseeing pearls of Troy and Pergamum through to Izmir and the rest. It is a good introduction to the delights of touring in Turkey.

Chapter Three
Istanbul

Introduction

For many travellers, impressions of Turkey start with Istanbul. The perfect approach is by ship: through the Dardanelles and across the Sea of Marmara, into the Bosphorus. There, stretching west, is the 4-mile Golden Horn: an inlet that offered the original Greek colonists of 7th century BC a safe anchorage, at the point where Europe almost touches Asia.

Dominating the skyline of seven hills is a forest of mosque minarets, more than 600 slim pencils that rise above Byzantine domes. At the extreme tip of the walled peninsula lies Seraglio Point, where the Ottoman Sultans ruled their sprawling Empire from an equally sprawling Topkapı Palace: a compound of apartments, pavilions, audience-chambers, kitchens, barracks and stables.

The alternative approach, by air or land, offers a totally different set of impressions. Within a few minutes' drive of the airport are the stupendous city walls that were subdued by the Turks in 1453, after the battlements had already served their defensive function for a thousand years. Today, half a millennium later, the colossal land walls still dominate the city outskirts. The four-lane London highway, jammed with cars, trucks and beat-up buses, plunges through the Cannon Gate towards the heart of old Constantinople - an extraordinary jumble of ancient and modern.

Depending on the traffic, other drivers choose an alternative highway which skirts the Sea of Marmara, with the fabulous city walls immediately on the left.

The raucous sounds of 20th-century Istanbul still leave little oases of tranquility where the traveller can recapture the mood of past civilizations. The main area of monuments is as tightly packed with sightseeing interest as classical Rome. Pleasant public gardens, bright with flowers, are set between the points of interest: the Topkapı Palace Museum, St. Sophia, elegant tiled fountains, a Roman hippodrome, the Sultan Ahmet Mosque, a Byzantine cistern with roof supported by several hundred columns, Istanbul University, the 3000 shops of the Covered Bazaar, more mosques. The dominating influences are Byzantine and Ottoman.

There is constant delight in browsing at random along the cobbled side streets. Children in pinafores play while mothers look out from wooden lattice-work balconies. A vendor with donkey cries his wares. The midday call of the muezzin, amplified by loudspeaker, competes with the wailing rhythm of Turkish radio pop music.

Carefully choose your tourist path, and you could say that little has changed. Equally, a 19th-century traveller on the Orient Express could still find his way around the central areas of the city without difficulty. But, in truth, there is constant change. If you already "know" Istanbul - from a visit ten years ago, or three years, or last December - your memories or impressions need updating. Right now, the pace of change is accelerating. New vistas open up, as the bulldozers march through broad swathes of Istanbul.

Consider this problem of living in one of the world's greatest tourist-potential cities, with remains from 2600 years of fabulous history. Add a population explosion which has boosted the city's inhabitants from one million in 1950, to something over 6.5 million today. The result is trouble.

Streets choke with traffic. Civic amenities are swamped. Population pressure leads to overnight erection of shanty dwellings on the city outskirts and on any available bare patch of land. Green countryside is paved over with concrete.

That has been the mammoth headache for Istanbul in recent years. Urban renewal was vital, but where does one start - or stop? From its former reputation among Europe's most beautiful cities, Istanbul was fast being overwhelmed by the 20th century.

At the start of the 20th century, the Golden Horn was still an inspiration for poets and painters. But then the waterside area crumbled, lined with tumbledown slum houses, decrepit workshops and small factories. The stagnant water functioned mainly as a dump for industrial effluent and sewage. Anyone who went swimming in the Golden Horn needed their brains tested, as part of the autopsy. The distant view remained superb. But close-up was less enchanting, rubbish and decay.

Enter a determined city mayor with ambitious clean-up programmes, and around $1.2 billion funds to carry them out. The result has been a massive exercise in city engineering, to tear down the waterside slums, wholesale markets and workshops, and replant with a green promenade of parks, children's playgrounds, well-stocked flower beds, informal areas for football, and facilities for pleasure boating. The target was to restore the crumbling glories of Istanbul, for the sake both of tourists and local residents.

Already the improvement clearly shows, with a wide ribbon of green along most of the southern shore of the Golden Horn. As each month passes, the gaps are filled with more greenery, as the bulldozers continue their work. Some 4000 eyesores have been removed, and hundreds of families rehoused.

This huge exercise in urban renewal faced great controversy, though the mayor certainly enjoyed immense popularity for his drive and achievements. Istanbul city-dwellers revel in the greening of the Golden Horn, along with similar programmes that have transformed the Bosphorus waterfront across on the Asian shore at Üsküdar. Likewise, Istanbul's 15 miles of mammoth city walls - dating from early 4th century AD - are being cleared of shanty settlements and scrapyard litter.

But some critics have argued that the bulldozer approach is too destructive, sweeping away many facets of Istanbul that were worth saving and restoring. Much of old Istanbul, and the European and Asian waterfronts of the Bosphorus, comprises a great open-air museum. But often there comes a clash with commercial interests.

31

The Bosphorus was famed for beautiful old wooden houses and mansions, where wealthier inhabitants would retreat during summer. Today, fast road access has transformed those waterside villages into desirable suburbs of Istanbul. The economic pressure is to tear down the old houses and build apartment blocks.

The graceful old houses are protected by a preservation order. But then they happen to catch fire, and the owner forgets to call the fire brigade until too late. And so another apartment block is built.

The alternative, less dramatic, approach is advocated by a greatly admired Istanbul personality - Mr. Çelik Gülersoy, General Director of the Turkish Touring and Automobile Club.

This remarkable man combines administrative ability with the vision of a poet or artist. He uses funds generated by the Automobile Association to rescue decaying Ottoman buildings, and restore them to new life.

First of the Turkish A.A.'s projects, in 1979, was the total restoration and refurnishing of the Malta Pavilion in Yıldız Park. Everything was done in superb taste, with the ground floor and terrace opened to the public as a café for light refreshments.

Likewise the Park itself has been completely transformed from a neglected wilderness into an elegant palace garden. The entire green hillside of lawns, trees, shrubs and flowers is now preserved much as it appeared in the 17th century, with beautiful views over the Bosphorus.

Similar work has restored the natural beauty of Çamlıca Hill, a famed viewpoint on the Asian shore. During the 19th century, it formed an integral part of Istanbul's social and literary life; but then became a derelict area of mud and shanty-building during the 1960's and 1970's.

Today, there is total restoration, with a delightful café in the traditional style of an 18th-century Turkish tea-house. You lounge on divans, and admire decorations which are completely authentic for the period.

Çelik Gülersoy gives personal attention to every tiny detail in these restorations. During a lifetime of dedication to Istanbul, he has collected a multi-language library of 6000 books that relate to the city: travellers' impressions, memoirs of diplomats, sketch-books of artists. His collection of prints can support every detail of the Touring Club's restorations.

Another transformation on the Asian shore is the Summer Palace of the last Khedive (viceroy) of Egypt. In 1937 it became the property of the Municipality of Istanbul, but was then left empty and neglected. Then in 1982 the Touring Club undertook the work of rehabilitation in art-nouveau style. Today it is a gracious hotel with beautifully furnished bedrooms, offering accommodation for 50 guests.

Istanbul is still changing, to meet the 20th-century needs of a thriving industrial and trading city. But the city planners, and the poets and dreamers, continue to work in their separate ways to preserve Istanbul's past for the future.

Getting Around in Istanbul

Information Bureaux (Turizm Danışma Büro) -
Hilton Oteli Girişi - at entrance to Hilton grounds - Tel 133 0592.

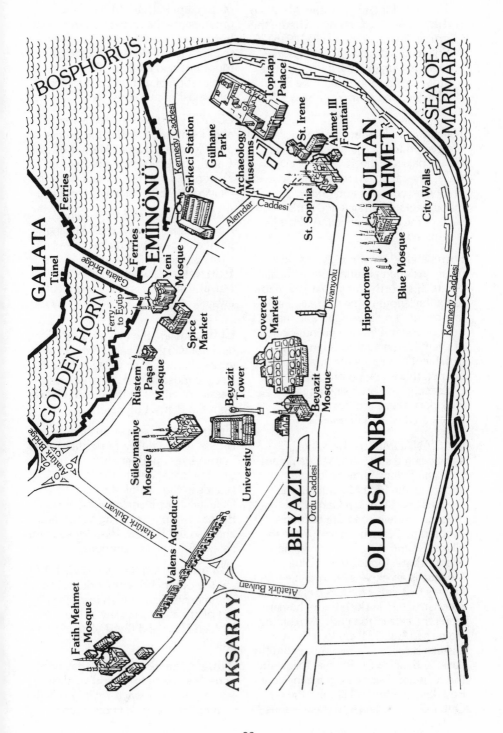

BOSPHORUS

GALATA

Tünel

Ferries

GOLDEN HORN

Galata Bridge

Ferry to Eyüp

Ferries

EMİNÖNÜ

Kennedy Caddesi

Sirkeci Station

Gülhane Park

Archaeology Museums

Topkapı Palace

St. Irene

Ahmet III Fountain

SEA OF MARMARA

Alemdar Caddesi

St. Sophia

SULTAN AHMET

Blue Mosque

City Walls

Yeni Mosque

Spice Market

Rüstem Paşa Mosque

Covered Market

Beyazit Tower

Beyazit Mosque

Hippodrome

Divanyolu

Kennedy Caddesi

Süleymaniye Mosque

University

Ordu Caddesi

OLD ISTANBUL

Atatürk Bulvarı

Valens Aqueduct

BEYAZIT

Fatih Mehmet Mosque

AKSARAY

Atatürk Bulvarı

Karaköy Limanı - at the Maritime Terminal at Karaköy where the cruise liners dock. Tel: 149 5776. Sultanahmet - Divan Yolu Caddesi, Otobüs Durağı Arkası - by the bus stops for St. Sophia and the Blue Mosque, on Divan Yolu Street. Tel: 522 4903.

The visitor to Istanbul cannot possibly see everything of the two fortresses, the six palaces, the 15 miles of city walls, several dozen museums, scores of towers, columns and other monuments, fountains and parks, and each of the 500 mosques. A short-list is required.

Fortunately the main highlights are neatly grouped around several focal-points. It's worth studying a city map, to fix the layout of these areas. Few taxi drivers speak English, and may not understand foreign pronunciation of even the most famous landmarks. But if you just name the appropriate district, there'll be no problem. Likewise, if you are using public transport, these are the names to check on destination boards.

SULTANAHMET is the prime sightseeing district. It takes its name from the Sultan Ahmet Mosque, known as the Blue Mosque. In the mosque precincts is a Carpet Museum, in two separate sections, devoted to Turkish carpets, rugs and kilims. Round the other side is the Hippodrome. Opposite the Blue Mosque is an expanse of greenery and flowers that sets off St. Sophia, with a reconstructed Turkish bath - hamam - along the side of the park. Across the main road called Divan Yolu is the Cistern Basilica (Yerebatan). From the park, and facing St. Sophia, follow up the right-hand side to the magnificent Fountain of Ahmed 111, and the Outer Gate leading into the grounds

of Topkapı Palace. Within these grounds are the ancient church of St. Irene, and - curving down a road to the left - the three Archaeological Museums and Gülhane Park. Exploration of all these riches could take most of two days.

BEYAZIT district likewise is named after its mosque, and is the access point for the Covered Market (Kapalı Çarşı), the University and Beyazit Tower, and - on the north side of the University - Süleymaniye Mosque.

Fatih Mosque and the Valens Aqueduct is the next main staging-point along a broad highway leading towards the city walls at **Edirnekapı,** where the Kariye Mosaic Museum is just a few blocks away.

Eyüp, outside the city walls, is a long haul but worth visiting if time permits, for its characteristic wooden houses, historic mosque and cemetery, and classic viewpoint of the Golden Horn from the Pierre Loti café.

Eminönü is the area around Galata Bridge, where public ferries start their journeys up the Bosphorus, across to the Asia coast and to the Princes Islands in the Sea of Marmara. Definitely worth seeing is the Spice Bazaar and the adjoining Yeni Camii; and also the Rüstem Paşa Mosque for its exquisite tile decorations.

Karaköy - also known as GALATA - at the other end of the bridge, is a commercial district with few "sites" but offers a historic view of the Golden Horn and the skyline of Old Istanbul.

Tünel, like most tunnels, has two ends. It's one of the world's oldest underground railways, built in 1877 by French engineers: a two-station

Métro, 600 yards long, from just near Galata Bridge to BEYOĞLU on the hilltop above. Running every ten minutes, it saves a very steep climb.

The area at the top end is called Tünel, and begins the mile-long İstiklâl Caddesi which was the 19th-century high society Bond Street of Istanbul, leading to Taksim Square. Walk back the other direction to reach Galata Tower for a great viewpoint, particularly across the Golden Horn to Süleymaniye Mosque.

TAKSİM is the traffic hub of the European-style city, leading along Cumhuriyet Caddesi to all the newer areas of town which formerly were meadows. Half a mile away is the Soldiers' Museum, past the major hotels like Sheraton, Divan and Hilton. Apart from the usual weapons and battle scenes, the Museum features performances every afternoon of the richly-costumed Mehter Band which struck terror into the hearts of the enemy.

Kabataş is a major ferry landing-stage on the Bosphorus, with a shuttle service to ÜSKÜDAR on the Asian shore, and express services to the Princes Islands and Yalova. A short walk along the Kabataş waterfront brings you to Dolmabahçe Palace; then another quarter-mile to the Maritime Museum.

Üsküdar in Asia is a lively starting point for road transport to Asian-shore Bosphorus villages, to the Black Sea and up to Çamlıca Hill for its splendid viewpoint. Near the landing stage are two interesting mosques, a bustling Sunday-morning open-air fruit and vegetable market, and a pleasant waterside promenade.

Transport Strategy

On longer journeys across Istanbul, use public transport between the main destinations listed above. For shorter journeys, save holiday time by hopping in a taxi, at the cost of peanuts. Try to avoid wasting your time locked in traffic jams, which can be miserable at the main rush hours: before 9 a.m. and from 5.30 or 6 p.m. To dodge the evening rush, plan the day's circuit to leave you within easy reach of your hotel when the last museum closes. If you are in Istanbul during winter, and snow starts falling, return immediately to within walking distance of your hotel. During snowfalls, Istanbul transport totally collapses as cars skid down cobbled hillsides, and all cabbies go into hiding.

At summer weekends, thousands of Istanbul families head along the Bosphorus, to Kilyos on the Black Sea, and to the Princes Islands. Good strategy is to leave those overcrowded locations to the Istanbullu's and enjoy sightseeing in the historic traffic-free zone. At weekends, all museums are open, at half price, and are closed either on Monday or Tuesday. Those are the best days to pick for a Bosphorus cruise, or a trip to the Princes Islands.

Visiting a Mosque

Turkish mosques are open to all. Visitors are welcome, regardless of faith, but are asked to conform to a few basic rules of etiquette. Firstly, remove shoes and either carry them with you or place them on low shelves. Sometimes over-slippers are provided, and a small contribution to the mosque is expected. During prayer time, do not walk around inside the mosque, but preferably wait quietly outside until prayers are over. Don't take photographs during prayer time. Inside the mosque, sit according to Turkish traditions, and especially do not lie down on the carpets in order to examine the ceiling. Women should cover their heads and arms, and not enter with shorts or mini-skirt. Sometimes the attendant will lend a robe. One mosque ends its four-language reminder of these rules with the line: "Thank you for your coordination."

Mosques follow a set pattern. In a spacious courtyard there are fountains for ritual ablutions before the faithful go in to pray. Rich carpets totally cover the floor. A niche called mihrap indicates the direction of Mecca. From an elaborate pulpit, the imam delivers the Friday sermon. Many mosques are beautifully decorated with tiles, but the Koran forbids any representation of living creatures. Walls are often adorned with verses from the Koran in Arabic calligraphy, which few Turks can read, but which look very pretty.

Which Istanbul Hotel?

Istanbul itself is Turkey's greatest single tourist attraction - the focal point which theoretically should be supplying 70 per cent of Turkey's tourism, in line with demand. Through lack of suitable hotels, the city can meet only a fraction of the requirement. However, several large hotel building projects are in the pipeline.

Most of Istanbul's top-grade hotels are closely grouped in the newer part of the city, close to Taksim Square on a hilltop overlooking the Bosphorus and the Asiatic shore. Hilton, Sheraton, Divan and Etap Marmara (formerly Inter-Continental) are the principal hotels for business traffic, expense-account conference delegates and for tourists who can afford de luxe accommodation. Their price levels are international rather than Turkish, with room rates quoted in US dollars.

Pioneer of the de luxe hotels was the Hilton, which opened 1955. The Hilton has proved to be a national training-ground for staff who have later moved on to management and executive positions in other Turkish hotels. The original 300-room hotel has since been extended by another 110 rooms. It is a well-established part of high-society Istanbul life, and is a frequent venue for major conferences.

On more intimate scale is the Divan Hotel, with a restaurant that is considered by local gourmets to be the best in town.

The two relatively newer additions are the Sheraton and the Etap Marmara - skyscrapers which jut like sore thumbs from the Istanbul skyline. They are completely in the international idiom. For a splurge with a fabulous view, treat yourself to a drink or a meal at their rooftop bar or restaurant.

In between the few hundred yards that separate these four hotels is the main centre of more sophisticated Istanbul life: airline offices, discos for the jet-set, night-clubs and pleasant small restaurants and boulevard cafés.

Several smaller three-star hotels are likewise very centrally located off Taksim Square - such as Dilson, Keban, Eresin, Kennedy and the two-star Santral.

Two first-class hotels face one another in the Tepebaşı district overlooking the Golden Horn: Pera Palace and Etap Istanbul (not to be confused with the Etap Marmara, operated by the same French international group which also has similarly named properties in Ankara and Izmir).

The rococo-style Pera Palace is the old-time great hotel of Istanbul - built 1892 to serve passengers of the Orient Express. During both World Wars, the hotel was setting for numerous scenes of international cloak-and-dagger intrigue, with leading embassies and consulates only a few minutes' away.

Kemal Atatürk frequently resided at the Pera Palace, and his suite has been officially designated as a museum. The rooms include the original furnishings, and a collection of Atatürk's personal belongings. On the crime front, Agatha Christie wrote her thriller "Murder on the Orient Express" while staying at the hotel, which also was setting for the opening scenes. A mysterious 11-day disappearance of the author is commemorated in Room 411.

Preserved like a museumpiece, the Pera Palace rates high in the nostalgia business. It's worth dropping by for a drink at the bar, looking around the salons, and admiring the elegant lift, like a small drawing-room that moves sedately between the floors.

Thanks to cheap and frequent transport, it's quite feasible for holidaymakers to stay in hotels along the Bosphorus, while commuting in for sightseeing.

Leading establishment is the Grand Hotel Tarabya. This hotel is highly popular during summer with Arab tourists from the Gulf. It overlooks a delightful fishing harbour, lined with restaurants. Evenings and weekends are lively with Istanbul families and groups, enjoying an outing.

Smaller hotels at Yeniköy likewise offers splendid views of maritime traffic along the Bosphorus.

On the other side of Istanbul, beside the Sea of Marmara, is the de luxe Çınar Hotel - very useful as an overnight stopover a few minutes from the airport.

Finally, many small and medium-size hotels are grouped in the areas of Aksaray, Lâleli, Beyazit and Sultanahmet - the historic older sections of Istanbul, with the great monuments and Covered Bazaar within brief walking distance. They are more convenient for sightseeing than the luxury hotels around Taksim Square. Well-chosen hotels in this sector are used by package tour operators. Budget travellers can also find very low-cost accommodation in the rambling side streets. During high summer, student accommodation is available in dormitories near Istanbul University at Beyazit.

For the most beautiful taste of Old Istanbul, the Turkish Touring and Automobile Club has converted a 19th-century mansion into a small hotel with modern plumbing and prices. Antique furnishings give guests the flavour of elegant living. The Yeşil Ev - the Green House - forms a little oasis of tranquility, where travellers can recapture the mood of past generations, sleeping in brass bedsteads. The location is perfect. Just along the street is the main entrance to Topkapı Palace Museum. Over the rooftops of a large Turkish baths is a view of the dome and minarets of St. Sophia. In the other direction is Sultan Ahmet, the Blue Mosque. Lunches and refreshments are served in the walled garden, which makes a peaceful retreat on the tourist circuit.

Close by, just behind St. Sophia and tucked beneath the walls of Topkapı Palace, is another of the Touring Club's imaginative projects. A row of old houses has been restored for use as guest-house accommodation. Called Soğukçeşme Sokak - Cold Fountain Street - the brightly-painted wooden houses have become part of the tourist itinerary, a hundred yards of pastel-coloured pictures. Several of the houses serve refreshments and light lunches.

Getting Your Bearings in Istanbul

Galata Bridge

To most first-time visitors, Istanbul is confusing. So let's start with an exercise in orientation: no museums on the first day, but just getting the "feel" of this vibrant trading city of 6.5 million inhabitants. What's it like, to live in Istanbul? Begin at Galata Bridge, Karaköy side. Just stand and stare in all directions, absorbing the atmosphere of one of the world's great history-packed locations, still bursting with vitality.

Away to the left is the Bosphorus, with Asia on the opposite shore. The bridge itself crosses the turgid waters of the Golden Horn, a five-mile fjord-like inlet from the Bosphorus. The original settlement of 7th century BC was just across the bridge, where seven hills dominate the skyline. Over the past 2,000 years, each of those hills has been crowned with majestic buildings. At the extreme tip is Seraglio Point, where the domed rooves of Topkapı Palace rise amid the surrounding trees. The walls and turrets are beautifully floodlit at night. From that strategic position, three great Empires were ruled - Roman, Byzantine and Ottoman - from 330 AD until new palaces were built elsewhere in the 19th century. It's curious to think that, during the 4th century AD, a remote island colony called Britain

was administered from this New Rome capital of Constantinople.

The next silhouette is St. Sophia - an incredible building erected almost 15 centuries ago when the Byzantine Empire was at its peak. The Islamic minarets are a newer addition, only 500 years old. Then comes the majestic outline of the Süleymaniye Mosque, the finest in Istanbul, with the Tower of Beyazit close by. Further along the skyline is the mosque of Selim 1, who conquered Egypt; and then the Fatih Mosque built by Sultan Mehmet 11 soon after he conquered Istanbul in 1453. All that side of the Golden Horn is Old Stamboul, where most of the tourist sightseeing awaits.

Karaköy

The Karaköy side - originally known as Galata, and the name persists - was a more recent development: a Genoese trading colony established in 1082, with exemption from customs duty. More Italian and other traders arrived over the centuries, settling up the hillside towards a new foreigners' section called Pera (present-day Beyoğlu), which became the prime district for embassies in large garden compounds.

Today, the entire area has a run-down appearance: ready for the bulldozer, and renewal in glass and concrete. Virtually all the larger companies have now moved out to prestige locations elsewhere in Istanbul - particularly along a long highway called Büyükdere Caddesi, with which business visitors soon become familiar.

Formerly, all the banks had their head office in this area, and bank publicity signs dominate the Karaköy square facing Galata Bridge. Several maintain branches on Bankalar Caddesi, which starts top left of the square, the former banking centre of Istanbul. But this is no longer the Wall Street of Turkey, and only a couple of head offices still remain. Yet this whole area is still packed with small traders and merchants, shipping companies and import-export firms, to make it one of Istanbul's busiest commercial centres. Thousands of commuters come pouring in every day aboard the ferry-boats, particularly from the Asian side of Istanbul. In fact, now's the time to get acquainted with these ferry services, which continue to flourish from docks at both ends of Galata Bridge.

On the Karaköy side, Dock no. 8 serves Haydarpaşa railway station -the Asian departure point for the original 19th-century German project of a through service, Berlin to Baghdad. Ferries from Dock 7 likewise serve the Asian shore, to Kadıköy (which should not be confused with Karaköy).

Destinations are sign-boarded in very large letters at the entrance to the landing stages. So there's not too much excuse for getting aboard the wrong ferry! For a quick scenic round trip, board whichever ferry comes first. Buy a token called by the French word 'jeton', to pass through the turnstile. The ferries steam very close to Seraglio Point, giving superb views.

Serving all the commuters and local workers, dozens of quick eating places are located opposite this ferry terminal. The food is more appetizing than the appearance of the restaurants, but prices are about the cheapest anywhere. For a gourmet lunch, go about 200 yards past the ferry landing-stages to the Maritime Terminal - where, incidentally, there's a Tourist Information Office. Ask for Liman Lokantası - it means Harbour Restaurant - perched on the top floor of the Terminal, accessible by a sedate

lift. A window-seat view is fantastic, unless blocked by a cruise-ship moored alongside.

Meanwhile, between Galata Bridge and the ferry docks is another characteristic Istanbul sight. Along the bank, small boats are deeply laden with gleaming, silvery fish. The boatmen sell their catch direct, at prices that seem remarkably cheap. They wrap the fish in plastic bags, two or three kilos, and deftly toss the bundles to their customers on the quayside above. That's something different for your movie camera! Sometimes they organise an on-board fry-up, serving each piece of fish in a hunk of bread. Delicious!

The fish theme continues. On both sides of the bridge, anglers stand shoulder to shoulder, catching fish about the size of large sardines. Despite the muddy look of the water, good catches are made. Sometimes fishermen haul in their line with several fish squirming on the hooks. It seems quite incredible that stocks are so prolific. Imagine similar scenes on Westminster Bridge!

Eminönü

As we cross Galata Bridge towards the Eminönü district, the hooting ferry-boats to the left are constantly coming and going across to Asia and up the Bosphorus, trailing their wind-socks of belching smoke. Here is one of Istanbul's major transport interchange points: ferries, buses to everywhere, longer-distance mini-buses in a rambling open space near the Spice Bazaar, streams of taxis and private vehicles - all adding to a colossal traffic jam every morning and evening, with cabbies waving their fists and hurling insults.

A few hundred yards further round

towards Seraglio Point is Sirkeci railway station, built 1890 as the terminus of the Orient Express. The train links with the rest of Europe still continue, usually arriving hours late. But the railway brings in far more commuter traffic from the suburbs, adding to the morning chaos.

Meanwhile, pedestrians are firmly barricaded away from all this traffic mayhem. Footbridges from the Golden Horn waterfront offer a safe crossing to the precincts of a splendid imperial mosque called Yeni Cami. That means New Mosque, so named when finally completed in 1663. The minarets, slender against the sky, are a popular camera subject.

In front of the mosque is one of Istanbul's liveliest areas, an unofficial open-air market packed with street traders. Little clusters of potential customers listen to salesmen making their pitch. It's worth just watching the faces, engrossed in the sales story. A knife-sharpening machine perhaps, or a patent lemon-squeezer? Or why not invest in a gadget to cut your own hair?

You can buy underwear, pyjamas, sticky cakes, nuts, simit rolls, sweaters and socks, cigarettes and lighters, watches, calculators, shoes, candles, hairbrushes and combs, leather belts, note-books and envelopes. At a basic level, it's all part of the Orient. Trade has been the function of this area for the last 2600 years. Only the costumes have changed. These vignettes of Turkish life are often more memorable than visiting yet another mosque.

A characteristic street trade is shoe-shining. With a box of brushes, a variety of polishes and waxes, and a few pieces of rag and velvet, a shoeshine boy is in business, maybe with a sideline like selling telephone tokens - jeton - at a small mark-up. The shine you get from an experienced man is superb: eight minutes' intensive work for under 20p.

Yeni Cami

Like most Turkish mosques, Yeni Cami is a popular feeding-ground for pigeons. You can buy little trays of bird-seed: a great favourite with children, who also love scattering the pigeons as well as the bird-seed. The birds are so well fed that quantities of seed are left uneaten on the ground.

In contrast to the noise and bustle outside, the Yeni Mosque has a very peaceful courtyard with a central ablution fountain that is worth a closer look. Tiles on the courtyard walls have seen better days. Many are faded and broken, but are originals from the 17th century. Restoration has brought out the bright colours of the arcaded roof. Within, the Yeni Mosque is lavishly decorated with İznik tiles, carved marble and stained glass doors. Enormous green and red carpets cover the floor.

Spice Bazaar

Walk back through the courtyard of Yeni Cami, out the other side, and you emerge onto a busy little park, with the domed Egyptian or Spice Bazaar (Mısır Çarşısı) running L-shaped around two sides. Shops and stalls that lean against the wall of the Spice Bazaar are devoted to gardening products: shrubs, flowers, pot plants, and sacks of bulbs.

All the activity in this garden centre is a reminder that the Turk's main interests are centred on home, family and garden. He has a love of flowers, and names like Tulip and Rose - Lale and Gül - are popular for girls. Quite apart from the more luxuriant gardens, heavy with the perfume of lilac, mimosa and honeysuckle, even the poorest home has pots of geraniums on the window-sill. Truck windscreens are often garlanded with roses. At the first sign of spring, Turkey seems to explode into colour.

Inside the Spice Bazaar is even more lively and colourful than the famous Covered Bazaar, though it's much smaller. It was built in 1660 to provide the Yeni Mosque with a steady income - quite a normal Ottoman arrangement for the funding of religious buildings and charities.

Great sacks and jars of spices, condiments and henna tickle the nostrils with their penetrating aromas - paprika, ginger, cinnamon, shredded coconut. Traditionally the spices were also used as ingredients for an enormous range of medicaments. In Ottoman times, merchants would grind up their folk remedies on the spot, all ready for kitchen or medical use. Today the market is filled with shoppers for every kind of food, not just spices. But, as a survival from former times, one shop proclaims that it sells "Aphrodisiac des Sultanes". No harm in trying, see what happens. A neighbouring shop sells Korean red ginseng, famed in Asia for a similar potency to make life more spicey.

Maybe try a few other purchases: authentic Turkish Delight, for instance, called lokum; or nuts, dried figs or candied fruits. Turkey excels in these natural products. The piles of comb honey are a bee-keeper's dream: produced on very large frames, and every cell completely filled and sealed. The bazaar has also diversified into other products like toys, clothing and even jewelry, but still keeps its unique character. Don't miss it!

For a lunch-stop of great charm, try to find the Pandeli Restaurant in the Spice Market. Go back to the main entrance; and there it is, hiding on the right hand side, up a flight of stone steps, with blue tiled walls.

All this Eminönü area is thick with markets. Another exit leads uphill into Istanbul's main sector for the textile trade, wholesale and retail. But specially colourful is a fruit and vegetable market which runs along the other outside wall of the Spice Bazaar - that is, the other side from the garden centre. It starts with shops that sell cheese, olives and sunflower-seed oil. Then come the fruits and vegetables, stacked high. The quality is first-rate, and everything is grown within Turkey itself: beautiful lettuces, huge horse radishes, prize-winning leeks, Brussels sprouts and spring onions; bananas, cherries, strawberries and the citrus fruits. Nothing is imported, except perhaps the odd coconut from India.

Rüstem Paşa Mosque

A short distance further along, past the Spice Bazaar and moving further up the Golden Horn direction, comes first a car park, then the domes of a mosque rising above the smaller domes of merchant storehouses. That is Rüstem Paşa Camii, which must be rated as Istanbul's prettiest mosque, utterly perfect. Don't miss this treasure. Get your bearings from a distance, and then try to home in.

Up a narrow side street, there's an entrance up a stone staircase to reach the Mosque itself, built on an upper level, above the surrounding warehouses and shops. If you have difficulty in finding it, don't give up. Use your smattering of Turkish to ask the way.

Rüstem Paşa Camii - named after the son-in-law of Süleyman the Magnificent - was built around 1550 by Sinan, the greatest architect of the Ottoman Emperors. In this delicate miniature, he brought ceramic decoration to perfection. The entire building is covered floor to ceiling with superbly-coloured tiles from İznik - every one an individual hand-painted masterpiece of tulips and carnations. As you stand admiring the detailed craftsmanship, the smell of oriental spices comes wafting in from a 16th-century caravanserai next door, used as a storehouse.

Take a look over the courtyard parapet, and you'll see dozens of interesting little scenes in the streets below - men working, gossiping, bargaining, drinking tea, or just sitting. Out the back, a narrow street returns to the Spice Bazaar. Specializing in household goods of every type, the alley is lined with tiny stores and metal-bashing workshops where the 20th century has not yet arrived.

Golden Horn (Haliç)

For a change of pace, let's take a half-hour cruise on the Golden Horn. Until 1988, no guide-book would have dared make such a preposterous suggestion. From a blissful 19th-century romantic dream, the Golden Horn and the buildings each side had become a derelict industrial zone with an unrivalled stench. But thanks to City Hall's clean-up policy, the journey is becoming more of a tourist attraction as each month goes by.

Make a beeline from Rüstem Paşa Mosque to the Golden Horn, and reach the landing stage marked Haliç İskelesi. Several private vessels offer ferry services; or you can wait for the main ferry which plies according to very punctual schedule, up and down the Golden Horn, 10p any distance through to Eyüp.

Shortly after the boat leaves, keep alert for a view of the Valens Aqueduct, on the left just before you sail under Atatürk Bridge. Immediately after the bridge is a long white four-storied building with a red roof: one of the Turkish Monopoly's cigarette factories. From then onwards, the ferry zig-zags from shore to shore, with brief stops. Local people use the ferry like a bus.

The entire left side of the Golden Horn has been transformed into a broad promenade, from Galata Bridge to Eyüp. It's an incredible change from the slums and primitive workshops that formerly lined the embankment. Even on the northern side of the Golden Horn, which still remains industrialised with working shipyards, green areas are taking over the shoreline.

Just before the final Haliç bridge called Fatih, look back to the left, for a glimpse of the Byzantine walls which played such a major role in the city's history.

The motorway crossing the Horn is the E5 highway which connects Istanbul to London: one international road the whole way, through Bulgaria, Yugoslavia, Austria, Germany and Belgium. This London Road is called just that: Londra Asfaltı. The other direction, over a Bosphorus Bridge, leads across Central Turkey until the road forks at Ankara to Iran, or to Syria and Iraq. It's the most important overland route to the Middle East, carrying an unending stream of heavily laden international juggernauts.

Just past Fatih Bridge, the ferry ride ends at Eyüp, which is worth an hour or two. Meanwhile, a minor mystery: why is it called Golden Horn? The 'Horn' is understandable, particularly just by Eyüp, where the waterway curves neatly into horn shape. But the colour? Some people say the reflection of the sunset sky gives the Horn a yellow or golden colouring. Or could it relate to the city's superb trading location, which made it the medieval world's greatest golden treasure house? Pick your fancy.

Eyüp

Located outside the Istanbul city walls, Eyüp is a village which became a suburb, while still keeping some of its original atmosphere. At the landing-stage, trees and shrubs have been planted, grass sown: all part of the Golden Horn's renewal programme. The waterfront area is lively with children playing, while more sedate citizens sun themselves comfortably on park benches. Many of the older private houses are of traditional Ottoman style with wooden balconies, often crumbling but still very picturesque.

Despite its modest appearance, Eyüp enjoys great renown for its mosque, which rates high among the major holy sites of Islam. It is the burial place of the standard bearer to the Prophet Mohammed, Eba-Eyüp-el Ensari, killed here in battle during the 7th century. Eight hundred years later, Mehmet the Conqueror built a mosque around the Saint's tomb, which has been a place of Islamic pilgrimage ever since. In the approaches to the mosque, shops and stalls sell religious souvenirs.

On accession to the throne, every Sultan came here to buckle on his sword. The present mosque itself dates from 1800, replacing the original, destroyed by earthquake. Inside the

small, tiled building which shelters the Eyüp tomb, the faithful stand in silent prayer. All around, and high up the hillsides, has long been a prestige burial ground for the mighty and the famous - from sultans to poets and politicians - almost every tombstone crested with a turban.

Pierre Loti Café

The classic tourist viewpoint, north of Eyüp Mosque, is up a long steep hill to Pierre Loti Café, where the French novelist rhapsodized over the idyllic scene above the Sweet Waters of Europe, a hundred years ago. The entrance to the cobbled way through the cemetery to Piyer Loti is tricky to find, but local people will point the way. A taxi saves the uphill climb, at modest cost, leaving you an easy walk down.

From the terrace, you get superb views of the Golden Horn, and can see the effect of the clean-up process - areas of parkland alternating with sectors which are still a muddle of dereliction. However, green is winning. It's a pleasant spot for tea, coffee or a reflective naghile.

From Pierre Loti Café the panoramic cemetery walk gives plenty more angles on the Golden Horn. Closer to Eyüp, you get pigeon's-eye views of the mosque minarets and domes, with white tombstones standing erect like a ghost army. By moonlight the effect can be spooky.

Transport back to central Istanbul? Catch bus 39A or 99A which return to Eminönü via Edirnekapı (hop off for the City Walls and the Kaariye Mosaic Museum, if closing time permits), Fatih Mosque, Beyazit and Covered Market. Or number 55 goes to Taksim Square, taking around 45 minutes.

Topkapı Palace

If you're an individual traveller, not part of a tour group, it's worth planning your moves to be one jump ahead of the traffic stream. Here's how to operate for the prime area of Topkapı, St. Sofia and Blue Mosque.

Start early and arrive just before Topkapı's opening time. Check whether that is 9 a.m. or 9.30, according to season. Many tourists and groups start first at St. Sophia, followed by an uphill walk to the Palace. Instead, save your legs (you'll need them for the rest of the day) and take a taxi direct to the ticket booth of Topkapı, located inside the First Courtyard next to an exchange bureau and close to the toilets. A word of warning: make sure the cabbie understands you want the Palace. Istanbul has another Topkapı - it means Cannon Gate - which is a long-distance bus terminal on the city outskirts. Tell the driver "Sultanahmet - Topkapı Sarayı."

Passing through the turnstiles at the entrance Gate of Salutations, you come into the Court of the Divan with choice of four paths. Ignore everything. Instead, hurry along the path straight ahead, through another gate, and bear right to the Treasury. You'll then be among the first of the day's visitors to view the jewels, and the famous emerald dagger which starred in the film 'Topkapi'. Maybe you'll have 20 minutes to admire the collection in tranquility, before the tour groups come thundering in. By mid-morning long queues have built up, and it's miserable, trying to admire the treasures as part of a milling crowd.

Across the centuries the Ottomans acquired vast hoards of loot or tribute from their Empire - emeralds and jade by the hundredweight, enough to turn any multi-millionaire green with envy; diamond-encrusted thrones; the arm and hand of St. John the Baptist; the pear-shaped 86-carat Spoonmaker's Diamond (found by a pauper who swapped it for three wooden spoons). Candlesticks were a hundred-weight of solid gold encrusted with 6,666 diamonds. Chinese porcelain was studded with precious stones on gold. Thrones, armour and ceremonial swords and pistols were all items of the jewellers' craft rather than of the furniture or armaments manufacturer.

The next sightseeing priority is to make early reservation for visiting the Harem. Guided groups of maximum 50 persons pass through every half hour, spaced through the day for Turkish, English, French and German. Tickets are sold, stamped with a reserved time, to save queuing. The ticket booth is located back in the Court of the Divan, half left from the entrance Gate of Salutations. Far more people want to see the Harem than can be funnelled through. You may hear squawks of dismay from tour groups when they discover that entrance to the Harem is not included in their itinerary. If you leave getting your ticket till later, you'll find that the day's allotment is sold out. No use protesting that you've travelled 2000 miles solely to visit the Harem!

Certainly the visit is eminently worth while, offering some insight into the home life of the Sultans, with a village of up to 200 concubines to tend their needs. It was quite unlike the home life of our own dear Queen Victoria. The Harem quarters have been extensively renovated. The visit includes the guards' quarters - first the white eunuchs, and then the black eunuchs (only the latter having access to the Harem, and touching not allowed).

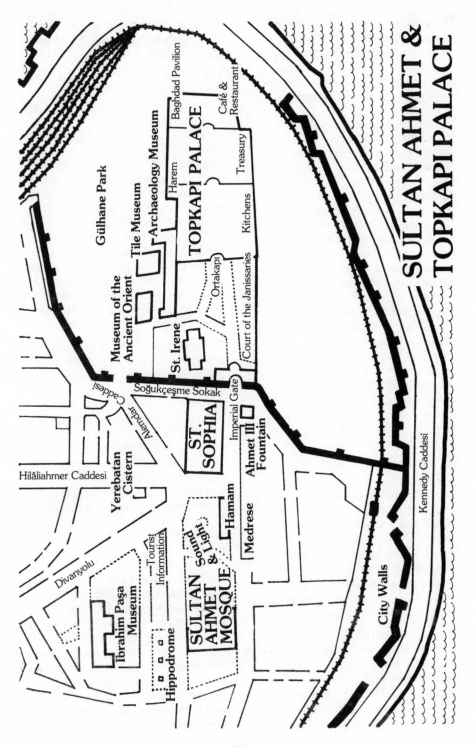

SULTAN AHMET &
TOPKAPI PALACE

Baghdad Pavilion

Café & Restaurant

TOPKAPI PALACE

Harem

Treasury

Archaeology Museum

Kitchens

Tile Museum

Ortakapı

Museum of the Ancient Orient

Court of the Janissaries

Gülhane Park

St. Irene

Soğukçeşme Sokak

Alemdar Caddesi

ST. SOPHIA

Imperial Gate

Ahmet III Fountain

Hilâliahmer Caddesi

Yerebatan Cistern

Hamam

Medrese

Sound & Light

Tourist Information

SULTAN AHMET MOSQUE

Divanyolu

İbrahim Paşa Museum

Kennedy Caddesi

Hippodrome

City Walls

45

The principal royal apartments are fully furnished and restored, including an audience chamber, bedroom, prince's quarters and the Pasha's mother's bedroom (where a personal slave girl slept over the canopy of her four-poster bed).

Mehmet the Conqueror laid out the original palace plan in the 15th century, and lived there with his court. Over the centuries, his successors added more and more buildings until Topkapı was finally abandoned in 1853, when Sultan Abdül Mecit moved house and harem to Dolmabahçe Palace on the Bosphorus. For many years the palace grounds were then left derelict, until re-opened as a museum in 1924. In recent decades the palace buildings have been completely restored, to house rich and varied collections: the imperial carriages; Turkish glassware; a wardrobe of imperial costumes; Turkish and Persian miniatures; sacred relics of the Prophet Mohammed; watches, clocks and musical clocks; hand embroideries; weapons; ceramics.

To the right of our Divan Courtyard is a group of buildings with enormous conical chimneys: site of the imperial kitchens, where over a thousand cooks and scullions served a palace community of 5000. Much of the design of the kitchens and chimneys in their present form is the work of Sinan, the greatest of Ottoman architects, who usually worked on major palaces and mosques.

From these buildings came most of the specialities which form the base of Turkish cuisine, with its influence spread throughout the Balkans and Middle East. But the influence was two-way. Dedicated chefs brought back recipes from outlying parts of the Ottoman Empire, and introduced them to their colleagues, to tempt the royal appetite.

Today, the vast kitchens house one of the world's rarest collections of Chinese and Japanese porcelain and Celadon ware. While admiring that collection, consider the layout of the buildings in their original role as palace kitchens. Look at each individual section, and imagine all the bustle of a thousand kitchen hands, preparing a meal for the Sultan and his court. Each department had its individual central fire, around which work revolved. In a couple of sections, a massive iron bar still reaches out for suspending huge cooking pots over the flames, with the smoke escaping through the chimney high above. Boiled egg for breakfast? No problem!

In the end kitchen is a splendid collection of cooking utensils. There are jumbo cooking pots, great spoons and ladles, tureens, mortar and pestles for grinding and pounding ingredients before the days of food mixers; massive tongs for lifting food away from the flames; frying and cooking pans of all types. It is less glamorous than the porcelain collection, or the Treasury. But it helps recapture something of the grand atmosphere of Ottoman times, when this palace was also the administrative centre of a great empire.

Feeling hungry? Even if time is only 11.30, strategy now demands a coffee break or a light lunch. It may sound early, but the clued-up visitor will get seated well before 12 noon. There is only one restaurant in the Palace grounds, and virtually all tables are block reserved for tour groups from midday till 2 p.m. or later. If you're not one jump ahead, then expect a long long queue.

Past the Treasury in the righthand corner of the Third Courtyard, go down steps to the Konyalı restaurant and a lower-level café. Here is a magnificent Sultan's-eye view of the entrance to the Golden Horn, the Bosphorus and its pageant of passing maritime traffic, and the Sea of Marmara with hazy outline of the Princes Islands.

Immediately below are the railway tracks that lead within the city walls into Sirkeci Station, terminal since the 1880's of the Orient Express. Just outside the wall is the highway that leads round the waterfront. Ferry-boats shuttle back and forth from Europe to the Asian shore, with a splendid view across the water to the barracks at Üsküdar where Florence Nightingale made her name during the Crimean War.

Looking out from his hilltop Palace, the Emperor could sit and contemplate his dominions. During the peak period of the Ottoman Empire, the territories ruled from Topkapı Palace included all countries of North Africa from Morocco to Egypt; most of the Middle East, including modern-day Lebanon, Syria, Israel, Jordan, Iraq and the Red Sea coast of Saudi Arabia. Northwards, the Empire embraced all the Balkans: Greece, Yugoslavia, Albania, Bulgaria, much of Romania and Hungary. Even the entire Black Sea was an Ottoman lake, with the present-day southern territories of the Soviet Union under Ottoman rule.

Having contemplated the Empire, finish your plate of Spaghetti Bolognaise, stroll through the Fourth Courtyard to the Baghdad Kiosk and complete the Palace tour.

Back into the First Courtyard - the Court of the Janissaries - there is

choice of two routes: bear right, downhill to the Archaeological Museums; or go straight ahead, back through the main gate to St. Sophia.

First, though - before quitting the Court of the Janissaries - take a glance at one of the world's most ancient church buildings, just there in the corner: the domed basilica of St. Irene. The site has had a changeable history over the centuries, quite apart from the normal hazards of fire, earthquake and plunder. Originally a Roman temple dedicated to Aphrodite, it was converted to Christianity by the Byzantines and remained the city's cathedral until the building of St. Sophia in the 6th century. Under Turkish occupation, the church was used by the Janissaries as a palace arms depot until the end of the 19th century, when it became an archaeological museum. That episode in St. Irene's life-story was followed in the 1920's by service as a Military Museum, until 1946 when St. Irene was given another face-lift with major restoration. Today the building is used as a concert hall, particularly for recitals during the annual Istanbul International Festival.

As you emerge from the main palace gate, with its framed view of Sultan Ahmet Mosque a few hundred yards away, look left at the splendid four-sided Fountain of Sultan Ahmet 111, built in 1729. The decorative verses in Persian script were written by the Sultan himself. Thanks to the Turkish love of running water, the lavish building of fountains was always a high priority of the Ottoman public works department.

On the other side of the main gate, the street called Soğukçeşme Sokağı - Cold Fountain Alley - is lined with reconstructed wooden houses which make a popular colour shot for tourist cameras. Several of these houses, now used as guesthouse accommodation, serve refreshments and snacks.

Because Istanbul is not fed by a river, the city has always depended for its water supply either on springs or aqueducts, with the water stored in depots and cisterns. These were built first by the Romans, then by the Byzantines. At the bottom of Soğukçeşme Street, on the right, is a below-ground restaurant called Sarnıç which means Cistern.

Peep inside, or stay for a meal. Originally this was a typical cistern dating from the 6th century AD - the same era as the building of St. Sophia Cathedral across the street, for which it served as a water depot. Over the centuries, this former underground cistern which stored the Cold Spring waters filled up with mud and rubble. Until 1986, the derelict site was being used as a backstreet car repair workshop, with only two metres of the original columns appearing above the debris below.

Then the Turkish Touring and Automobile Club took it over, excavated five metres down, and converted the original columned structure, over 1400 years old, into a delightful restaurant seating 120. For lunch or dinner, it's pricey by Turkish standards. But it's an enjoyable experience, with good food served by waiters in şalvar baggy trousers and black tunics, with classical background music or a live guitarist most evenings.

Aya Sofya

Istanbul's most awe-inspiring monument is St. Sophia, called Aya Sofya in Turkish. It was built in 6th century AD by Emperor Justinian, who aimed to eclipse all former buildings in size and magnificence. This was the golden age of the Byzantine Empire, when art and science had reached a brilliant peak. When the city became an imperial capital two centuries earlier, craftsmen and architects had flocked to Constantinople from East and West - from Persia and Syria, Greece and Rome. From this architectural marriage, a Byzantine style was born. Its characteristic feature, the dome, was essentially the work of Eastern craftsmen. From Asia, too, came the purely decorative and non-representational art so typical of early Byzantine interiors.

To build St. Sophia, the finest materials were gathered - columns of white or green marble, from Syria and Egypt or recycled from Ephesus; doors of ivory, amber and cedar. Ten thousand men laboured six years. The cost was such a drain upon the treasury that Justinian had to stop the salaries of government officials, and raise new taxes. Architecturally, everything was subordinated to the primary object of supporting the vast dome: 175 feet from the ground, 107 feet in diameter, 46 feet high.

The Byzantines built well. For over 1400 years the cupola of St. Sophia has continued to dominate the skyline, to inspire later generations in the design of both church and mosque. Despite several earthquakes, St. Sophia has survived almost miraculously into the 20th century. No visitor to modern Istanbul can ever forget that incredible interior: the dome poised above a golden sea of mosaic, lit dramatically by sunbeams' gleaming down through stone latticework. St. Sophia is undeniably the world's greatest Byzantine monument.

In the use of mosaic, St. Sophia is a masterpiece. Decorations cover four acres of walls and ceilings. The mosaics were formed by about 6,000 tiny fragments to the square foot. Plaster was first applied to the brick wall. Then the thousands of fingernail-size stones were embedded into the plaster, to form a picture that reflected light without distorting the design. Precious metals, too, were used. The Byzantines discovered a technique of gilding a cube with gold leaf, and fixing it with a molten film of glass.

When the Ottomans conquered the city in 1453, St. Sophia symbolized for the Turks the triumph of the Crescent over the Cross. They converted the church into a mosque, added Islamic minarets, and covered the Christian mosaics with plaster. Ironically, that was a work of preservation, compared with the actions in year 1204 of the 4th Crusaders, who looted the gold and silver treasures and plundered everything they could lift.

Then, in 1931, the Turks decided that St. Sophia belonged not merely to themselves as conquerors, but to the whole world, regardless of creed. They gave permission to an American expert, Professor Whittemore, to strip off the plaster, uncover the murals and restore them. His work revealed such treasures that the Turkish government decided in 1935 that the building should no longer be used as a mosque, but be secularized into a museum. There, Christian and Moslem alike could marvel at the building planned by Emperor Justinian "to surpass the glory of Solomon."

In the ensuing years, the task of restoring the mosaics has quietly continued, to reveal new splendours. When Professor Whittemore died in 1950, his place was taken by Professor Paul Underwood, another American authority on Byzantine art and archaeology.

Conservation is a constant battle. For years on end, parts of St. Sophia are blocked by scaffolding as renovation continues. Quite often, slabs of mosaics are stacked against the walls, awaiting expert attention. Some of the best of the mosaics are located in the upstairs gallery. Tastefully lit, these glorious mosaics are still as bright and sparkling as the century they were made (principally 10th to 12th). But for long periods access to the gallery is closed for repairs.

As consolation, look back at the magnificent 10th-century mosaic over the exit door at the far end of the vestibule. Emperors Constantine and Justinian are portrayed presenting a model of the city and one of the church, to Jesus and Mary. Effectively it symbolizes the two great pivotal events in the city's early history: Constantine's adoption of Christianity as the state religion in AD 330; and Justinian's building of St. Sophia in AD 537 as the culminating achievement of the Byzantine age.

The Sultan Ahmet Area

The entire Sultanahmet area is packed with sightseeing interest. Obviously a first-time visitor concentrates on the great highlights: Topkapı Palace, St. Sophia and Sultan Ahmet Mosque itself. It is tempting to tick off the big three, and then whirl off to the Covered Bazaar, just over half a mile away. But numerous sights remain, to justify at least another leisured day to explore the district in more detail.

The Sultanahmet district revolves around the small park that stretches between St. Sophia and the Blue

49

Mosque. The gardens set off both monuments beautifully, with well-watered grass thick with daisies, and luxuriant beds of flowers to provide photographers with foreground interest. Weekends, Turkish couples and families stroll around the central pond, admiring the flower displays.

Off to one side, with the entrance facing St. Sophia, is a long low building with domes: Hürrem Sultan Hamam, a Turkish bath built by architect Sinan in 1556. This was commissioned by Süleyman the Magnificent, in honour of his wife Roxana. It is a solid building which has been beautifully restored. Look inside, to get a clearer idea of the layout of a traditional hamam, which played such an important part in the Islamic rituals of bodily cleanliness. Friday, particularly, was a good day for a steam clean, at a time when bathrooms were unknown in Europe - forgotten since Roman times.

Round the other side of the hamam is a side street distinguished by a green wooden mansion which has been converted into an elegant hotel, with a peaceful garden that serves refreshments and meals. Next door is a converted medrese - a religious school - based on the classical model: a one-storeyed building with central courtyard and porticoes, with rooms leading off from the courtyard. From 13th century onwards, all religious schools were built precisely on this pattern.

This medrese fell into disuse in mid-19th century. A tasteful reconstruction has given the building new life. Along the street front are attractive stores, operated by the Turkish Touring Club, exhibiting high-class products at fixed prices: local guide-books, carpets, brassware and pottery. Unlike the merchants in the Covered Bazaar, the staff make no attempt to hustle you into buying. Specially delightful is the candy shop, where tourists can buy all the typical sweets and Turkish Delights of old Istanbul.

Rooms surrounding the interior courtyard have been sub-let as studios to artist craftsmen who produce 20th-century masterpieces of calligraphy, illuminated miniatures, lacework dolls and individual designs of costume jewelry. Visitors are welcome to watch, without sales pressure. A charming spot!

The Sultanahmet area is well supplied with open-air cafés where tourists can ease their aching feet. Opposite the medrese is a pleasant café with view of the Blue Mosque. Within the periphery of St. Sophia is the Café Sebil, meaning Fountain. Despite the tourist location, prices are reasonable. For a budget-price lunch, cross the busy main highway called Divan Yolu. Several fast-food restaurants face the park, including The Pudding Shop - a famed hippy rendezvous in the days when Istanbul was a staging-point on the annual migrations between Europe, India and the low-cost hash of Nepal. Today the bearded overlanders are few, and the clientele is mainly Turkish and tourist.

Just around the corner of Divan Yolu and Hilâliahmer Street is the Cistern Basilica, called the Sunken Palace in Turkish -Yerebatan Sarayı. Built during the reign of Emperor Justinian in the 6th century, the Cistern is another Byzantine monument that ranks close in grandeur to St. Sophia across the road. The brick vaulting is supported by 336 Corinthian columns which came originally from an on-site Basilica built by Emperor Constantine, and recycled when Justinian needed to enlarge an adjoining reservoir.

Measuring 154 yards by 77, the Cistern - which still holds water - was used during Ottoman times to keep the Topkapı Palace gardens green during the dry months of summer. Today, the Cistern earns its living from tourist entrance fees.

Now dodge back across Divan Yolu to Sultan Ahmet Square, site of the ancient Hippodrome, built by the Romans in 203 AD, using the model of Circus Maximus in Rome. Later, Constantine the Great enlarged the facility. Here was the setting for all major sport events, wrestling matches and chariot races, with the Stadium richly decorated with statues of bronze, copper and marble. During Byzantine times, the supporters of rival Green and Blue chariot teams would occasionally go berserk, even worse than football fans. Blues and Greens were separated on opposite sides of the arena, and the emperors themselves backed one team or other.

The riots became political. The climax was a full-scale rebellion in 532 AD, when a day at the races ended with 30,000 corpses heaped near one of the Hippodrome gates. Some historians put the body count as high as 60,000. That protest was mainly against high taxes, imposed by Emperor Justinian to finance the building of St. Sophia.

Today there's not much to show of the original Hippodrome, though the outline is recognizable. Only three monuments remain: the Obelisk of Theodosius (an Egyptian souvenir, originally carved in 1500 BC); the bronze Serpentine Column (which was removed from the Temple of Apollo at Delphi); and the Obelisk of Bricks (a local production). Everything else was destroyed or looted, particularly by the Fourth Crusaders. Part of the Venetian share of the booty was the Quadriga - a team of four bronze horses - which adorns the entrance of St. Mark's, Venice.

During Ottoman times, the Hippodrome was used for javelin practice on horseback. The area continued to be an occasional centre for popular demonstrations. In 1826, the Janissary troops rose in protest against a decree to abolish them. In fighting and executions that followed, 30,000 were killed, mainly in the Hippodrome grounds. The latest major riot was in 1909, which led to the overthrow of Sultan Abdül Hamid 11. He is remembered on the German Fountain in the Hippodrome, presented by Kaiser Wilhelm 11 as a memento of his State visit to Turkey at the turn of the century, when the two emperors met. The Fountain marks the location of the original Royal Box in chariot-racing days.

On the western side of the Hippodrome is the İbrahim Paşa Palace, built in 1524 by the Grand Vizier and son-in-law of Süleyman the Magnificent, who later had him executed. This sumptuous private residence was built of stone - not of the usual timber - which explains its unusual survival into the 20th century. Today the palace houses the Museum of Turkish and Islamic Arts - especially Turkish and Persian miniatures, Seljuk tiles and antique carpets. The collection covers from the earliest days of Islam, 8th century to the present.

Blue Mosque

Facing the Hippodrome, and St. Sophia, stands the majestic Mosque of Sultan Ahmet - a gem of dome design, unique in the world with six minarets. It was built in seven years, 1609-1616, by a pupil of the great architect Sinan.

Blue-tinted light reflected from over 20,000 İznik tiles has given it the popular name of Blue Mosque.

The work of restoration and upkeep continues year after year. Colours of the ceiling decorations have been awakened into vivid life. The best effects come when the sun beams down through windows high above.

Within the confines of the Blue Mosque is a two-section museum - kilims and flat woven rugs in one location, and carpets in another. Antique kilims are mounted on boards and displayed around the walls of a barrel-vaulted basement. The massive stonework makes an impressive setting for the collection. The origin and century of each exhibit is clearly labelled. The display is well worth seeing, even if you whizz round in ten minutes. Then return to the front of the mosque. A stone ramp leads up to the Carpet section of the Museum, which formerly was the way in for sultans on horseback.

The Archaeological Museums

Three museums for the price of one entrance fee, half price on Sunday: it's hard to get a better deal except at the British Museum, which is free. Understandably the Turks complain about the rapacity of 19th-century British and German archaeologists who dug classical sites, and shipped everything moveable back to London or Berlin. By the time more stringent laws were applied, Turkey had been thoroughly looted.

Since then, much more detailed and scientific excavations have unearthed great treasures from the wealth of Anatolian civilizations. Dating from 1881 with the appointment of an

energetic Director called Osman Hamdi Bey, a collection of antiquities was greatly enlarged and later housed in the purpose-built Archaeological Museum. The Director himself organised excavations in Ottoman territories, including Sidon in present-day Lebanon. From these sites he brought back major finds which can possibly counter-balance some of Turkey's earlier losses. Today the Archaeological Museums at Istanbul can take high place among the richest in the world.

The three museums are grouped in one compound, reached either from Gülhane Park, or downhill from the first courtyard of Topkapı Palace and through a narrow archway which is just wide enough for tour buses to scrape through. At the approaches, a number of spare tombs and sarcophagi are laid out beside the walls. Collections are divided between the Museum of Classical Antiquities, the Museum of the Ancient Orient and the Çinili Köşk Tile Museum.

Sarcophagi were Hamdi Bey's great speciality. Even the basic design of the main Museum of Classical Antiquities was inspired by his two greatest finds: the Alexander Sarcophagus and the Sarcophagus of Mourning Women. These burial monuments from the Royal Necropolis of Sidon, dating from 4th century BC, are incredible in their detail - dramatic hunting and battle scenes on one; the grief of eighteen weeping women on the other. Even if you are desperately pressed for time, visit the Museum just for those two works of art alone: though you'll probably be tempted to stay longer, to inspect all the other riches on show.

Opposite is the charming Çinili Köşk, housing the Tile Collection. The kiosk is Istanbul's oldest non-religious building erected by the Turks, dating from 1472, soon after their capture of the city. Quite apart from the beautiful tile displays, just enjoy the building itself, and its light and airy interior. Half an hour will give you deeper understanding of the decorative role of ceramics in Turkish architecture. There are tiles in greens and blues and yellows, decorated with splendid examples of calligraphy. İznik tiles from the 16th century offer glowing reproductions of flowers - every tile an individual work of art in itself. Many of the İznik techniques still have to be rediscovered.

Covered Bazaar and Old Istanbul

Istanbul's famous Covered Bazaar - Kapalı Çarşı - is a small city in itself, with 4,000 shops under one roof. Streets and alleys are roofed with vaults and domes, and the wider thoroughfares with columned arcades. Entire sections are devoted to each trade. Jewellers' stores stand shoulder to shoulder, each window glittering with gold bracelets, brooches, rings and cuff-links. There are whole streets of oriental rug merchants, furniture dealers, tinsmiths. You-name-it, it's there.

Founded in 1461 by Mehmet the Conqueror as a trading centre, the Grand Bazaar has several times been damaged by fire or earthquake, and rapidly rebuilt without changing the basic layout. The most recent disaster was a big fire in 1954. Rebuilding introduced the 20th century. Strip lighting and plate glass have become a normal feature in the more opulent sections. Occupying an area a mile in circumference, the Bazaar remains the biggest covered market in the world. The Western tourist can enjoy

strolling through the 67 streets of all-pedestrian shopping malls, savouring the highly coloured sights, sounds and smells of the Orient, while returning to his familiar Western hotel comforts when the day is ended.

The Grand Bazaar is not just a survival, protected for tourism. The streets are busy any time with Istanbullu's, shopping for jeans, bathroom scales, buttons and thread, a new kettle or a child's toy. During the great days of the Ottoman Empire, this was a fabulous treasure-house of silks and pearls from the East, clocks from Germany, steel from Sweden, woollens from England; and was one of the world's richest centres for jewelry business. Today, the super-luxury trade has moved elsewhere. But the Grand Bazaar is still a thriving shopping centre for the average Turkish family.

Making a special pitch for the tourist traffic are stores that display sheepskins, suede and leather coats; brassware; Meerschaum pipes; kaftans and blouses; shoes, beaded slippers and sandals. Another section is loaded with mass-produced ceramics, alabaster giftware and chess-sets. Some of the shops are little more than tiny cubby-holes, with a craftsman who sits and works; or just sits, and waits, like a spider ready to pounce.

For casual browsing, head for 'the old bazaar' or İç Bedesten, where all the clutter of the centuries is located, dead centre in the labyrinth. This building is the original, from 1461. Traders sit patiently cross-legged upon soft cushions, all set to haggle over their antique carpets, rusty swords and weapons, camel-bells, tiles painted with texts in Arabic calligraphy, Istanbul glassware and dust-clogged jewellery. An antique-hunter's paradise - especially for those who are willing to play the Oriental game of haggling!

The Grand Bazaar is the bargaining capital of the world. The merchants are wily characters who live mainly off their wits to win the hearts and foreign currency of every passing tourist. Within minutes of entering the Grand Bazaar you are likely to be charmed into the store of a carpet seller, or a Meerschaum pipe merchant, or a leather shop. Most of the merchants have at least a half-dozen languages at their command, and can make their sales pitch equally well in any of them. They weigh up your potential with lightning speed, and give price quotes accordingly. The dealers have numerous price scales, depending on whether you are a personal friend, a local Turk, an Arab, a foreigner living in Turkey, a tourist, or an American tourist.

A basic rule is to avoid buying at any shop into which you are steered by a guide or hustler. "Straight" dealers claim that these middlemen expect anything up to 35% commission on your purchases. Even if they don't remain in the shop with you, the merchant knows they are hovering outside, waiting to collect their slice later.

Hence, all price bargaining has to take account of that reserved commission. Avoid touts, however plausible and friendly, and enter shops entirely of your own accord. You will then have better chance of driving a more reasonable bargain. You can always get endless glasses of tea by dropping in to carpet shops. But it could be an expensive way of quenching thirst.

There are plentiful little buffets and coffeeshops for snacks and refreshments. If you want a full lunch of Turkish specialities in a non-tourist traditional setting, try to find the Havuzlu Lokantası: quiet and lofty, with marble floors and walls, and even some stained glass. Ask for the Post Office -called PTT - and it's right next door, in the area of Bodrum Han.

Don't worry about getting lost in all the confusion. In fact, the Covered Bazaar layout is more or less a grid system. To escape, just keep going uphill until you reach the main wide street called Kalpakçılar that is loaded with jewellers. Go right, and you'll emerge at Beyazit, to pick up transport to anywhere. Besides, there are hundreds of sales people around who speak English, and who cheerfully give directions. There is an information centre for lost tourists, but how to find it?

Even outside the confines of the Covered Bazaar, surrounding streets are filled with all kinds of trading activity and little workshops. At the Beyazıt exit, it's worth turning right on Çadırcılar Caddesi and then fork left into the charming Old Book Bazaar (Sahaflar Çarşışı). Mostly the books are Turkish, but there's still some pleasant browsing for bibliophiles among the English-language stacks. Continue through the courtyard and you emerge into a popular tea-garden, much used by Istanbul University students, just behind Beyazıt Mosque. The monumental gates to the University and the central administration block were built in 1870 for the Ministry of War - now, of course, located in the capital, Ankara. Today's University comprises more than 30,000 students, with faculties scattered in several parts of Istanbul. Beyazıt Tower in the University grounds offers the finest viewpoint of Old Istanbul, 280 feet high, originally built in 1823 for fire-watch duty.

Kariye Museum

It's a longish taxi ride to the outskirts of the old city, to reach the Kariye Camii Museum close to the Byzantine city walls. But the journey - costing maybe £2 from more central locations - is eminently worth while. Here are the best-preserved Byzantine mosaics and frescoes of anywhere in the world, dating from early 14th century - probably all created between 1310 and 1320.

The original church was built as a monastery, outside the existing city walls of Byzantium, mid-4th century. During the following century, the site was enclosed within an extension of the city walls, which are those which remain today. Then came the usual history of periodic earthquakes and destruction, so that the present physical building with its six domes is mainly 12th century. A minaret was added later when the building was converted to Islam.

Splendid frescoes, richly coloured and lively, are of the same style and period as those of church decorations in Italy by Giotto, but the artist is unknown.

The mosaics were covered by wooden partitions during the building's 400 years as a mosque (unlike the mosaics of St. Sophia which were plastered over). The whole rich splendour was brought magically to life by two American specialists in Byzantine Studies during the period from 1948 to 1958. Since then, the museum has been a major tourist attraction.

Floodlighting brings out the fantastic detail of mosaics that cover the domed and vaulted ceilings. Every detail of clothes, trees, birds and scenery stands out vividly, as a lyrical masterpiece of the Byzantine Renaissance.

There are dozens of scenes from the life of Christ, and of the Virgin Mary, presented in chronological order: a complete golden story-book of the New Testament, illustrated in the dress and style of the early 14th century. Portraits of saints and martyrs form a complete portrait gallery of early Christian history.

It is well worth lingering in the area, which has been beautifully transformed by the Turkish Touring Club into one of the most charming corners of old Istanbul. Pastel-coloured wooden houses are set along a few cobbled streets, barred to traffic. The scene is quite untouched by the 20th century - flowers everywhere, and the sound of birds.

Then stroll up to the city walls, and follow them left till you reach the Edirnekapı Gate. There, bus and dolmuş traffic streams back along Fevzi Paşa Caddesi, dead straight to Beyazıt. Meanwhile, as you walk along, look closer at the walls - one small part of Istanbul's historic 15-mile defensive system which included 400 towers and 50 gates. Just here saw some of the fiercest fighting in 1453, and the final breakthrough of the Turkish forces.

The promise is that all these crumbling ramparts will be restored, as Istanbul aims to salvage the legacy of past centuries. A huge task! Just within the walls, many of the two-storeyed wooden houses are falling into ruin. But it takes a big injection of money and good taste to revitalize them on the model of the Touring Club's restorations. Maybe some Turkish yuppies could gentrify the neighbourhood, before the bulldozers move in?

Fatih Mosque

En route back towards Beyazıt, consider a stop-off at the Fatih Mosque, marked by a very long and high wall on the left. This gigantic mosque complex was built between 1463 and 1471 at the command of Fatih Sultan Mehmet (otherwise known as Mehmet the Conqueror). Having captured Constantinople in 1453, he found a run-down city, which had long out-lived its Byzantine glories. Within ten years, building began on the vast ensemble, on a hilltop formerly occupied by the ruined Church of the Apostles (which was a model for St. Mark's, Venice).

The new mosque was surrounded by a variety of charitable and religious buildings which mostly still stand today: a complete cultural centre, with a library, a hospital, an asylum for the mentally sick, schools for primary and advanced studies, free lodgings for travellers and their servants, and alms houses for the poor.

A stroll around the precincts gives a good idea of the scale of these social institutions, dating from the 15th century when much of Europe was living in a benighted state. The buildings themselves are still in active use, though their functions have changed. Today, children play in the grounds, while venerable old men with knitted caps and beards gossip as they warm their bones in the sun. In one of the garden courtyards, the tomb of the Conqueror is housed beneath an immense cupola, lavishly decorated.

Valens Aqueduct and The City Museum

From Fatih Mosque, take a short downhill walk from the side entrance - keeping parallel with Fevzi Paşa Caddesi - until you get your bearings on the Aqueduct of Valens, which dates from the 4th century AD. Cut across leftwards, beneath one of the arches, and follow it along. About half a mile of the enormous construction still survives, towering sixty feet high. A major highway - the Atatürk Bulvarı - passes beneath its arches, which seem to survive that constant vibration, quite unforeseen by the original builders.

Tucked close to the aqueduct at the Atatürk Bulvarı crossing is the small marble-domed Municipal Museum, which houses a variegated collection of bits and pieces, mainly from the 18th and 19th centuries. If the museum door is closed, ring for entrance. It's worth a 15-minute stop, specially for its period paintings of old Istanbul, from costume to traditional wooden houses.

Süleymaniye Mosque

The mid-16th century Mosque of Süleyman the Magnificent is the finest work in Istanbul of the architectural genius, Sinan, who built mosques, bridges, palaces and aqueducts by the hundred during an incredibly active life. Completed in seven years, it is a splendid achievement in dome design. In the forecourt are the tombs of Süleyman and his favourite wife Roxelane, subject of the monarch's most lyrical love poems.

Walk round the precincts which formerly housed all the peripherals of this major mosque: hospital and theological school, student hostel, alms houses and soup kitchens for the poor. From the broad terrace at the rear, where boys play football and stray cats bask in the sun, there's a fine view down to Galata Bridge, the Golden Horn and the Bosphorus.

From that vantage-point over domed out-buildings and crumbling walls, you can get your bearings and walk down the stepped hillside on a short cut to Galata Bridge. But the route goes through a grotty district of small workshops, which mainly contribute heaps of rubbish to the scene rather than local colour.

The Modern Town

Taksim

While most of Istanbul's tourist interest is tightly packed in "Old Stamboul" on the southern side of the Golden Horn, many of the leading and middle-grade hotels are bunched around the Taksim area. That is the traffic focal-point of the newer districts, which particularly began developing in the 19th century, then rocketing over the past 20 years.

To get your bearings in Taksim Square, stand with your back to the tall, rectangular Hotel Etap Marmara, rising at one end of the square, with the other tower block, the Sheraton, facing across Taksim Park. To the right is the modern glass and concrete Atatürk Cultural Palace, also known as the Opera House - a principal venue for performances during the summertime Istanbul Festival.

Take any of the streets leading out of the right-hand side of the square and park, and you can walk downhill to the Bosphorus, with dramatic views over a football stadium to the first Bosphorus Bridge, with Dolmabahçe Mosque and Palace at the water's edge. En route, particularly near the Sheraton Hotel, you may be accosted by a dancing bear and its gipsy master. At first sign of a foreigner, the bear is forced to rise onto its hind legs. This barbaric display is kept going by tourists who pay to take a picture.

Back to our position in Taksim Square: at the near left-hand corner is the beginning of İstiklâl Caddesi. During 19th century, this was the elegant main street of 19th-century Pera (now called Beyoğlu), where major embassies were located. The former embassies - British, American, French, Russian, Swedish - still function as consulates, and have been tastefully redecorated in pastel colours. Otherwise, İstiklâl Caddesi looks very run-down, though bursting with vitality. It's no longer the Bond Street of the Ottoman Empire, but is still packed with everyday shops. For textiles and clothing - non-boutique style - İstiklâl Caddesi offers wide choice at reasonable fixed prices, no haggling. At night, street lights are dim, but there is bonus illumination from low-life cabarets that wink from the side streets.

Although the whole area each side of İstiklâl Caddesi is "new" compared with Old Stamboul, that means it's mainly 19th century, over a hundred years old, due for bulldozing. Here's another example of the clash between conservation and city engineering. To relieve the appalling traffic jams that clog the district every day, a broad new boulevard has carved out chunks of 19th-century architecture. The huge plus point of the project is that İstiklâl Caddesi has become a pedestrian precinct.

Yet there is great character in those cobbled side streets. Many critics - and even hard-headed investment bankers - feel that numerous historic buildings could be cleaned up and converted to tourist accommodation. There's a wealth of Victoriana in the architectural details, dating from when Pera was where the rich lived: merchants, foreign traders, bankers, diplomats. Take a look while it's still there! You could easily imagine yourself in one of the older quarters of Paris, rather sleazy.

Meanwhile, back at our position on Taksim Square, we can look straight ahead to a broader boulevard called Cumhuriyet Caddesi, leading past airline and travel agency offices to the Hilton Hotel. At the entrance to the Hilton grounds is a helpful Tourism Information Centre, and a bookshop with yesterday's English newspapers.

Military Museum – Askeri Müzesi

Continue past the Hilton Hotel for another half mile, and there's the Military Museum on the right. Even if you don't thrill to the sight of swords and Gatling guns, there are other items of interest. Every afternoon the Janissary military band - called The Mehter - gives a short concert in their full Ottoman costume. The band is 30 strong, heavy on drums, cymbals, wind instruments, bells and voice.

You can imagine the scene during the triumphant days of Ottoman conquest. In their magnificent uniform, with tall hats to enlarge an overall impression of great ferocity, they would parade through a newly-conquered city, playing their instruments and singing, instilling the local inhabitants with awe and fear. If you likewise want to frighten the neighbours, two cassette recordings are available at less than £1 each.

Other non-lethal items on display include a superb collection of Ottoman costumes, civil and military. There are the costumed models of such dignitaries as the Prime Minister, the judge, the archive official at the Foreign Ministry, or the Chief of the Descendants of the Prophet

Mohammed. On a more humble level are members of Topkapı Palace staff - the water distributor, the chief cook, the buffoon, palace guards, and the chief of the men charged to administer the bastinado.

Another section of the museum is devoted to historic military tents, made of cotton and silk, richly embroidered and decorated. Several magnificent royal tents are the size of a ballroom, at least twenty feet high.

To summarise: don't let the Military Museum title put you off. Many of the exhibits would be more appropriate for Topkapı Palace itself, if there were room available.

Nişantaşi to Şişli

Just past the Military Museum the main road forks. This district is a good hunting-ground for shopping at middle-income price levels, Oxford Street style. Either take the left fork called Halaskârgazi Caddesi for a mile of shops; or right fork on Valikonaği Caddesi, and then left at the crossroad chaos, bringing you back up to Halaskârgazi Caddesi. Halfway along that long street - number 250, on the right - is the house where Kemal Atatürk lived before he became world famous. It is open daily except weekends, and contains photographs, furniture, documents and personal items that relate to different periods of his career.

Further along to the very large Şişli Mosque, the highway then continues to the new business sectors of Istanbul which have migrated from the overcrowded downtown locations. This area has nil tourist interest.

Dolmabahçe Palace

The palace of Dolmabahçe stands on

what formerly was a Bosphorus cove, used as a harbour. During early 17th century, the bay was filled in with rubble dumped from the hillside above, where the present football stadium is located. A garden was planted. Hence the Turkish name of Dolmabahçe, meaning "stuffed" or "in-filled" garden. The present palace was built in 1853 by Sultan Abdülmecit, who transferred his court and his affections to this site, while draining the Turkish Treasury to meet the cost. The marble quayside alone comprises over one-third of a mile of prime waterfront. The main building material was glistening white marble, to make an enormously long wedding cake. The 365 rooms of the Palace are stuffed with all the European luxuries of the Victorian age. No expense was spared, to cover every square inch with lavish, ornate decoration.

Tours are in groups, conducted by a Palace guide. Visitors wait - appropriately enough - in the reception hall used during Ottoman times as a waiting room for foreigners. There are Victorian chandeliers to admire while passing the time. That may be 20 or 30 minutes, before your language is called.

The Palace divides into several sections: the sultan's apartments; official reception rooms and eight large halls used for ceremonial purposes; the quarters of the sultan's mother, who traditionally was the power behind the throne; apartments of varied court officials; and the harem department. The main staircase is roofed over with glass rather like a greenhouse at Kew Gardens. In the largest hall is a little present from Queen Victoria: a chandelier weighing 4½ tons. The Russian Czar's contribution was two polar-bear rugs.

With so many rooms and corridors to decorate, the sultans were massive supporters of local and foreign artists and craftsmen. Two hundred metres of corridor lead to the Harem section - enough to keep a Sultan in trim, if he needed even more exercise. Along the way he could indulge in art appreciation of battle scenes galore, with dead and dying soldiers in the foreground to complete a decorative composition. Within the harem quarters, the art-work becomes more bucolic, with deer crossing forest paths, cows grazing, camel caravans passing over bridges, old Turkish houses, and rather fewer battle scenes.

In display cabinets are items of household crockery: dinner settings of solid gold, a tea service encrusted with precious stones, porcelain fruit bowls and dinner services with lace decoration. Doubtless, all this was very pleasant while it lasted. But the Dolmabahçe Palace helps one understand why Turkey finally became a Republic.

In severe contrast is the relatively spartan suite of Kemal Atatürk. His bedroom is still furnished as on the day he died - 10 November 1938. To mark the hour of his death, every clock in the Palace is permanently stopped at 9.05.

The full guided tour takes 80 minutes, leaving you free afterwards to enjoy the gardens and the quayside views of the Bosphorus. Toilet facilities at the exit are palatial, well worth visiting.

Naval Museum (Deniz Müzesi)

Reasonably close to Dolmabahçe Palace is the Naval Museum, a 2-minute taxi ride or 15-minute walk along Dolmabahçe Caddesi to Beşiktaş - a busy intersection, with a Bosphorus ferry landing-stage and numerous cafés and eating-places. For a gourmet lunch, try the Motorest Restaurant, just by a pedestrian footbridge and next to a gas station. It sounds an unlikely location, but Motorest is among the best lunch-spots in town.

The museum contains a standard selection of naval hardware: side-arms, grenades, cannons in assorted sizes, cutlasses and other carving utensils; torpedoes and mines in the basement. This museum should appeal to anyone interested in naval architecture, with some splendid models of warships.

In a separate building (with a separate entrance fee) the Historical Caiques Gallery houses a selection of boats, skiffs and royal barges used by the sultans, other nobility and court officials. On the imperial level, royal barges were propelled by 13 oars each side, while the emperor's ladies were protected from plebian gaze within the State Cabin at the rear. Elsewhere in the Naval Museum, nineteenth-century paintings depict the royal progress along the Bosphorus from one palace to another. Other paintings and prints give more impressions of old-time Istanbul.

Along The Bosphorus

The 19-mile Bosphorus that links the Black Sea with the Sea of Marmara, and which separates Europe from Asia, must rate supreme among the scenic waterways of the world. A Bosphorus boat excursion is an unforgettable highlight of any holiday in Istanbul. The trip can be done luxury style in sleek white-painted vessels, purpose built for the higher-priced end of the tourist trade, and operated by Hilton, Sheraton or Etap group hotels. But the classic formula is to make the journey by regular ferry-boat which zig-zags to villages on both shores, during a two-hour journey from Galata Bridge to within sight of the Black Sea. For under a pound, you get transport, scenery and first-hand experience of an authentic Bosphorus ferry.

During the tourist season the Bosphorus-trip ferries are extremely crowded, usually departing from Dock 4, nearest to Galata Bridge on the Eminönü side. Check the timetable, and aim to be aboard 30 minutes before departure to pick the seat location you want: sun or shade with the boat travelling due north; or left side for European views, right for the Asian shores. Before the ferry sets off, there'll be standing room only unless you have chosen a foggy day in November.

An alternative, with better chance of less crowding, is to reverse the itinerary: take road transport to Sarıyer or Rumeli Kavağı by bus or dolmuş, and catch the ferry on its return.

Immediately on departure from Galata Bridge, the boat offers a fantastic panorama up the Golden Horn: hillsides stepped high with ancient and modern buildings, mosque minarets and towers. Very soon there's a superb view of Dolmabahçe Palace, spread along half a kilometre of prime waterfront. The brutal modern buildings which dominate the skyline above are the hotels Etap Marmara and the Sheraton. The Hilton is less obtrusive. Soaring ahead is the first-ever inter-continental suspension bridge, sixth longest in the world and partly British built, opened in 1973 on the 50th anniversary of the Turkish

Republic. The newer bridge further upstream is a joint Japanese, Italian and Turkish construction, stretching almost 1200 yards across from Europe to Asia, 130 feet wide.

Meanwhile, more palaces: on the European side is Çırağan, built 1874 for Sultan Abdül Aziz but burnt out in 1910. The empty hulk then remained like a grim skeleton until quite recently, when permission was given for complete renovation, with a luxury 300-room hotel complex alongside.

Immediately behind are the park grounds and imperial pavilions of Yıldız Palace. Make a mental note to break away from the streets of Istanbul and restore sanity with a couple of hours in Yıldız Park, a gardeners' paradise which most tourists miss.

Dwarfed by the Bosphorus Bridge, on the Asian side, is Beylerbeyi Palace - built 1865 as a summer residence for Abdül Aziz and a guest-house for visiting royalty, on the site of a former wooden palace which caught fire. If time permits, this marble gem is worth a visit (but is closed on Monday and Thursday). The Terrace Gardens, also known as Cruciform Gardens, are a pleasure in themselves. Small pavilions in the park complete the complex. Sultan Abdül Hamid II, deposed by the Young Turks in 1909, was left in this palace to console his final years with no wives, just his cat.

The Bosphorus varies from half to 1½ miles wide, with occasional bends in the north-south line. Although the current runs at seven knots, it seems more like the middle of a calm lake, surrounded by hills. Compared with the turgid Golden Horn, the Bosphorus sparkles with non-polluted water from the Black Sea. The massive input from the drains of Istanbul comes lower down. Occupants of waterside villas - called 'yalı' - have no hesitation about taking a morning dip, and little strips of beach are always crowded in summer.

Every few minutes, yet another ferry boat heads towards a landing stage, or casts off. A myriad smaller craft and fishing boats go about their business, dwarfed by rust-coated tramp steamers and trim well-painted cruise ships. As an international highway linking the Black Sea with the Aegean, the Bosphorus carries a high proportion of East European shipping. The traffic rules were switched in 1982, so that even the hammer-and-sickle vessels keep to the right.

Meanwhile, tea sellers are circulating with their trays, or offering yogurt, sandwiches or chocolate bars. Other peddlers come round with everything from knitwear to postcards and guide-books. It's all part of the ferry-boat atmosphere.

Stops are made on each shoreline, giving close-up views of delightful waterside villages. Two-storey wooden houses with carved beams huddle along the zig-zag cobbled streets. Many of the crumbling wooden summer houses and villas have been completely modernised inside, and the exteriors refurbished, to make elegant year-round apartments. But their days are numbered, as owners find there is more money in concrete.

However, photographers still have plentiful colour subjects: blue and yellow houses, green fishing boats, and timber restaurants and tea-houses built out on piles over the blue Bosphorus. The atmosphere is tranquil. Outside sheltered coffeehouses elderly Turks sit thoughtfully with their hubble-bubble pipes. At the water's edge, anglers with just a single line and hook make a small catch every minute: enough for a family meal in half an hour.

Innumerable fish restaurants are packed at weekends, and on most summer evenings, thanks to easy transport from the centre of Istanbul. Arnavutköy and Bebek are specially popular.

Look again to the Asian shore: a wide expanse of greenery marks the Sweet Waters of Asia, a high society picnic spot in Ottoman times. Here's another of Sultan Abdül Mecit's little palaces, small enough to be called the Küçüksu Pavilion, but also known as Göksu Palace. Built 1857, it was used for hunting and relaxation. Like the Beylerbi Palace, it is open daily except Monday and Thursday, 9 a.m. till 4 p.m. The setting is beautiful. Located on the Üsküdar to Beykoz main road, it can be reached by public transportation, with a bus stop near the Pavilion.

Next, at the narrowest point of the Bosphorus, are two castles which played a key role in the Turkish conquest of Constantinople. Even 60 years before the capture of Istanbul, the Turks controlled the Straits and its maritime traffic to and from the Black Sea. To enforce that control, the Asian-side castle - Anadolu Hisarı - was built by Sultan Beyazit the Thunderbolt in 1395.

Then came the final seige under command of 21-year-old Mehmet the Conqueror. He drew the net tighter by building the Rumeli Hisarı fortress on the European side. Construction was completed in the incredibly short time of 19 weeks, with a work-force of 1000 skilled masons and 2000 labourers. The castle saw no fighting, but certainly played a key strategic role in

choking off aid from the Black Sea, and in undermining Byzantine morale. As military architecture, Rumeli Castle is a gem. Today the inner courtyard is used for open-air theatre, concerts and folklore shows.

Here onwards, it's mostly villages to admire: Kanlıca (locally famed for its yoghurt), Beykoz and Anadolu Kavağı on the Asian side; Yeniköy, Tarabya, Sarıyer and Rumeli Kavağı on the European shore. Past there, the end of the Bosphorus is a closed military zone. Tarabya is the liveliest centre, with a colourful boat harbour, a first-class hotel, dozens of fish restaurants, plentiful evening music, and thronged all summer with Arab families on lengthy holidays from the hotter areas of the Middle East. Certainly worth an evening visit!

Each of the fish restaurants has a barker standing outside, doing his best to haul in customers - mainly in Turkish, but also in German and English. Just by the entrance, a selection of fish is artistically displayed: sea-bass and tuna, crabs, sturgeon, bream, shrimps. You point to the seafood you want, ask how much, and decide. A typical restaurant has 17 varieties on its menu, ranging from grilled anchovies to swordfish. Lobster costs a fortune, but you always get free toothpicks with your bill.

A go-it-alone tourist can easily make a whole-day circuit - boat trip to the end of the Bosphorus, fish lunch, then shared dolmuş taxi from Sarıyer through the Belgrade Forest to the Black Sea beach of Kilyos, and finally back to Istanbul.

Çamlıca Hill

Built on a series of hills, Istanbul has no shortage of superb viewpoints.

Among the best is Çamlıca Hill on the Asian shore, offering a gorgeous view of Istanbul from across the Bosphorus. You can readily spot this hilltop from the European side, by looking for the TV tower which rears up against the skyline.

From Çamlıca you can see right over Old Istanbul to the Sea of Marmara, dotted with moored freighters. Further round are the Princes Islands that seem to be floating in the haze just off-shore. To sit watching the sunset over the minarets of Istanbul is quite unforgettable. Straight down is a magnificent view of the Bosphorus Bridge, looking like a civil engineer's mock-up with traffic pouring back and forth between Europe and Asia.

The hill is also a wonderful bird-watching location during the spring and autumn migrations. Millions of birds know that here is the easiest commuters' route between Europe and Asia and Africa. From mid-September to October 10, huge flocks make the crossing, including many thousands of storks every day. Here's the chance, also, of seeing eagles, buzzards, kites and vultures.

The Çamlıca tourism development opened in 1982, and has become a favourite outing among the local citizens. There are ornamental gardens, woodland walks, and white-marble tea and coffee pavilions furnished in traditional style with brass tray table-tops. Horse carriages - called fayton - are available for rides, like those on the Princes' Islands where motor cars are forbidden.

At weekends, Turkish family groups sit cross-legged around a carpet, for a simple picnic: a domestic scene that has not changed for centuries. Thus they pass a whole afternoon in gossip, tea-drinking and tranquility, while children play amid the trees and bushes.

Many of the half-day coach tours include Çamlıca Hill, for a taste of Asia. On your own, the easiest route is by ferry from Kabataş to Üsküdar, then a taxi.

Üsküdar

What else to visit, along Istanbul's Asian shore?

Üsküdar itself is specially lively around the landing-stage of the ferry from Kabataş. At a Sunday-morning market, farmers arrive in large trucks laden with several tons of produce, and use the lorry tail-gate as a drop-down counter.

Just past that market centre is the Yeni Valide Camii, built by Sultan Ahmet 111 for his mother. The great architect, Sinan, followed a similar size and design to Rüstem Paşa Mosque in old Istanbul, but without that overall covering of tiles which is the great appeal of Rüstem Paşa. For antique hunters, there's a flea market close by.

Along the shoreline promenade, you get more views across to Old Istanbul. Rod fishermen try for the bigger game of the Bosphorus - but not, apparently, with so much success as the amateurs who dangle their lines in the more dingy waters of the Golden Horn at Galata Bridge.

Üsküdar and neighbouring Salacak are suburbs where many people commute to earn their living in Europe; returning each evening to their Asian retreat. Upper-income Turks have a flat on the European side, where they stay in winter. Then they have an Asian summer house, preferably with shady garden, for the warmer months.

63

Walk along the promenade towards the white building offshore, called Leander's Tower, or the Maiden's Tower in Turkish. It comes with a suitable fanciful legend about a maiden who lived there for fear of death by snakebite. However, as Eve found, there is a strong link between fruit and potential disaster. A peddler arrived by boat and sold her a basket of grapes, which regrettably contained a lurking snake. End of maiden. There are several variations of this legend around the Turkish coast. Maidens never learn.

Pleasant cafés and restaurants are strung along this waterfront, more tranquil than on the European side. A glass of tea or a light lunch offers the bonus enjoyment of watching the never-ending passage of maritime traffic.

The Princes Islands

Nine islands in the Sea of Marmara are a favourite haven for Istanbullu's in search of clean air, a beach and a picnic spot among the pine trees. Four of the islands are inhabited, and can be reached within an hour by express ferry to the largest island called Büyükada; or 1½ hours by a slower boat which stops at the smaller islands en route. For visitors to Istanbul, a day or half-day excursion makes a pleasant break from city sightseeing and the smell of exhaust fumes. On the Princes Islands, all motor traffic is banned. Transport is by horse carriage or donkey.

During summer weekends, you can expect the Princes Islands to be very full. Better policy is to choose a weekday, using the 9.30 a.m. express ferry from Kabataş to Büyükada. Alternatively, go to Number 5 Dock at Sirkeci - at the far end from Galata

Bridge, past the railway station itself. Board the ferry at least twenty minutes before departure, unless you prefer to stand. On departure, there's a classic close-up view of the green park areas around Seraglio Point, below the city walls and Topkapı Palace.

The first island stop is called Kınalıada - smallest of the four inhabited islands with wealthy-looking houses and low-profile apartments grouped around the sailing-boat harbour. Next stop is Burgazada, with the dome of a Greek Orthodox church rising behind the waterfront buildings.

The third island is Heybeli, derived from a Turkish word meaning "saddle-bag", based on the shape of the pine-forested hills. Left of the landing stage is the Naval Officers Academy, the frontage covered by an immense mosaic mural with a maritime theme. The Academy was founded in 1773. Beautiful houses reach towards the peak, all with amphitheatre views of the sea.

Most of the organised tour groups go to Büyükada, which means Big Island, with a one-hour horse-and-buggy (fayton) tour, a fish lunch, time for shopping or swimming, and back. It's a good formula, which can be copied by individual travellers either on Heybeli or Büyükada (also known by its former Greek name of Prinkipo). You can cover both options by landing first at Heybeli, continuing to Prinkipo by a later ferry. Don't expect too much of the beaches, which are shingle or pebble, no sand.

On both islands, restaurants and cafés line the waterfront by the landing-stage. It's delightful to sit there with a beer, watching the boat traffic, and looking across the water to the Asian shore. The restaurants have no need

Istanbul
One of the world's greatest buildings,
the 6th century St Sophia with its
mosque minarets added 900 years later.

A professional shoe-shine man takes pride in his gleaming equipment.

Bodrum
The classic view of the harbour
protected by the Crusader Castle
of St Peter.

Pamukkale
The "Cotton Castle" - terraces and
snow-white stalactites of calcium
deposits from hot springs above.

of big signs: the tantalising smell from open grills is publicity enough. Well-fed cats preen themselves, while waiting with total confidence for their share of fish-bones.

There are all kinds of tranquil vignettes. A street sweeper leans on his broom as he discusses purchase of a lottery ticket, while waiting for the odd bit of litter to drop. Children pedal past on their tricycles, with no need of anxious mother to cluck about the traffic. Young couples and family groups stroll along the waterfront.

A typical "big tour" around Heybeli by horse-carriage lasts an hour. A superb panoramic carriageway leads through pinewoods, with an occasional pause at hilltops to give the horses a breather, and to admire the view. It must rate very high among the tourist drives of Europe, with just the jingle of carriage bells to compete with bird-song. To save on street cleaning, every horse is fitted at the rear end with a canvas crap-catcher for the droppings. A very practical arrangement: nosebag at the front, garden fertility at the rear, and one horse-power in between.

An alternative is a donkey-ride through the woods. The donkeys don't take their job too seriously, thinking that a stroll with a passenger aboard is merely an excuse for eating grass and wild flowers along the way. This relaxed view of life is typical of the Princes Islands.

Where Are Beaches?

Nobody goes to Istanbul for a beach holiday. But, within easy reach, a few beach areas are available for anyone who wants a break from sightseeing.

The best-developed beach is at Kilyos on the Black Sea coast, 22 miles from the city centre. Take public transport to Sarıyer and then dolmuş or a slow 151 bus. A vacation village is operated by the Tourism Bank chain, with total of 304 beds, sea-view restaurant and disco. The white sands get very crowded on summer weekends, when it's better to leave all beaches to the Istanbullu's.

Several small patches of sandy beach are also spread along the Bosphorus (which, fast-flowing, is tolerably free of pollution). Go on a weekday afternoon to Sarıyer, and stay for a fish dinner. As an added touch of the exotic, this is the most popular resort for Arab families, but they don't come for the sand.

The Sea of Marmara coastline, close to the industrial zones of Asian and European Istanbul, is less attractive. On the Princes Islands, however - easily reached by ferry - there are several delightful small beaches and lidos.

Another sandy-beach favourite for Istanbul residents - particularly those who live on the Asian side - is Şile on the Black Sea coast, 45 miles by regular bus from Üsküdar bus station. Reckon just over a pound return. Hotel resources are rather limited, but there are plentiful restaurants, guesthouses and pensions. The village has the remains of a Genoese castle, but otherwise not much reminder of a history that goes back to the 7th century BC.

Nightlife and Dining Out

How to spend the evenings in Istanbul? Mostly the choice wraps around some variation on eating and drinking. So let's launch our survey on that theme. The high-rise hotels - the two Etap properties and the Sheraton - have rooftop bars that offer tremendous sunset views. Another good sunset-viewing location is the Galata Tower, where later in the evening they feature a Turkish floor-show with dinner; or with drinks alone from balcony seats above. Reservations are essential for dinner, as most tables during the summer season are advance-booked for tour groups. The food gets a thumbs-down signal from local gourmets.

At the low-life end of the scale, visit one of Istanbul's most colourful beer-drinking haunts: the Çiçek Pasajı halfway along Istiklâl Caddesi at Galatasaray. Around the corner are the lofty gates of the British Consulate (formerly Embassy) which faces a lively fish, flower and vegetable market. Stroll through, and you'll come to this courtyard jammed with tavern tables.

Early evening the Passage is crowded with standing drinkers, who may later sit down for a lengthy meal of Turkish meze and fish. Less crowded tables are usually available inside the tavern restaurants, but the preferred position is outside, for a ringside seat on all the exuberant activity: waiters, peddlers, gipsies, and strolling singers and musicians who render old Turkish folksongs. The customers become part of the entertainment, bursting into maudlin song or an attempt at belly-dancing. Maybe it's too raw and noisy for some tastes, but you can always just walk through, for the experience. Highly recommended are the deep-fried mussels (midye tava), eaten as a passing snack.

On a more sedate note, try the bar or restaurant of Pera Palace Hotel, five minutes away, where a Victorian Orient Express atmosphere is carefully preserved. More inspiring food is served at the Four Seasons

Restaurant at 509 Istiklâl Caddesi, near the Tünel subway terminus. You could easily pass it by, the facade is so discrete, with no flashing signs. The owner's wife, who takes orders, is English; but cuisine is Turkish, French and international. A famous Russian restaurant called Rejans still keeps its old-time emigré decor. The hard-to-find location is near the Çiçek Pasajı described above. Just ask for Rejans, and people will point the way.

All along Istiklâl Caddesi, up to Taksim and in the side streets, are innumerable average-grade restaurants, some with a three-piece group of Turkish stringed instruments and a drum. The seedy appearance of these restaurants is not always inviting, though the food can be good. About the best, with quite moderate prices, is Hacı Baba at number 49, offering classic Turkish cuisine. On a warm evening, there's a delightful terrace out back, overlooking a Greek Orthodox churchyard.

Side streets off Istiklâl Caddesi are filled with tenth-rate night clubs and clip joints. Best policy is to steer clear. If you do venture, first establish the price of each and every item of food or drink, particularly if any friendly ladies are helping you sink a bottle of wine or rakı.

From Taksim Square and along Cumhuriyet Caddesi, the restaurant picture brightens. Here begins the jet-set territory of the big hotels, with dinner-dancing and floor shows at the Etap Marmara, Sheraton and Hilton. Clientele is upper-crust Turkish, not just tourist and expense-account businessmen. Hence the shows are quite often international - such as Filipino dance groups - rather than the folklore and belly-dance that visitors expect. The Divan Hotel restaurant (no floor-show) gets highest rating for its Turkish and French cuisine; and the Pub Divan is likewise popular with local Turks for a faster meal in up-market coffeeshop style.

If you want a change from Turkish menus, this area offers several alternatives. In the side turning just behind the Divan is the Ristorante Italiano; next side turning along is the Swiss, with a well-known Swiss Pub downstairs. China is located at 17 Lâmartin Caddesi (an oddly elusive street to find in the dark, slanting down from Taksim). German and Russian cuisine is the speciality of Fisher, opposite the German consulate at 51 Inönü Caddesi, which curves down the other side of Taksim Square. French nouvelle cuisine is featured at the Orient Express restaurant on the lobby floor of Etap Marmara Hotel. McDonald's is across Taksim Square, at the beginning of Cumhuriyet Caddesi, where competing fast-food outlets enliven the scene at Istanbul's busiest bus-stops. The French type Boulevard Café is good for a light meal.

Several up-market discos and jazz clubs operate in the zone between Divan Hotel and the Hilton. Try Club 33, Hydromel or Regine. In the same area, top of the night clubs is the Kervansaray, which offers the full tourist treatment of dinner and floor show with belly-dancers and Anatolian folklore. Fifty yards away is a cabaret spin-off from the same organisation, with two shows nightly - Les Parisiennes and Crazy Horse. Prices are reasonable for that kind of deal; and probably come cheaper at check-out time than venturing into the dubious joints around Istiklâl Caddesi.

Still in quest of food, nobody should miss spending a leisured evening at one of the Bosphorus fishing villages. The atmosphere is delightful. Many restaurants have music, over-loud if you prefer conversation with your seafood. Other restaurants start quiet, and then suddenly explode into life with the arrival of a tour group who are cajoled into singing and dancing Turkish style. Restaurants at Arnavutköy, Bebek, Tarabya and Sarıyer are so thick on the ground that part of the fun is just strolling along, inspecting the fish on display, and choosing which establishment will have your custom. Take a ferry back to central Istanbul, for a Bosphorus view of the lights.

Gazino

Along the Bosphorus and in other locations are open-air night-spots called Gazinos. They have no connection with gambling. They are a cross between music hall and night club, offering Oriental-style cabaret with a Turkish orchestra and popular singers. Shows continue at least four hours, while you pick your way through a dozen platters of variegated Turkish food, washed down with a bottle of wine or rakı. Worth trying, for one of your spare evenings. You can always leave early, if you get bored.

Belly-Dancers

An old Turkish saying, roughly translated, is that "beauty in a woman is measured by the kilo" - though the younger generation has switched to the Western taste. A well-rounded belly-dancer can arouse great excitement in night-spots with 90% hard-drinking male audiences; or more restrained enthusiasm in respectable establishments where men dine out with their own wives. The best dancers perform in top night clubs and gazinos, where the act is regarded as a folklore art-form somewhat akin to flamenco. The proper (or improper) way of showing appreciation is to stuff banknotes into the dancer's bra or wherever. Response to this titillation depends on the size of the banknote. If it's big enough, she'll probably dance on your table.

Folklore Shows

During the summer season, from the last week of May until the end of September, students at the Eminönü Halk Eğitim Merkezi usually give a 2½-hour folklore performance every evening at their centre in Cağaloğlu - the newspaper district of Istanbul, adjoining the Sultanahmet area. Check first on starting times, which vary from month to month: usually from 7.30 p.m in the light evenings until early August; 7 p.m. for the remainder of August; 6.30 or 6.00 p.m. during September. If this group isn't operating, ask a Tourism Information Office for an alternative show. The wealth of traditional dances reflects Turkey's regional diversity in costume, climate, way of life, legends and wedding rituals.

Most of the tourist-oriented nightspots include Anatolian dances in their floor show. Particular favourites are wooden spoon dances from Silifke on the Mediterranean coast, Elaziğ candle dances from Eastern Turkey, Hora from the Black Sea, sword and shield dances from Bursa.

Folk and classical music likewise offer rich variety of instruments, rhythms and modes - strange to the Western ear, but can be addictive. Traditional folk songs and their updated pop versions are often a cocktail of agony: soulful ditties about young men and village maidens who pine for each other and finally commit suicide.

Sound and Light

A free Sound and Light show outside the Sultan Ahmet Mosque rotates on a 4-day cycle between Turkish versions, English, French and German. The season goes from May through September. Usually the English-language version is presented on 2-6-10-14-18-22-26-30 of each month. Times vary according to month: 9 p.m. from mid-May until the first week of August; earlier hours for the remainder of the season. Check during your daytime sightseeing from a notice board in Sultan Ahmet Square, where the benches are permanently in place. The presentation is by courtesy of the Tourism Bank.

Istanbul Festival

The city's most important cultural event is the Istanbul Festival, which runs every year from mid-June and throughout July. The star-studded programme has international status, with performances from leading European symphony orchestras, chamber groups and soloists. It has become traditional for Mozart's "Abduction from the Seraglio" to be performed in the grounds of Topkapı Palace, which inspired the original work. (The word 'Seraglio' is derived from Turkish 'Sarayı', meaning 'Palace'). Pop and jazz, ballet and dance, Turkish classical music, folk dances, Whirling Dervishes and art exhibitions are all part of this considerable Festival. The principal venue and box office is at the Atatürk Culture Centre in Taksim Square. Other events are held in historic sites such as Rumeli Castle and the church of St. Irene.

Casinos

Live casino gambling in Turkey is limited by law to five-star hotels, with access restricted to foreigners, using hard currency. Only two hotels have taken up the option: Hilton and Etap Marmara. One-arm bandits are open to everyone, including Turks. Around two dozen slot machine halls are spread around the country.

A Day Out From Istanbul

Istanbul is so packed with sightseeing that it seems wasteful to take day trips away, unless you are staying at least a week and yearn for some countryside. However, for the independent traveller, three suggested destinations - Yalova, İznik and Bursa - can each be treated as a long one-day trip, or (much better) combined in a two-day swing. One-day Bursa is promoted by travel agents, but the logistics are against the D.I.Y. tourist: there is so much to see, scattered around Turkey's 5th-largest city. Either buy the package, or stay overnight - hotels are plentiful.

The most pleasurable routing is by express ferry from Istanbul's Kabataş dock to Yalova, giving a two-hour Sea of Marmara cruise via the Princes Islands. For anyone geared to overnight stopovers, consider spending part of the day enjoying the Princes Islands. Then continue by later ferry to Yalova.

At the Yalova landing-stage, connecting buses await for just over a one-hour drive to either İznik or Bursa. To complete the triangle, İznik-Bursa or vice versa is another 90-minute bus journey. Each road sector passes through supremely beautiful countryside - green rolling hills, olive groves, vineyards and fruit trees

everywhere. Anyone pressed for time could use one of the daily 30-minute flights from Istanbul to Bursa. Another higher-speed alternative: check on hydrofoil timings between Kabataş and the Marmara port of Mudanya, which is then only 30 minutes' bus to Bursa.

Yalova

If you want directions or advice, ask at the Tourism Information Office just there at the landing-stage. Turn right, and a pleasant tree-lined promenade leads to a somewhat littered People's Beach, with rowing boats drawn up on the sands. Yalova is a favourite resort for Arab family holidaymakers, and many shop and restaurant signs are in Arabic. Evening time, the promenade is the focal point for local residents and visitors, out for a stroll or a meal.

Yalova has been in tourism business since Roman times, thanks to hot-spring sulphurous mineral waters which gush from a forested hillside 12 kilometres away. It's worth spending an hour or two at the spa. Just ask for "Termal Minibus" in your best Turkish, and a beautiful ride past orchards, market gardens and small farms will cost you maybe 12p.

The main baths are in Byzantine style, reflecting the spa's long history. Take a swimsuit, to sample the large open-air pool fed by waters that originate at 140° F. In the Sultan Banyo you can hire a cubicle for two, and wash away your rheumatism. The 230-bed hotel is modern, opened in 1984, replacing the original Grand Thermal Hotel. Café Çınar is part of the complex, and offers a tranquil tea or snack beneath the spreading branches of an enormous 180-years-old plane tree. The surrounding hills make beautiful walking country, with plentiful marked paths. A substantial summer house was built for Kemal Atatürk in 1929, and is open to visitors.

İznik

Located beside a deep freshwater lake, İznik was settled in prehistoric times and developed in 316 BC by Antigonus the One-Eyed, one of Alexander the Great's generals. Another general took over a few years later, and named the city after his wife, Nikaia. That became Nicaea under the Romans, who renewed the present-day city walls and gates.

The town became famous in church history as the meeting-place of the First Ecumenical Council - the Council of Nicaea - which laid down in 325 AD the first universally agreed doctrine of Christianity, the Nicene Creed. The meeting was convened by Constantine the Great, who was not a Christian at the time, just a good friend trying to be helpful. Among the 300 participants was the Bishop of Myra who later became St. Nicholas, better known to future generations as Santa Claus.

During Byzantine times, particularly in 5th century under the reign of Justinian, the city continued to prosper. Then came a period from 1078 as a capital of the Seljuk Turks, until Crusaders restored Nicaea to the Byzantines in 1097, when a new revival began. Finally the Ottoman emperors captured the city in 1331, and changed its name to İznik.

During late 14th century, a porcelain industry was established and grew rapidly thanks to constant demand for ceramics to decorate mosques, palaces and other buildings. A glaze technique was introduced, to brighten up the colours: blue, green, red and black. Then, in 1514, Sultan Selim the Grim transplanted Persian ceramic craftsmen from Tabriz to İznik, to upgrade the industry still further. Architects for prestigious construction jobs would automatically specify İznik tiles - Rüstem Paşa Mosque in Istanbul is a prime example.

All that history is the background for present-day İznik. When the great wave of Ottoman building subsided, tile-painting went into decline, and techniques were forgotten. İznik has slumbered since then: a pleasant small town that is market centre for a prosperous and beautiful fruit-growing area.

The basic Hellenistic city-grid street layout is unchanged from two thousand years ago. Likewise, most of the historical monuments have survived: Roman gates; remains of a Byzantine aqueduct; the 6th-century basilica of St. Sophia, much altered over the years by Seljuks and Ottomans; a turquoise-tiled Green Mosque, and an adjoining 14th-century Soup Kitchen and Dervish Hospice now used as a museum which is strong on ceramics.

Close by is the Tourism Office at 168 Kılıçaslan Street - named in honour of the Seljuk ruler called Lion of the Sword, who murdered his father-in-law at a banquet. If you are staying the night, several motels and fish restaurants are located on the lake shore, which is the best place for viewing the sunset. Tourism has helped revive the tile-making craft, and good reproductions are available at reasonable price.

Bursa

Information Bureau (Turizm Danışma Büro) - Atatürk Caddesi 82 - near Ulu Mosque. Tel: 12359.

Bursa is Turkey's most pleasant industrial city. It spreads with 1.5

million inhabitants along the foothills of an 8300-ft mountain called Uludağ. Bursa's colour code is green: trees everywhere, hillside views across to open countryside, and even its most famous mosque and mausoleum with walls of green - the favourite colour of the Prophet.

In 1326 Bursa became the first capital of the Ottoman dynasty. A desert people, these early Turks loved the sound of rippling water, and used the snow-fed streams of the Uludağ mountain to grace the town with some two hundred fountains. As a thriving spa town with hot springs, Bursa already had a long history as a thermal resort, with baths established by Justinian in 6th century AD.

Transport to the tourist highlights of Bursa is quite easy by dolmuş. The arrival bus depot is called GARAJ. To reach the town centre, board a dolmuş with the destination board of HEYKEL. Everything radiates from Heykel, the Piccadilly Circus of Bursa. Heykel means Statue, which inevitably is Kemal Atatürk on a horse.

If you want to go up the Uludağ mountain, get a connecting dolmuş labelled TELEFERIK. The spa suburb is ÇEKIRGE. For the renowned Green Mosque, find a dolmus called EMIR SULTAN, and request a stop at Yeşil Cami.

Along Atatürk Caddesi, the main street that runs from Heykel, is a huge mosque called Ulu Cami - a superb building from 1399, with a roof comprising twenty domes. Most unusual, the ablutions fountain is placed within the prayer hall itself, instead of in a courtyard outside.

Next to Ulu Cami is a pleasant public area of fountains and park benches. The long, elegant building is Koza Han - centre of Bursa's traditional silk bazaar - dating from 1490 but reconstructed. It's worth strolling through, whether you wish to buy silk cloth or not: just to get an idea of Bursa's most important traditional industry. Every shop accepts Visa.

The adjoining Covered Bazaar has been rebuilt since a big fire in 1958, and much of the fun went with it. Street markets outside have a more lively atmosphere. But it's still worth exploring the various Hans - mostly of 15th-century origin. They make good settings for a restful glass of tea.

Bursa's greatest sightseeing highlights are its Ottoman mosques and tombs. Of these, the supreme treasures are the Green Mosque (Yeşil Cami) and the neighbouring Green Mausoleum (Yeşil Türbe). Completed in 1419, the Green Mosque is renowned for its 15th-century six-sided tiles and exquisite 17th-century square tiles with a carnation and tulip motif - all made in İznik, 50 miles away.

The magnificent Green Tomb across the road dates from 1421. The mausoleum was built for Sultan Mehmet Çelebi, which means Gentleman, who regained power after a long civil war with his brothers. (Succession to the throne was not automatically to the first-born son. Civil war or fracticide was a means of settling the problem.) A notice at the entrance says: "It was the noblest tomb the dynasty had yet achieved." Look particularly at the superbly carved walnut door.

Next to the mosque is a pleasant terrace café where you can enjoy a good view over Bursa, while sipping tea or elma çay (apple tea). Close by is the Turkish Islamic Art Museum, a former medrese - Moslem theological college - founded in 1414. Many renowned scholars were educated here. The museum courtyard is charming: a central fountain, beds of flowers, and tables and chairs in the shade of overhanging trees. Birds twitter, and all is peace, undisturbed by traffic roaring along the main street outside.

For non-Moslems, the museum's most unusual exhibit is the display of a Circumcision Room: the instruments used; and a specially decorated bedroom for the boy - usually between 7 and 10 years old - where he could rest and welcome his friends and relatives. The lad wears a red fez, heavily decorated with stars and spangles.

Also exhibited are early ceramics from İznik, regional costumes, and a room devoted to characters from the Karagöz shadow play, which local people claim to be of Bursa origin.

Elsewhere, in the Çekirge district of Bursa, is a lively memorial to Hacivat and Karagöz - two incorrigible jokers who were executed by Sultan Orhan for distracting fellow building workers with their incessant patter and repartee. Afterwards, the Sultan was struck by remorse. To console him, a shadow play was devised, in which the two clowns resumed their dialogue. Ever since, Karagöz shadow plays have flourished as a popular folk entertainment, a Turkish Punch and Judy.

Çekirge is the hot-spring suburb of Bursa, located on hill slopes that lead up to Uludağ in the background. Spa hotels in all price ranges are strung along the main highway. The peaceful atmosphere is remarkable for a thriving industrial city specializing in car and textile manufacture, silks and Turkish towels.

Many of the spa hotels and guest-houses include a mineral bath in the tariff. Look for the sign saying Çelik Banyo, which indicates that the establishment has its own mineral spring facilities. Hot taps in individual bathrooms are often supplied by the mountain, using waters that gush out steaming. Some hotels even run central heating from the same source. Most of the older hotels have been modernised in recent years. Similarly, restoration work has been progressing on the Eski Kaplıça Bath, established 1400 years ago by Justinian the Great and claimed as the oldest bath in the world to be in continuous use.

Leading hotel is the Çelik Palace, modernized in 1983, where temperature of the mineral spring water is 117° F. A Roman style marble pool has all ancillary facilities alongside: solarium, sauna, fitness room, ping pong. After a swim, a pool attendant can give a firm-handed massage. In a matter of minutes, knotted nerves and muscles are soothed away.

Uludağ

The easiest route up Bursa's mountain is by dolmuş from Heykel to the cable-car station called Teleferik. From there, the cable-car brings you to the Uludağ National Park. The forested hillsides show no sign of Europe's devastation from acid rain. Every tree is green. Wintertime, it's like a corner of Austria, with Uludağ rated as Turkey's leading ski resort. Even in mid-June, patches of snow still remain on the higher slopes.

During summer, tables and chairs are spread among the trees, so that outdoor restaurants look like garden picnic areas. Most of them offer "et mangal" - cook-it-yourself barbecued meat, with tempting aromas wafting along the mountainside. If you're not hungry, at least try a bright red toffee apple.

Edirne

A trip from Istanbul to Edirne - provincial capital of European Turkey - is just about feasible in one long day. The road journey is 150 miles along the very busy E5 highway. Reckon four hours by bus, much slower by train. There are frequent departures from the long-distance bus terminal at Topkapı Otogar - the city gate, not the Palace! The route passes through miles of sunflower country, gorgeous when in full bloom. Otherwise, the flat scenery is not wildly exciting.

Edirne is a frontier town, close to the Bulgarian and Greek borders. Founded 125 AD on the banks of the Maritza River by Roman Emperor Hadrian, the city was named after him as Hadrianopolis, which foreigners cut to Adrianople. Captured by the Ottoman Turks in 1362, the city was renamed as Edirne and became the Turkish capital until the capture of Constantinople in 1453. Thanks to that high status, Edirne is liberally endowed with some of Turkey's finest monuments: baths, mosques, caravanserais, bridges and fountains.

Today the city is dominated by the Selimiye Mosque, rated as architect Sinan's greatest masterpiece. Completed in 1575, when the architect was 84 years old, the Mosque is fitted with a triumphant dome that rivals that of St. Sophia in Istanbul. The spacious interior is lit by precisely 999 windows. Four slender minarets complete a perfect picture.

Quite apart from the rich sightseeing, Edirne has a colourful old town section in the original grid-plan district formerly surrounded by Byzantine city walls. A curiosity of Edirne is that an estimated 30% of the population is of gipsy stock. They add their individual sparkle to the scene, every day a carnival.

Even more of a carnival atmosphere prevails every year during a week devoted to the Kırkpınar Greased Wrestling Festival. The joker is that the huge wrestlers are smeared in olive oil, and heave and grunt away to the incessant beat of drums and the excitement of wind instruments. Sometimes twenty wrestlers are fighting simultaneously. Contests continue until a wrestler accepts defeat, or is counted out "while his belly sees the sun." The event - one of the most popular folk festivals in Turkey - has continued virtually every year since 1361. There's all the atmosphere of a country fair, with plentiful sideshows, folk-dance performances, open-air eating, buying and selling.

Check the Festival dates from a Tourist Information Office. Theoretically it runs June 30 to July 6, but dates can change. If you're in Istanbul at the time, a one-day trip to Edirne would be an unforgettable experience.

Chapter Four
The Aegean Coast

Turkey's Aegean coast comprises the entire western shoreline of Anatolia, facing most of the Greek islands. Geographically the region runs from the Dardanelles in the north, down to the tip of the Datça peninsula where officially the Aegean Sea meets the Mediterranean. However, in the world of tourism, the Aegean area is often stretched round to include Marmaris and Fethiye.

This entire region captures the bulk of holiday traffic to Turkey, outside of Istanbul. Including major resorts like Bodrum and Kuşadası, the Aegean coast features a good range of developed beaches, with the bonus of great scenic beauty far removed from industrial pollution.

The region is particularly rich in historic interest: 5000 years that started in mythology, and then developed into the classic civilization of the Greeks. As reminder of that age, numerous Greek and Roman sites have been excavated, with reconstructions that can give great pleasure even to the layman. In more modern times, history of the area has come closer to Britain, Australia and New Zealand, with memories of the World War 1 battles at Gallipoli which aimed at gaining control of the strategic Straits of Dardanelles.

Close by is Troy, legendary site of the Trojan Wars which most likely were fought for similar strategic reasons, rather than for the love of Helen of Troy.

Today, the tourism focal point of the Aegean coast is Izmir, Turkey's third largest city, and second port after Istanbul. Izmir airport is the main arrival point for holidaymakers on package tours, either by charter flights, direct scheduled services, or on a connection from Istanbul.

At the airport, coaches await to transfer beach holidaymakers to their chosen resorts. Several holiday resorts are easily reached from Izmir, including the Club Med beach village at Foça to the northwest; Çeşme due west; Kuşadası; and Bodrum much further to the south. Clients on a self-drive package can pick up their cars at the airport or at their overnight hotel. Likewise, many coach tours around Turkey have Izmir as the starting point.

Izmir is an ideal excursion centre for archaeology enthusiasts. Around twenty sites are within day-trip range, including the Seven Churches of Revelation.

Ephesus - 46 miles from Izmir, but only 7 miles from Kuşadası - ranks as the most important site of biblical and tourist interest for a one-day trip, while the dedicated archaeologist could keep plodding around indefinitely. Thirty miles south from Kuşadası are several more major classical sites: Priene, Miletus and Didyma. On a lightning-tour basis, a whole-day excursion from Izmir can include these sites, as an extension to Ephesus. But, like most sightseeing, slowing down the pace is much more rewarding.

East of Izmir is Sardis, where rich King Croesus minted money. North is Pergamum - medical centre of the ancient world.

Of course there's much more scenic and general interest to this region than just the classical sites. The Aegean coastal region includes some of Turkey's most fertile agricultural areas, where prosperous peasant farmers produce grapes, tobacco, cotton, figs, apricots, nuts and honey. Each crop contributes to the variety and beauty of the landscape. Especially in late summer, there is great pleasure in watching the traditional harvest scenes, with every form of transport pressed into service. Regrettably for shutterbugs, however, camels have been phased out.

The Aegean Beach Resorts

Çeşme

Information Bureau (Turizm Danışma Büro) - Iskele Meydanı 6 - at the port landing-stage. Tel: 6653. 84 kms Izmir to Çeşme, about 90 minutes' drive.

The road due west from Izmir to the resort of Çeşme fringes the coastline of a peninsula that juts 50 miles into the Aegean Sea. Just past the outskirts of Izmir, a major Army base is backed by hills covered in green scrub. Occasional shingle beaches are faced with a ribbon development of cafés and modest restaurants, a few small hotels and campsites. Typical is Güzelbahçe, with a small harbour, and a narrow pebble beach alongside. It's a typical working fishing village before tourism takes over: a good stopping-point where self-caterers can buy fresh fish. But most travellers whirl past, bound for the broad sands of the Çeşme area.

Çeşme itself is a small resort nestling below bare limestone rocks. The village centre revolves around a diminutive port, a Genoese castle, and a caravanserai which has been given new life as an elegant 32-room hotel. One main tourist shopping street and a wide waterfront promenade lined with pleasant cafés and restaurants complete the picture. The harbour is scheduled for later development as a holiday marina. Meanwhile, yachtsmen can enjoy the excellent harbour facilities of the Altın Yunus (Golden Dolphin) complex. From the port, ferries operate daily during summer to the Greek island of Chios. Day excursions are available aboard the Ertürk 11 ferryboat whenever they schedule a morning departure - depart 9.30, return 19.30.

Çeşme village is short of beaches, except for a strip of sand just past a little pleasure harbour. Instead, the resort can be regarded as a transport focalpoint to reach a selection of charming bays with patches of sand. The prime beach is at Ilıca, virtually a resort in itself, a five-minute cab-ride away.

Çeşme's splendid 14th-century Genoese castle is open 9 till 1, and 2 till 6, and is certainly worth the modest entrance fee. In excellent condition, the castle was restored and enlarged by the Ottomans in the 16th century. A mini-museum is devoted to mini-finds from Erythrai: nothing over 6 inches high. These finds date from the Hellenistic period of 4th century BC, and later finds from Roman times through till AD 395. Par for the course is ten minutes round the one-room collection. Elsewhere in the fortress is an Ottoman Arms Museum.

An annual pop-song contest is held in the castle courtyard at the end of June, beginning of July, with participants from some 20 countries: a

75

Turkish type of Eurovision Song Contest. That coincides with the Çeşme Sea Festival, when national and international folklore groups throng the streets in colourful costume. A good time for a festive atmosphere, but check dates! Adjoining the castle is a beautiful exercise in reconstruction: the ancient caravanserai which was converted in 1986 into a hotel called Çeşme Kervansaray, operated by the Golden Dolphin holiday resort. The original building dates from AD 1528, in the reign of Süleyman the Magnificent. Dining in the courtyard is a delightful experience in itself. In high season, they give a twice weekly Turkish folk show including belly-dancing. Other hotels put on similar shows.

Çeşme doubles as a spa resort. At the wide and sandy mile-long beach of Ilıca, hot springs bubble direct into the sea, just offshore. Dominating the end of the bay is one of Turkey's most ambitious developments - the completely self-contained Golden Dolphin holiday village.

The 508-room complex is a semi-circle of three first-class hotels - Dolphin, Mermaid and Marina - overlooking a well-designed Marina of international calibre. The basic architecture is of whitewashed concrete, like a long and low-profile wedding cake. Sugar-cube apartments are neatly stacked along three or four terraces. Each apartment has its individual sun balcony, overlooking the "village" of restaurants, cafés, pool, shops and supermarket. Craft moored in the marina are elegant yachts, catamarans and gulets.

The complex includes all the usual sport and entertainment facilities required by holidaymakers. The Golden Dolphin puts major accent on sport, with facilities for all the water-sports, horse-riding, tennis, cycling and winter boar-hunting. Utilising the natural thermal waters, a Fitness Centre includes indoor and outdoor thermal pools, steam bath, sauna and solarium. For evening exercise, a Casino is equipped with the Las Vegas style of one-arm bandits. During summer there's a popular moonlight cruise with wine, music and bellydancer.

The Çeşme area is not so good for yachting in comparison with the Marmaris and Bodrum regions. But it's worth taking a one-day cruise, to visit the little beaches that are scattered around the peninsula.

A typical boat trip visits a tiny yachting centre called Dalyanköy. Total peace prevails, far removed from the world of organised tourism. The waters are totally unpolluted, emerald-green, with a sandy bottom.

Another charming stop is at Ayayorgi - nothing but a little bay, minute stretches of sand, and a few modest open-air restaurants. Simplicity is the keynote. Residents at Hotel Ertan in Çeşme get free minibus transport to the beach.

Altogether there are now 2500 touristic (i.e. graded hotel) beds in the Çeşme area; plus double that number in pensions and motels. Longer-stay visitors have wide choice of villas and apartments, mostly in uniform block developments which still need time to mellow. Along the main waterfront of Ilıca small hotels, cafés and restaurants are lively with evening music.

At the up-market Turban hotel, catering for international visitors, the wide beach is superb: fine white sands, water shallow enough for children, and thatched umbrellas to shelter sunbathers from the sun. Topless is acceptable. The public beach on either side, frequented by Turkish families, is of comparable quality. Only the beach umbrellas and sun-loungers are missing, but not bikini tops.

Ilıca started in business as a hot-spring resort, which is certainly what pulled in the Romans. To find the curiosity of hot water bubbling into the sea, walk to the end of the furthermost breakwater which shelters Ilıca's harbour. Near the tip, there are usually several Turkish bathers' reclining blissfully in rock pools. Every few moments, bubbles sparkle up from between the rocks, and the water is temperature of a hot bath. Surrounding rocks are coloured red, ochre and green, in contrast to neighbouring grey. Even mid-winter there are off-shore patches where bathers can swim without getting goose-pimples. Just behind the main street of Ilıca are two stone-built tanks where more mineral water bubbles constantly into an extremely hot pool.

The principal public beach at Ilıca stretches from the little port, right along to Grand Turban Hotel; and then still further beyond. There the beach is even wider, with white powdery sand. That section is backed by low-profile and well-matured villa developments which do not offend the eye - which is more than can be said for other developments around that stretch of coastline.

A few miles further along, at Şifne, is another location where a mineral spring warms up the sea, just off-shore. The main hotel at Şifne has only a tiny sandy beach for children, but there is pleasant swimming in sparkling waters.

Because of its location at the tip of a peninsula, Çeşme is not a good centre for exploring the classical sites of the Aegean coast. To visit Pergamum, Ephesus or Aphrodisias, there's a 100-mile round trip to and from Izmir before you are really launched. However, local travel agencies operate whole-day tours throughout the season, though the mileage is obviously uncomfortable in the summer heat.

An alternative is to visit two classic sites located on the peninsula within easy reach of Çeşme. Erythrai and Teos are two of the dozen cities which formed the Ionian League in 9th century BC. They are lesser known 2nd-Division sites, but have great charm in their beautiful natural settings. Some local agencies offer excursions. Otherwise it's worth hiring a car for the day. At both sites one can capture something of the simple innocence of amateur archaeology, before the ancient cities became part of travel business.

Fifteen miles from Çeşme is Erythrai, which has been partially excavated since 1966. It occupies a beautiful hillside with panoramic views of four small off-shore islands, looking like a family of hippos - which is precisely what the ancient Greeks called them. In classic times, Erythrai was a thriving town of 30,000 people. Archaeologists hope to uncover much more of that city, at present mostly buried beneath fields of wheat, aniseed and artichokes.

In today's village of 70 houses - 350 inhabitants - many of the houses and barns are built from the original Greek remains: bits of stone-carved fountains, pediments, blocks of marble. Columns are used as corner-stones, or are cemented into garden walls. The agora, former heart of the ancient city, is a wheat field. Close by they are growing melons and beans, or maize for the cattle. In the most populous part of the original town, a goat is tethered to a Greek column in the shade of a fig tree, grazing in a nanny-goat's paradise.

In another direction are rolling hills, where partial digs have uncovered ancient Greek and Roman houses in a natural rock garden of aromatic plants, herbs and shrubs. A Roman villa reveals part of a mosaic floor which still awaits expert attention. One wonders what glories are buried in this entire city, which formerly was enclosed by three miles of city walls.

A semi-circular hillside, partly excavated, is the setting for an ancient theatre which formerly could seat 10,000. Costly work remains to be done. But already the majesty of the site shows through the overgrowth of shrubs and wild flowers. The whole area is a naturalist's dream, with great variety of plants and wildlife. Every field is brilliant with poppies, self-seeded from the time when poppies were a major cash crop.

A similar experience awaits at Teos - another prosperous city which formerly housed up to 30,000 inhabitants. Teos was founded around 900 BC and flourished during the same period as Ephesus, Miletus, Samos and Erythrai.

Access is easy: turn off at Güzelbahçe for the 12 miles to Seferihisar, and then another five miles to Teos through groves of oranges and mandarins. Near the site, picnic tables are set out in the shade of pine trees.

All that has been uncovered is a Temple of Dionysus, a theatre, an odeon and several streets. Broken columns and massive stoneworks are scattered around the site, interspersed with olive trees. Wild flowers and insect life alone would keep any naturalist happy. Birds sing, and there is total peace, with no other tourist in sight or earshot. Solitary visitors can enjoy feeling like pioneers who have "discovered" a treasure from the past. There are no entrance fees, no watchmen, no guides, no postcard salesmen or soft-drink vendors. Just walk in, stroll around, and go, silently. A lovely spot.

Close by are superb beaches. In that area of the southern shore of the peninsular are some 17 miles of fine-sand beaches, still only in early stages of development. A few holiday settlements, camp-sites, cafés and restaurants have been established. Otherwise, all is tranquility. The nearest village is Sığacık, entirely located within its original fortress walls which were rebuilt in 16th century by courtesy of Sultan Süleyman the Magnificent.

Kuşadası

TRAVEL: from Izmir, 2 hours by bus Information Bureau (Turizm Danışma Büro) - İskele Meydanı - by the port Customs Office at the landing-stage. Tel: 1103.

Kuşadası means 'Bird Island' but it's really a charming seaside town, sixty miles from Izmir. The original impetus for its tourist growth came from proximity to Ephesus and other classical sites. Thirty years ago, when the road from Izmir was a bumpy ordeal and further south was a hellish ride in a cloud of dust, the little harbour of Kuşadası solved a logistical problem: how to transport luxury-loving cruise passengers to those classical sites with minimum discomfort. The answer - pioneered by

Swan Hellenic Cruises - was to make special arrangements for passport control at this tiny fishing village.

Since then, Kuşadası has become one of Turkey's major ports of entry. Tourist arrival numbers are greatly swollen during the seven-month season with the daily arrival of between two and six cruise ships. Passengers stream ashore for their one-day exposure to Ephesus.

The standard cruise-ship programme is to arrive early morning, disembark into waiting coaches immediately after breakfast, do Ephesus before the midday sun makes everyone droop, then back to town with time for shopping. Sometimes, for dedicated culture-vultures, there's the option of a fast half-day swing to Priene, Miletus and Didyma.

But it's the shopping potential which made eyes glitter. All those hundreds of people coming ashore, eager to make best possible shopping use of their few hours in Turkey, so famed for low prices . . . Seeing a great opportunity, merchants have opened carpet shops by the dozen; leather and suede boutiques; jewelry stores; every type of sales outlet for luxury goods and giftware. The bazaar area by the landing-stage has become one of Turkey's leading shopping precincts, with an international turnover that can make shopkeepers in Istanbul's Covered Market envious. Prices are geared to well-heeled customers who have no time for comparison shopping or for the bargaining ritual. Fortunes have been made.

Other transformations have come to this simple fishing village.

There is now a superb marina at Kuşadası, used by a very international collection of yachts from all over Europe, particularly Germany, Britain and France. The Marina is quite unpolluted, teeming with small fish in the clear waters. Yacht owners winter their craft here, because of Kuşadası's sheltered weather conditions. Prices for all Marina services are claimed to be much lower than those of competing marinas in neighbouring countries like Cyprus, Greece and Yugoslavia.

In recent years, the marina has blossomed. The former bare concrete has matured with flower beds, shops, café and restaurant, sport arrangements like tennis, evening entertainment, swimming pool, and all necessary facilities for servicing and wintering boats. There is room for 600 yachts, but the capacity is filled most of the time. An extension will increase berths to 750.

Every night they have entertainment at the swimming pool and restaurant with pianist. Often there are special programmes of dance music, folk show with belly dance, fixed meal and a bottle of wine at remarkably low cost. Facing the Marina is a long line of restaurants and cafés, all ready to slake the thirst and hunger of yachtsmen from those 600 vessels. There are numerous discos. Pigeon Island - reached by a causeway - is particularly lively at night, and the birds just don't get any sleep.

History, archaeology and tourism come together at the Öküz Mehmet Paşa Kervansarayı in the centre of town: a restored Ottoman caravanserai which has partly reverted to its original concept with luxury stores around the courtyard, a restaurant in the centre and hotel rooms upstairs, but no parking for camels. The atmosphere is delightful. Stroll in, look around, and possibly have a drink at the Barbaros Bar. Restaurant prices are higher than elsewhere in town.

Today's holidaymakers demand sand, but there's no beach in the centre of Kuşadası itself. Along the main Kordon Promenade, stretching to the Marina, is a made-up area of sand for children and sun-bathers. The principal public beach is about two miles from the harbour area: a stretch of gently sloping sand called Kadınlar Denizi - "Ladies Beach". Years ago, the beach was reserved for women only, but is now completely co-educational. It is very crowded in high season. Otherwise, most of the beaches are operated by outlying hotels or holiday villages, easily reached by bus or dolmuş.

Tusan Hotel and BP Mokamp are located about four miles from the centre, along the road to Ephesus. Several other prime developments are about four miles in the other direction. Top of the market is Club Méditerranée, which has the two best sandy beaches in the area. Quite apart from the food, wine, pretty girls and entertainment, Club Med is paradise for sportsmen and body-builders. Among the facilities on offer are archery, windsurfing, volley-ball, tennis, muscle-building, jogging, bridge, scrabble, aerobics and midnight ping-pong.

Further round the bay is the Club Diana, with about 400 chalets that cater principally for Turkish guests; and another 150 double bedrooms of higher grade for international visitors. Occupying a lengthy stretch of sand, the Club is open to non-residents who buy about £4 of beads at the entrance, for spending on food and drinks with

no refunds. The aim is to prevent overcrowding of the beach facilities. It's worth trying, for anyone staying in a pension in central Kuşadası.

But the main object of choosing Kuşadası is to take full advantage of the sightseeing potential. No other resort is so well located for reaching the classic highspots of the Aegean coast, and inland to Aphrodisias and Pamukkale. Guided or do-it-yourself, there is wide choice of organised tours or public transport. Renting a car is ideal, with good roads and light traffic through gorgeous scenery. The bad old days of bouncing along on washboard corrugations are over - at least on the main highways. Worth visiting is the Dilek National Park, a haven for some of Turkey's rarer mammals including wild horses and the Anatolian Cheetah. Finally, you can always pop across to the Greek island of Samos for a day or two.

Altınkum

About five kilometres from the Apollo Temple at Didyma is an up-and-coming resort called Altınkum, which means "Golden Sand". The beach must rate 10 out of 10. It is very wide, with broad golden sands, and paddling depth for children for at least a hundred yards out to the safety line. Further offshore, the water level suddenly goes deeper, and is used for water sports. In the centre of the beach, Turkish families predominate, sheltering from the sun beneath hired umbrellas. The verdict: a wonderful beach; the centre is rather crowded; in the restaurants you share your meal with hungry flies; the resort is still being built. Otherwise, top marks for the sand. A few hours on the beach of Altınkum is often included on coach tours to the classical-site trio of Priene, Miletus and Didyma.

To stay at Altınkum for an entire holiday fortnight may be fine for the bucket-and-spade clientele. However, for those who want something more than a sandy beach, this resort is right at the end of the transport line, with very limited entertainment.

Bodrum

Information Bureau (Turizm Danışma Büro) - 12 Eylül Meydanı - on main harbour square, by the Castle wall. Tel: 1091

TRAVEL - 4 hours from Izmir by bus; or 165 kms from Dalaman airport - 3 hours' bus

SITES to visit: Didyma/Miletus/Priene two hours north; Ephesus 220 kms; Knidos - day trip by boat

Bodrum today is Turkey's liveliest holiday resort. Yet Bodrum town itself is just a shallow piedish around two small bays, with no building allowed more than two storeys high. The winter population of 15,000 jumps to 25,000 in summer, but that doesn't make it another Torremolinos.

What the travel-agency brochures promote as Bodrum is really the entire Bodrum Peninsula, which juts out westwards towards the Greek island of Kos (only 3 kms away at the nearest point). Officially, Bodrum includes that whole area - a 250-square-mile department in the province of Muğla. Located on the southern neck of the Peninsula, Bodrum town is the focal-point and market centre for a dozen satellite beaches and fishing villages which take the accommodation overspill, and which are zoned for expansion. That is certainly enough space for holidaymakers to spread out without getting that Torremolinos feeling.

Because of the local ban on high-rise development, accommodation in

Bodrum town is in very charming pensions, villas, self-catering apartments and quite small hotels: all right there in the heart of the nightlife action, or stepped up the hillside with sea views.

The fulcrum point of Bodrum town is the Castle of St. Peter, built on the isthmus that separates the two semi-circular bays. The fortress faces the sea on three sides. The west bay is the ancient harbour from 2500 years ago, with a modern marina packed with elegant yachts. A wide concrete promenade is lined with open-air cafés and a mosque, faced by ship chandlers and yacht brokers.

A little further round, westwards, is Bardakcı, which means water-seller, mythical site of the Fountain of Salmacis. According to legend, the son of Hermes and Aphrodite fell in love with Salmacis. Bathing in her stream, he became "neither man nor woman, being something of both" - a hermaphrodite. Grief-stricken, he begged his parents to cast a spell over the waters, whereby every man who bathed there would lose his male vigour. To console him, they granted his prayer. The legend is hardly the means of promoting a 20th-century tourist beach, but Bodrum caters for all life-styles.

In the other direction, along the east bay was a former Greek enclave of cubical houses, with their appearance protected by a preservation order. By municipal decree, owners may paint their buildings any colour they like so long as it's white. Brilliant flowers drip from every balcony.

The charm does not extend to the town beach, which is grotty, and the murky water not for swimming. Instead, for daytime beaches, swimming and watersports, there is

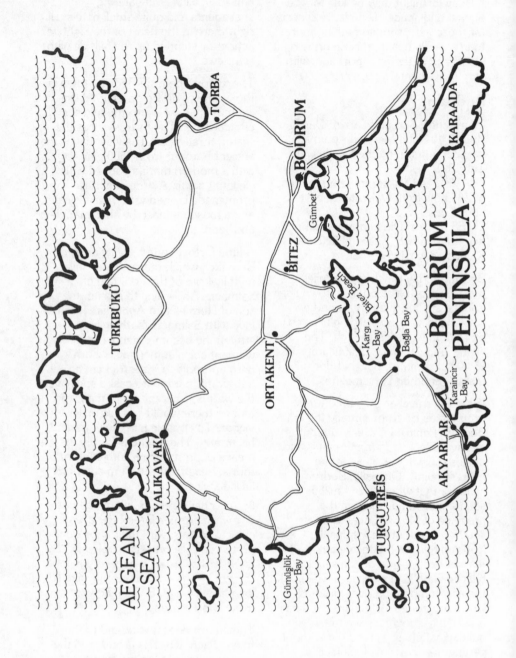

plentiful choice of boat rides or shuttle-service dolmuş jeeps and mini-buses to supremely beautiful coves around the Peninsula.

Clockwise around the coastline, Gümbet is 3 kms from central Bodrum; Bitez 8 kms; Ortakent beach 10 kms; Turgutreis and Gümüşlük facing due west 20 kms; Türkbükü on the northern shore 18 kms; popular Torba 9 kms away across the Peninsula neck; and Güvercinlik, further along the northern coast, on the main highway out from the pensinsula, 20 kms from Bodrum.

Nobody staying in these outlying villages need feel cut off from the pleasures of Bodrum town. Just like anywhere else in Turkey, dolmuş transport prices are unbelievably cheap. Holidaymakers can pop in and out of Bodrum with no financial pain, enjoying the scenery as compensation for being the stuffing in a jeep: ten minutes from Gümbet or half an hour from the more distant villages. All road transport centres on the bus station, a five-minute walk from Bodrum waterfront.

Originally called Halicarnassus, Bodrum is famed for the travel-poster view of its harbour and Crusader Castle of St. Peter. The fortress was built 15th century by the Knights of Rhodes on the site of ancient fortifications already restored by the Seljuk Turks.

Building materials came principally from the enormous Tomb of King Mausolus. His name lives on, into the English language. The Mausoleum was one of the Seven Wonders of the ancient world, high as a 20-storey building, with a base that measured 400 feet square. Construction of the gigantic tomb began during the lifetime of Mausolus himself, mid-4th century BC, and the work was continued by his widow, Queen Artemisia, who was also his elder sister. Today, that site is just a very large hole in the ground, with a museum alongside. Statues of Mausolus and his sister-wife Artemisia, varied reliefs, and remnants of the four-horse chariot which topped the monument, were hijacked to the British Museum in 1846.

On a hillside close by - adjoining the main road around the peninsula - stands a well-preserved 10,000-capacity theatre which is still used today for festivals. The theatre was another project of King Mausolus, who specialized in major public works, financed by heavy taxation and even a special levy on those who wore long hair.

You can hardly blame the Knights for using the Mausoleum as a stone quarry. When they started re-fortifying an existing castle in 1402 AD, the memorial had long since been wrecked by earthquake. An estimated 160,000 rectangular stone blocks - three feet square, one foot deep - had been used in erecting the Mausoleum. The Knights - or, rather, the hired help - merely had to wheel the ready-cut blocks downhill.

Building the Castle was an international exercise - English, French, German, Italian - with a separate tower named for each nation, plus a fifth tower called Snake. Today the Castle has tourist appeal on three levels: as a splendidly-preserved Crusader stronghold, using state-of-the-art 15th-century military technology; for its inner-courtyard collection of plants and trees of classical or mythological significance; and particularly for its Underwater Museum of Archaeology, which attracts nautical archaeologists from around the world. During the Bodrum Art and Culture Festival every September, the northern moat doubles as a theatre.

The museum garden is unique in its concept, collecting together the regional trees and plants which relate to ancient times. The central plane tree was a symbol of kingship. The olive trees are evocative of that most Greek of all trees. Peacocks strut amid the oleanders, the sacred shrub from ancient times. There is myrtle and mandrake, pomegranate and mulberry.

Similar creative imagination has gone into the underwater archaeology displays.

Most of the Castle buildings are devoted to finds from seven shipwrecks that have been scientifically excavated along the south Turkish coast. Each wreck dates from a different age, to give a good cross-section from Bronze Age through to Byzantine, with all the artifacts appropriate to each century.

The oldest ship went down at the end of the Late Bronze Age, about 1200 BC. Copper ingots weighing 25 kgs each are stacked precisely as found by the divers. A more modern trading vessel sank about AD 1025, while carrying a mixed cargo of Byzantine amphorae, and broken Islamic glass destined for re-melting. It was excavated between 1977 and 1979. Coins, seals, pottery and food particles all offer rich scope for scientific study.

The English Tower has been renovated in original style, with flags and pennants in the majestic banqueting hall. On special occasions, wine is served by waiters in medieval costume, with appropriate background music.

A snag is that the Museum - like others in Turkey - is short of experienced staff. Each day in turn, different galleries are closed off. Visitors must go at least twice to see everything.

From the Castle ramparts, views are superb over the harbour, or across the Gulf of Gökova to Kos. Bodrum is one of the main departure points for a Blue Voyage, with each shore of the sheltered 45-mile Gulf offering a hundred idyllic havens for yachtsmen, with access to sandy beaches, sheltered coves, small uninhabited islands and a beautiful pine-wooded coastline.

Bodrum Marina - like Kuşadası, run by a subsidiary of the Tourism Bank - contains dozens of British boats operated by yacht companies on bareboat charter or for flotilla sailing. Local Bodrum gulets with crew wait for their charter passengers. Former sponge-divers have now switched careers, and have become Blue Voyage captains, utilising their intimate knowledge of the entire coastline between Bodrum and Antalya.

Tourism has given a major boost to Bodrum's boat-building industry. Using the local species of red, black or white pine, the shipyards were active even in the days of King Mausolus, and warships were built for the Egyptian Navy in 3rd century BC. For 2500 years ship-building traditions have been handed down from father to son. Today, in the Bodrum area's thirty small shipyards, there are constant reminders of that long history. It's worth taking a close look at a boatyard, just for the pleasure of admiring skilled wood craftsmen using techniques which have almost died out in higher-wage countries.

The yards specialise in the Bodrum 'gulet', a broad-beamed vessel that was originally used for fishing or coastal freighting. Starting from 1946, when a famous Turkish writer nicknamed the Fisherman of Halicarnassus first popularized the idea of Blue Voyage, these beautiful vessels were converted to pleasure use, fitted with cabins, saloon and sun-deck. From conversions, the shipyards have switched to purpose-built craft for the tourist trade, using ever more luxurious fittings.

Along the harbour waterfront, or from jetties along the east bay, there is good choice of all-day boat trips to various coves and bays and beaches. Boats can sometimes be crowded, but the value is unbeatable. A usual starting time in Bodrum is 11.30 - quite early enough for night-owls, and for those who commute in from the satellite villages - returning 6 or 7 p.m., with stops for swimming or refreshments and snacks.

The larger boats - the traditional gulets - are fitted with tables, a bar, and a loudspeaker music system (which could be a minus, rather than a plus point). To avoid the noise pollution, go up front of the vessel, where the sound of music gets lost.

Stops are made at coves where swimmers can plunge into pale turquoise water of unbelievable clarity - the kind of perfection which people dream about. Captain and crew join passengers in the water, except for cook who is slaving in the galley, preparing a meal of grilled fish with rice, salad and hunks of bread. Maybe half the passengers aboard are Turkish, conversation becomes multi-lingual and new friendships blossom.

After lunch, time for siesta, spread out on the vessel's roof and deck. Nobody has any desperate urge to move on somewhere else. Why move, when you are already in paradise?

Then, quite likely, the crew turn themselves into musicians, with a guitar, electronic organ, tambourines and a small drum. Everyone joins in, by then 4 in the afternoon, perhaps what the Brits might call time for a tea-dance, but Turkish style. Imagine a sultry-looking Turkish girl, black hair and flashing dark eyes, belly-dancing in her bikini. That vision alone is worth the fare to Turkey.

Finally, up anchor and away back towards Bodrum, with another swimming stop in an equally beautiful cove - time again to marvel at sea water of such total clarity that you can see every detail of the sea bed 20 or 30 feet below.

More music, drinking and dancing on the final lap into Bodrum; and you finally land with virtually every passenger having fully qualified for a belly-dancing certificate. It all makes our English hour aboard the 'Skylark', to the lighthouse and back, seem rather pale.

A combination of boat trips and dolmuş rides give access to every corner of the Bodrum area, somewhere different every day. Let's go clockwise:

Karaada - Black Island - lies 4 miles out of Bodrum harbour: a popular stop on boat trips to explore a warm-spring grotto where the mineral waters are reputed to beautify the complexion. Visitors daub themselves with yellow mud, rather like a face-pack, and emerge looking like Red Indians, just off to a scalping. Excursion boats also continue further

85

along the coast, and to Orak Island, for more swimming-stops.

Ada Boğazı is an island just off the tip of the peninsula that separates Gümbet and Bitez Bays. There is choice of several coves with water of unbelievable clarity - visibility 100 feet down - hence called "The Aquarium", with tourists instead of fish.

Gümbet is virtually a resort in its own right. Only 10 minutes by dolmuş from Bodrum, the little bay features all types of accommodation up the hillside, with more buildings under feverish construction. A rough road leads to the centre of the beach, where restaurants, hotels, camp sites and tea-gardens are spread along a good stretch of golden sands.

Small sailing yachts and windsurfers glide across the bay, while children paddle and scream with joy. When learner windsurfers fall off, the water is shallow enough to stand up and start again. It all makes up a traditional beach holiday, wrapped around sand and sunshine. Only 20 minutes' walk, and you can reach Bodrum Marina.

Bitez is around the next bay from Gümbet, with mixture of rocky shoreline, shingle and sand. A popular resort with a mosque right by the beach; pleasant low-profile restaurants and bars, some villas and small hotels. The beach also offers shade, which so often is in short supply. Wind conditions are good for sailboarders, with experts skimming along faster than a motor-launch. You can try your hand at scuba diving.

Just inland, background cypress trees make an attractive green setting for white buildings with red-tiled roofs. Venture up into the tangerine groves, and you pass traditional farm houses with riotous garden displays of

bougainvilia, hibiscus, oleander, roses and wisteria.

Ortakent village is a mile inland, with a Turkish tower-house that stands like a small castle above the village houses. The long sandy beach has a couple of resident camels, a boat-building yard, and restaurants well spaced out. On the outskirts is an Aktur Holiday Village, overlooking Bitez Bay with a good sandy beach, and the buildings reaching up the hillside - rather like duplexes, overflowing with bougainvilia.

Kargı and *Bağla* Bays are popular boat stops, but without direct road access. The next bay, called *Karaincir*, has a wide beach - rated among the most beautiful on the pensinsula.

Akyarlar is a tiny village, a half-hour 22-km drive from Bodrum, with less than 300 residents. Nearest neighbour is the Greek island of Kos, three miles away. Britain's Mark Warner operates the 80-guest Club Simin, specializing in watersport. The gently-shelving sandy beach is safe for children. In this tucked-away corner of the Peninsula, there are many small bays and secluded beaches along the coastal road to Turgutreis.

Turgutreis is a town named after a famed Turkish admiral who was killed in the Seige of Malta 1565. There's a mile-long beach, the usual fish restaurants and some holiday accommodation.

Gümüşlük is a delightful little village, half an hour from Bodrum, with sea water of crystal clarity. A few simple sugar-cube white houses step up from the small sand and shingle beach. Along the shore towards Rabbit Island, olive trees grow alongside the path. Offbeat and peaceful, yet only 30 minutes from the madding crowd, it's a good location for a family-style self-catering villa holiday, with sandy beach on the doorstep. Here is the simple-life Turkey of 20 years ago, before tourism arrived. By official decree, time is scheduled to stand still: the zone is covered by a preservation order as an archaeological site. The remains of ancient Myndos - dating from the 4th-century BC reign of King Mausolus - are scanty, mostly underwater and best seen by snorkel. The wildest form of nightlife is to watch the sunset, every evening a new spectacular, with octopus for supper.

Yalıkavak is where sponges are more important than tourists. The village is home base for sponge-divers who cruise the Blue Voyage route to Antalya and back, May through October. Holidaymakers can buy the processed sponges in Bodrum and elsewhere, but most of the haul goes for export. The harbour is a port of call for yachtsmen.

Türkbükü is approached through lush green hills, and then lemon groves, oranges and tangerines. A fishing village, Türkbükü is sheltered by two islands - one big, one little according to their Turkish names. The restaurants serve other food besides fish, but essentially they support the local industry. Resident fishermen have also diversified into tourism, splashing out into day trips. Accommodation for visitors is mainly in charming village rooms or pensions.

Torba is a small but fashionable fishing village with yachting and windsurfing facilities. There are self-catering studios in private villas, and a handful of small restaurants. Evening time, you can try your luck on the slot machines of the Casino at Torba Holiday Village.

Güvercinlik is an ideal bay for windsurfing, with calm waters, good breeze, warm water when you fall in, and scenery all around whenever you want to stop underwater goggling. The coastal views are superb, along much of the 20 kms into Bodrum. Britain's Mark Warner company operates a watersport centre at the Bargilya Motel, with lessons in windsurfing, water-skiing, sailing and snorkelling included in the price. This location is not suitable for small children, with swimmers' plunging straight down into deepish water from the wide concrete platforms. Around the bay, however, it shelves much less rapidly, and there's even a tiny strip of sand.

During a visit I made, a dolphin decided to join in the watersports. Just a few yards off-shore, playing amid the swimmers and the sailboarders, the creature gracefully rose above the water and dived, and then rose again in what seemed like active enjoyment of the facilities. This certainly doesn't happen every day. But, anywhere along this southern coast, playful dolphins can appear close to shore: another of the unexpected pleasures of a Turkish seaside holiday!

Entertainment

Shopping and nightlife in Bodrum town starts early evening, when shopkeepers put aside their backgammon boards and get ready for the peak trading hours from sundown till midnight. However, Thursday and Friday it's worth making a special daytime effort to visit the colourful farmers' market, just past the bus station. June or July there are great heaps of water melon, sweet melon, peaches, apricots, cherries, plums, bananas, oranges, lemons - all grown simultaneously in Turkey. Later in the summer come delicious fresh figs, and mountains of grapes.

Bodrum holidaymakers soon find their way into the narrow pedestrian precinct called Cumhuriyet Caddesi - otherwise known as Tourist Alley. The layout is that all the restaurants and bars on one side of the road have a terrace out back, direct onto the sea with Castle view, floodlit at night. Every summer evening it's the focal point for the friendly chaos of Turkey's most laid-back and Bohemian resort. The street bubbles with action: shops overflowing onto the pavement; street vendors of sponges, T-shirts, sandals, blue beads; hundreds of tourists and yachtsmen, cruising for a meal, a drink, a jazz bar, or just cruising.

There's every type of café-bar - indoor, outdoor, garden setting, on the beach, along the promenade - with choice of every type of background music: jazz, hard rock, Turkish or classical. If you yearn for international cocktails, instead of the Turkish mixtures, several bars can make a brave attempt. For something more sophisticated, try the Bodrum Yacht Club.

Stopping anywhere for a meal, you need three ears to get full benefit of the incoming sound waves: one for the music offered by your chosen restaurant, one for the jazz from the bar next door, and a third ear for the disco across the Alley. To chat up a girl, you need loud-hailers.

For a jet-set disco, try the Halikarnas, rated as one of Turkey's best night clubs. You don't need to ask the way: just home in on the sound. It offers a Hollywood stage-set version of a Roman amphitheatre: a melodramatic open-air setting with flares burning on the tops of columns, and in the background the magnificent view of Bodrum Castle, illuminated not by the disco owners but by the municipality. A laser light show somehow enters into the display, giving an added touch of authenticity. The £8 entrance includes the first Turkish drink. All the lucky residents of pensions in the area can lie abed and enjoy the music for free until 4 a.m.

One evening a week, there's a folk show instead: traditional music, folk performance and belly-dancing, with a Turkish-cuisine dinner.

Around Bodrum at one in the morning every friendly bar and disco is still swinging. With so much nightlife to enjoy, breakfast is any time till noon, and day-trip boat cruises do not start until late morning.

Bodrum people are very conservative - like following Ramadan faithfully. But they have come to accept the eccentric life-styles of the writers, pop stars and artists who first gave Bodrum its unconventional reputation. Sophisticated Turks call the resort Bedroom. With today's prosperity so dependent on tourism, Bodrum townfolk are very tolerant, even of slim young men who use lipstick.

Classical Aegean Sites and Sightseeing

Dardanelles and Troy

Çanakkale

Information Bureau (Turizm Danışma Büro) - İskele Meydanı 67 - opposite the ferry landing-stage. Tel: 1187 TRAVEL: 310 kms from Istanbul or 330 kms from Izmir - six hours by bus; 245 kms from Bergama, 3½ hours by bus.

Three great historic place-names are linked to the narrow fast-flowing waterway that separates Europe from Asia Minor: Dardanelles, Gallipoli and Troy. Here is one of the world's most strategic locations, controlling the passage between two continents and the seaway from Black Sea through the Sea of Marmara to the Aegean and Mediterranean. On today's Turkish map, the key town is called Çanakkale, sited on the Asian shore of the Dardanelles Straits.

Although Çanakkale does not feature in tour operators' programmes - except on some coach tours - the individual traveller could find the town a useful staging-point on a Turkish itinerary.

Thus, motorists driving across Europe on E5 - or arriving from Greece on E25 - can use the E24 highway and ferry crossing as a short cut to the Aegean coast, avoiding the roundabout journey via Istanbul. It's the preferred route used by German and Austrian motorists, heading for the southern and western beaches.

At Çanakkale three good-grade tourist hotels are located on the waterfront, close to the ferry landing-stage: Anafartalar, Truva and Bakır. Numerous smaller hotels and pensions are spread in the same area.

After the Germans, the most numerous visitors to Çanakkale are the Anzacs - the Aussies and New Zealanders. Owing to the key role of Anzac troops in the Gallipoli landings during World War 1, this tiny corner of Turkey has become part of their own legend and history, commemorated every year on Anzac Day. They want to see that piece of Anzac history for themselves.

Local travel agencies operate morning or afternoon battlefield tours by taxi or mini-bus, the price fluctuating according to the number of participants. If you plan to include this in your itinerary, first read Alan Moorehead's classic book "Gallipoli" which sets the picture.

In the War Museum and Castle at Çanakkale there is a considerable display of cannon, mostly as used in the Gallipoli campaign. On show, for instance, is a 40-cm calibre gun made in 1875 by Krupp's - a small gift to Sultan Abdül Aziz. Along the waterfront is a lifesize model of the mine-layer Nusrat, which played a deadly part in stopping the Allied fleet from moving up the Straits of Dardanelles on 18 March 1915.

On that historic day, Allied vessels entered the Straits, expecting a relatively clear passage through to the Sea of Marmara. Instead, they found that shore batteries which had theoretically been silenced were all in full operation, to pound them like sitting ducks. Theoretically, too, the Straits had been cleared of mines. But the minelayer Nusrat had crept out during the night and relaid mines which crippled three British ships. By the end of the day's carnage, one third of the Allied fleet had been knocked out. What began as a naval operation to force a passage through to the Black Sea - to help the Russian armies with supplies, and to block German access to the Middle East - was converted into a bitter campaign to capture the Straits by troop landings. Trench warfare led to total stalemate, until evacuation was ordered seven months later. Commanding the key sectors on the Turkish side was Kemal Atatürk, who became a national hero.

The bare hillsides that saw such grim fighting are now forested with pine trees. The whole area is protected as a National Park. The key place-names - Lone Pine, Chunuk Bair, Kabatepe, Johnson's Jolly and Suvla Bay - are stops on a scenic circuit. Arı Burnu, where the Anzac troops landed, has been officially renamed Anzac Cove since 1985, to mark the 70th anniversary. The total cost was a quarter-million casualties on each side. Today, the paying tourist can cross the Straits for 7p.

Troy

The 40-minute dolmuş ride to Troy (Turkish spelling Truva) starts at the Otobüs Garajı in Çanakkale, and passes through beautiful fertile countryside, parallel to the coastline, with views to the Dardanelles Straits. It's a typical village dolmuş, which operates regardless of tourists. Motels and camp sites are scattered amid pine trees alongside small beaches - Güzelyalı, for instance. The turn-off from the main E24 road to Izmir is 25 kms out, and then five kms to Troy.

The first view of Troy is like something out of Disneyland - a huge reproduction wooden horse, built according to Homer's description in the "Iliad", including a neat garden shed on top, presumably where the soldiers kept their spears. Steps lead into the interior of the Trojan Horse, but the entrance door is usually chained. Maybe that's to avoid disturbing the birds, who nest in the horse's thatched tail.

Considering the volumes of intellectual effort which have been expended on Troy, the site is quite small. Troy was just a mound, rising from the surrounding plain. But this small fortified city was highly strategic, commanding clear views to the Straits of Dardanelles.

Key to the problem was that the fast-flowing current and head winds from the Sea of Marmara into the Aegean made the Hellespont almost impassable by sailing-boats. Trading cargoes had to be off-loaded and carried overland for re-loading onto ships going north. The Trojans could 'protect' that overland passage, extracting a fee for the service. It's all surmise and mystery. But economic and strategic arguments seem a more logical basis for a ten-year war, than just Helen's pretty face. However, Homer's romantic version gave it more chance as a best-seller.

Part of the fascination of the site comes from realisation that nine separate cities are layered one above another, within the compass of a few hundred yards. The first settlement was dated 3000-2500 BC; Troy V11A was Priam's city which underwent the ten-year seige, in the 1200's; Troy 1X was the most enduring, 350 BC till 400 AD. On each section of the remains, helpful archaeologists have posted up which Troy it belongs to, and which century.

Within a few yards you can walk from one millennium to another, like something out of a Time Machine. Step back, and you are away into the deepest mists of pre-history, long before the Trojan War, which itself was something not so much of history, but of legend perpetuated by a blind poet who wrote 500 years after the event.

You climb past Trojan houses that date from 1900 to 1300 BC, up to the Temple of Athena of Troy 1X, offering a royal view over the surrounding countryside. Tractors and trailers chug back and forth amid the patchwork quilt of fields, each growing its individual crop. Early July, sunflowers explode into Van Gogh displays. You can people that flat countryside with a besieging army, which sat there impatiently for so many years, until the final collapse of Troy more than 3000 years ago.

A newly-built Archaeological Museum is located on the outskirts of Çanakkale, beside the road to Troy. The Museum's collection is mostly of finds from various minor sites in the Troas region: neolithic axe-heads, amphorae and bronze age pottery. It also has one of Kemal Atatürk's shirts.

Pergamum
Travel to Bergama

The ancient classical site of Pergamum is located outside the modern-day city of Bergama. Most tourist visitors arrive on excursions from the south, via Izmir, which is a 90-minute bus drive for the 100 kms. Cruise ships call at Dikili, only a 20-km coach ride to Pergamum.

If you travel from the north - from Çanakkale and Troy - the E24 highway passes around the Gulf of Edremit, facing the Greek island of Lesbos, alias Mytileni. A turn-off from E24 leads to the walled hilltop city of Assos, founded 8th century BC, where Aristotle lived for three years, and where St. Paul visited. Below is the present-day fishing village of Behramkale, now rapidly switching to tourism business.

Numerous small beaches are spread around this coast, which is not yet 'discovered' by major UK tour operators, though the Germans are there. Several resorts make attractive stopovers for self-drive visitors: Küçukkuyu, Altınoluk, Akçay and Ören.

On hill slopes near Akçay are hot springs and thermal baths. Legend relates that the world's first beauty contest was held beneath a plane tree at a picnic spot on Mount Ida (Kaz Dağı in Turkish). A handsome young shepherd called Paris adjudicated between three goddesses - Aphrodite, Hera and Athena. The judgement of Paris - giving the golden apple award to Aphrodite as the first Miss World - led finally to the Trojan War. The "Iliad" explains how it all happened.

Further round the Gulf of Edremit is Turkey's largest area of olive tree plantations, with production centred on the popular resort of Ayvalik. Avoid the town centre in late autumn, when primitive olive oil plants and soap factories discharge their effluent into the bay. Turkish city dwellers come here in large numbers during the summer season. The best golden-sand beach is at Sarmısaklı, five miles south. Along the coastline are plentiful tea gardens for watching the sunset over Lesbos. The favourite viewpoint is from a hill called Şeytan Sofrası - the Devil's Dining Table, composed of large flat boulders. The Devil also left his footprint there.

The journey itself is a pleasure, through all this fertile countryside with great diversity of crops: vegetables, fruit, maize, tobacco. Field work and family transport is still at the horse-and-cart stage. Farm carts are decorated in traditional style, with flowers painted in vivid primary colours. Horses are festooned with red pompoms and necklaces of beads, and trot along jingling with harness bells. Huge water melons are stacked high in a peasant market. A withered crone leads two sheep on a string to graze in a fenced orchard. Everywhere you look, there are characters and scenes to keep your camera clicking fast.

Pergamum

The essentials of Pergamum are widely separated: the Acropolis, five kms from Bergama; the Kızıl Avlu or Red Hall; an Archaeological Museum; and the Asklepieion, two kms from Bergama. Taxi transport is advisable from one main site to another, unless you are basically on a hiking holiday. Local cabbies are well attuned to shuttling tourists from point to point. Even then, plentiful walking is still in store.

Best views are from the Acropolis. Perched 1300 feet above the Caicus valley plain, the town-planned site included a royal palace, temples, a very steep 10,000-seat theatre, barracks and arsenal (which stored 100-lb stone missiles for use in the pre-gunpowder age of the ballista).

The most famous building was the Library, which once housed 200,000 books. The original works were written on paper made from the papyrus of Egypt. When that export was banned by the Ptolemies - jealous that Pergamum was rivalling their book collection at Alexandria - a new technology was evolved using sheep and goat skins: hence the word 'parchment' derived from 'pergamum paper'. A bound volume, a codex, had writing on both sides of the numbered pages - another innovation - all a great improvement on papyrus scrolls. Later, when the Library at Alexandria burned down, Mark Antony consoled Cleopatra by giving her Pergamum's entire book collection as a replacement.

Pergamum was also renowned as the great medical centre of the ancient world, with the Asklepieion dedicated to the god of healing. The therapy of water, mud-baths, massage, herbal remedies, country walks, diet, music, positive thinking, auto-suggestion and dream analysis were all part of the treatment. The healing snake symbol was adopted when the great physician named Galen discovered the medicinal potential of snake venom. That's one story: but there are several other explanations for the serpent associated with Asklepios. During Bergama's annual Festival - usually around late May, early June - folklore shows are performed in the adjoining Theatre.

To see the most magnificent remains is a much longer journey than the local cab-drivers can handle: all the way to East Berlin, where the world-famed Pergamum Museum was purpose built to exhibit the huge Zeus Temple, together with numerous other statues and monuments from the Acropolis. If you cannot face that journey, Bergama is a pleasant old city to explore for an hour, though hotel facilities are somewhat limited. The Ethnographic Museum displays local costumes and Bergama carpets. As you stroll around the town, you can peek through open doorways and see young girls weaving carpets and kilims to those same rich colours and patterns.

Izmir

Information Bureau (Turizm Danışma Büro) - Büyük Efes Oteli Altı 1/C - just past the Turkish Airlines office at the Büyük Efes Hotel. Tel: 142147. The airport bus delivers you right outside the door. All the 3-, 4- and 5-star hotels are within a 200-yard radius. Mid-range and no-grade hotels are grouped in streets that radiate from Basmane railway station. At the waterfront facing the Atatürk statue on Cumhuriyet Meydani is the central Post Office - PTT - which is open till midnight for international phone calls and currency exchange.

Founded 3000 BC, and claimed as the birthplace of Homer, modern Izmir spreads up piedish hillsides that overlook a perfect natural harbour. Although the city is a tourism centre, its income derives mainly from processing and shipping the farm products of the Aegean region: dried figs, sultanas, olive oil, tobacco and cotton.

Izmir - formerly called Smyrna - has survived a long and turbulent history. Located on its present site by Alexander the Great in 4th century BC, Izmir was captured in the 11th century by the Seljuk Turks; then back and forth between Byzantines and Seljuks. The Knights of St. John captured the city in 1344, and held it for 58 years. In 1402 the city was sacked and the citizens slaughtered by Tamerlaine, the 'Scourge of God'. When the Golden Horde rode back to Samarkand, the city reverted to the Seljuk Turks of the Aydin dynasty, who lost it to the Ottomans in 1415.

Destroyed several times over the centuries, Izmir has a variety of historical remains: a Hellenistic citadel, a Roman agora, Byzantine aqueducts, Ottoman caravansaries and mosques. The Culture Park is venue for an International Trade Fair, among the largest in the Eastern Mediterranean, held every year from 20 August to 20 September. Accommodation is very difficult to find during that period.

Let's start sightseeing in the 'new' area, at the Atatürk statue in front of Büyük Efes Hotel. The monument shows the Turkish leader as

Commander of the forces who drove out the invading Greeks in 1922. The statue commemorates a historic speech to his troops in the interior. Pointing towards the sea, he declaimed: "Men - your first destination is the Mediterranean . . . Forward march!"

Shortly afterwards, that command was fulfilled in Izmir, and Independence was won. During the final Greek evacuation, Izmir burned. Most of 20th-century Izmir has since been rebuilt with broad new boulevards lined with apartments and office buildings. Up-market bars and restaurants are strung along the seafront promenade called Kordonboyu, leading north - that is, right - from the statue.

To find old-time Izmir, head for the district called KONAK, which is the principal bus, dolmuş and ferry terminal for the downtown area. Facing the sea from the Atatürk statue, turn left for Konak, and stroll along the lively waterfront with its coffeeshops and middle-price fish restaurants. Fishing vessels and small coasters are tied to the quayside. Some of the boats badly need painting and de-rusting; but they are working vessels, rather than pretty-pretty pleasure craft.

Look in at the fish market, which hasn't changed for centuries. Fishermen in gumboots display their catch, everything from sardines to swordfish, crying their wares in age-old style. Don't miss it! The noise, the smell and the sea-gulls will point the way.

By the ferry-boat terminal at Konak, a charming clock tower stands on one side of an extremely busy highway, and a tiny mosque on the other. The highway is railed off, to prevent pedestrians from damaging the speeding traffic, and a modern concrete pedestrian bridge crosses to the bazaar area. From that bridge, just go straight ahead, and get lost in the maze.

The bazaar cannot match the full fascination of the Covered Bazaar of Istanbul, but certainly can run it a good second for colour and interest. Highly recommended! In this area, too, have survived the buildings and the atmosphere of Ottoman times. There are plentiful wooden houses, with balconies that reach over the street.

Don't worry about getting lost. Just remember that downhill will finally lead you back to Konak. Uphill you'll finally hit Gazi Osman Paşa Bulvarı, within short distance of the Roman Agora. Just say "Agora nerede?" and kind Turks will point the way. Or a taxi will drop you there for less than a minimum London bus-fare.

The Agora, located below Mount Kadifekale, is a little oasis of green amid the surrounding houses. A neat line of 13 columns has been restored. Elsewhere are scattered bits and pieces from Roman times - small statues and carved Greek inscriptions leaning casually against the walls.

This was the market place of ancient Izmir: a 3-storey building with a gallery 500 feet long. In 178 AD, Izmir was hit by an earthquake which ruined everything. Aid was granted by the Roman Emperor Marcus Aurelius, and the Agora was rebuilt. In more recent centuries, the area became an Islamic cemetery, until excavations were undertaken from 1927.

The view from the grassed area is magnificent. Castle walls rear high up on the hilltop above, past tier upon tier of housing. All this part of Old Izmir was originally protected by city walls which ran down from the castle to the sea. But those walls have almost entirely disappeared, recycled in the house-building of later centuries.

To save your breath, a cab-ride from the Agora to the hilltop castle of Mount Kadifekale is a worthwhile investment. If you are starting from Konak, take a dolmuş minibus labelled K-kale, short for Kadifekale, which means Velvet Castle.

The whole area within the fortress walls is a park, planted with trees, where families picnic. Children climb and play on the walls, first built by Alexander the Great in 4th century BC.

Nestling close to the ramparts are village-style houses with magnificent views, but looking very dilapidated. It's a complete pedestrian precinct. From above, the streets look perpendicular, with hundreds of steps leading way down. Chickens squawk on the rooftops, amid lines of washing.

A pleasant tea-house is perched by the entrance to the Castle, which is dramatically floodlit at night. Views are superb: over the Bay, active with shipping. Here you are well placed to catch the cooling afternoon sea breeze, called the Imbat. Stay till sunset for the evocative magic of the muezzins' call to prayer from a hundred mosques. Afterwards, you can easily get dolmuş transport, which shuttles back to Konak.

Close to Konak is the spacious new Archaeology Museum, looking out from above a waterfront park, where ultra-modern buildings finish and a more elderly sector begins. The museum mainly exhibits finds from excavations at Bayraklı - Old Smyrna - where the city was originally located.

For a final view of Izmir, try a round-trip ferry ride from Konak across the Bay. Buy a token - jeton - which lets you through the turnstiles. White-painted ferries shuttle back and forth on a regular schedule, at least every half-hour for the 15-minute ride to the suburb of Karşıyaka. The suburb need not detain you, so buy another jeton for the return. The trip will give your sightseeing feet a break, though your ears will be bent by very loud lo-fi music.

From the ferry you can look beyond the hillsides of Izmir to the dramatic hint of higher mountains in the background, reaching up to the Central Anatolian plateau. You can see why the Turks call it 'güzel Izmir' - beautiful Izmir.

Manisa and Sardis

Further down the list of places to visit from an Izmir base are Manisa to the north-east, and Sardis 90 kms due east along the E23 highway towards Ankara. Local travel agencies combine them in an easy day's circuit.

Sardis was capital of the ancient kingdom of Lydia, ruled by a wealthy dynasty who produced the world's first metal coinage around 600 BC. Primarily their steady income was in gold, washed down from Mount Tmolus by the river Pactolus, and caught in greased sheepskins - hence the probable origin of the legend of the golden fleece.

Last of the royal line was rich King Croesus, who reigned in the 6th century until captured and slain by the Persians. The city stayed prosperous under Persian rule, as the western end of their Royal Road which linked Persia with the Mediterranean. Sardis became Greek when Alexander the Great turned out the Persians in 334 BC. Excavations by American archaeologists have restored a section of the Royal Road paved with marble, and a small area of Roman shops, gymnasium and a synagogue. The temple of Artemis was among the largest Ionic temples in the Greek world.

Travel agencies often link Manisa with a tour to Sardis. Manisa is market centre for a fertile fruit-producing area, and contains some fine Seljuk and Ottoman mosques.

Ephesus

Turkey's most famous and most accessible classical site is Ephesus, only an hour's drive for the 46 miles from Izmir, along a good road. Several cruise-ships call every day during the season at Kuşadası, 7 miles away. Ephesus can also be reached on a longer drive from the southern resorts of Bodrum and Marmaris.
Selçuk (Ephesus) Information Bureau (Turizm Danişma Büro) - Atatürk Mah. Efes müzesi Karşısı 23 - opposite the Museum at Selçuk. Tel: 1328 or 1943.

The remains at Ephesus include several distinct cities, built by Greeks, Romans and Byzantines. Ephesus was capital of Roman Asia, and its wealth is reflected in the scale of the public buildings. Among the Seven Wonders of the ancient world was the Temple of Diana, also known as Artemis - a fertility-cult goddess equipped with three rows of breasts. The temple once attracted 700,000 visitors in a single season.

When St. Paul preached to the Ephesians in the well-preserved

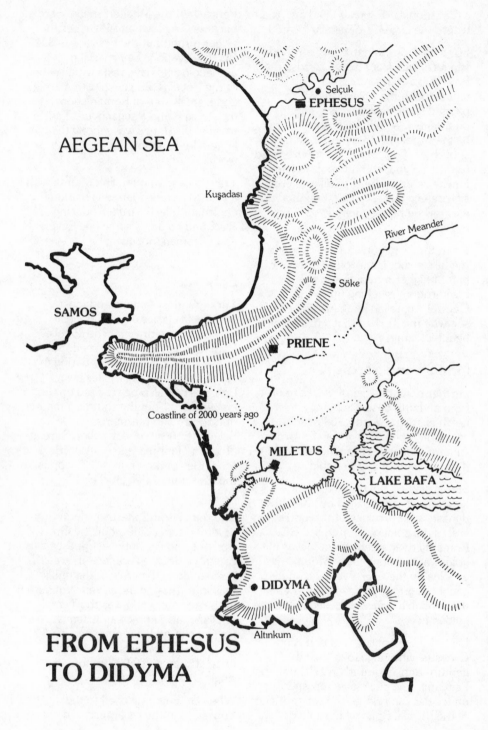

AEGEAN SEA

Selçuk

EPHESUS

Kuşadası

River Meander

Söke

SAMOS

PRIENE

Coastline of 2000 years ago

MILETUS

LAKE BAFA

DIDYMA

Altınkum

FROM EPHESUS
TO DIDYMA

Near Fethiye - a secluded sandy
cove, accessible only by boat trip.

Fethiye
Year round, the fruit & vegetable
market has colourful displays
of local produce.

Ölü Deniz

The narrow entrance into the lagoon, now barred to vessels. On the seaward side is a long beach with great potential for water sports.

Friendly villagers in Hisaronu,
above the resort of Ölü Deniz.

Theatre that seats 25,000, he was shouted down by local silversmiths who feared that his attack on the worship of graven images would hit their souvenir trade in replicas of Diana. The riot of the silversmiths is dramatically reported in Acts 19: 23-41.

St. John, too, visited the town, and stayed. According to tradition, Mary went to Ephesus with St. John and lived in a safe and lonely place on the Aladağ mountain. There, about five miles from Ephesus, the reputed house of Mary is situated in a spot called Panaya Kapulu. A church was built over the site in the 5th century. Since rediscovery of the site in 1892, a tiny rebuilt church has become a centre of pilgrimage, particularly since the visits of Pope Paul VI in 1967 and Pope John Paul in 1980. A commemoration service on August 15 each year draws thousands of worshippers.

An even earlier church, built at Ephesus during the 4th century, was dedicated to Mary. Ecumenical Councils were held there in 431 and 439. Attended by two hundred bishops, the Third Ecumenical Council of 431 AD proclaimed the dogma: "Mary, the Mother of God."

In the present-day town of Ephesus (now called Selçuk), a small but excellent museum houses archaeological treasures, of which several have become familiar on travel posters: the bronze Boy on the Dolphin, and two marble statues of Artemis. Begin the day with a Museum visit, as it puts the surrounding sites into context for the splendours of Ephesus itself. Finds are well displayed, with English notes to help understanding. A typical display shows how oil lamps were made - preparation of the clay, shaping of lamps, and final glazing and firing. The biggest flashing of tourist cameras is aimed at the many-breasted statues of Artemis, otherwise known as Diana, and formerly as Cybele - the fertile but virgin goddess whose worship so aroused the wrath of St. Paul.

The cult of the Mother Goddess originated in Anatolia, and spread to all Mediterranean countries. The earliest finds in Asia Minor date from 6800 BC. The various forms of fertility goddess were shaped in different ways, mostly as very heavily pregnant figurines. But finally Cybele evolved into the 37-breasted Artemis of Ephesus, in direct descent from the Anatolian Mother Goddess of thousands of years before.

From the museum, best strategy is then to visit Ayasoluk Hill which dominates present-day Selçuk. During the reign of Byzantine Emperor Justinian (527-565), the citizens of Ephesus finally gave up struggling against the silting of the harbour on which their trading prosperity depended. They abandoned the city and moved to the higher ground of Selçuk. Building of a huge Basilica dedicated to St. John marked the new era. For the requisite marble they used the pagan Temple of Artemis as a stone quarry. In later centuries the Turks converted the church into a mosque, which in turn was destroyed by earthquake followed by the even more destructive Mongols of Tamerlane.

Today, excavation continues steadily on Ayasoluk Hill, with restoration of the 6th-century Basilica undertaken by the Ministry of Culture and Tourism, and funded by the George B. Quatman Foundation of Lima, Ohio, USA. It looks like a complete rebuild, which hopefully will last for the next thousand years.

The hilltop terrace gives good views over the Isabey Mosque just below. A panorama plan depicts the gradual retreat of the sea through silting of the River Maeander's flood-plain. It meant the death of Ephesus - now 3 miles inland from the coast - but brought fertility to fields which formerly were part of the shallow sea.

Past the Basilica, a path leads up to the Citadel - a landmark visible long before arrival in Selçuk. It's well worth the few minutes' extra climb. Steps have been relaid to make a complete walk around the ramparts. They offer a tyrant's view of patchwork agriculture in every direction, with little dots of human beings toiling in the fields.

Next stop: Temple of Artemis. All that survives of what formerly was rated among the seven wonders of the ancient world - four times the area of the Parthenon - is just one tall solitary column. During my most recent visit, the column was topped by a storks' nest with a resident family - curiously appropriate in the home temple of the Mother Goddess! In the background is a dramatic view of the Citadel, the Isabey Mosque and the reincarnation of the St. John Basilica.

En route from the Artemis Temple site to the Magnesian Gate at Ephesus, a turning to the right indicates the Cave of the Seven Sleepers. According to legend, seven Christian youths fled from persecution. Together with their dog, they took refuge in the hillside cave and fell asleep. When they awoke, one lad went into town to buy bread. When he offered the baker out-dated coins, it was realised they had slept for 200 years. By then,

Christianity had become official. A miracle was declared; upon which, the seven youths went back to sleep in their cave, for ever. It has been a place of pilgrimage ever since.

The Magnesian Gate is the better of the two entrances into Ephesus, as it's then downhill all the way. Visitors can finally exit at the car park past the Theatre, where coaches and taxis patiently wait for their clients.

From the entrance, just follow the crocodiles of tourists. To see Ephesus in detail would take an enthusiast several days. But the average visitor is content with a gentle two-hour amble, or three hours to include readings from the helpful booklets on sale at the entrance. Each building or monument is labelled.

Starting at the top end, there's the Upper Agora with a Temple of Isis, and an adjoining 1400-seat Odeon, Town Hall, Temple of Domitian and several fountains. Then comes Curetes Street, mind-blowing in its magnificence: everything marble, 36 feet wide, a proper drainage system beneath the paving stones, and lined with monumental fountains, temples and baths, with side-turnings to terraced houses.

Extra packed with interest is the area near the bottom of the slope, where Curetes Street veers right at the Library of Celcus into the Marmorean Way, and where most guides take their groups for a quick five minutes in the brothel.

Stop to admire the superb mosaics, roped off on the left of Curetes Street. Just there, a path climbs steeply up a hillside. For a modest extra fee, one can now visit reconstructed middle-class houses, covered by a special roof as protection against weather and earthquakes. Rooms are decorated with beautifully restored mosaics and frescoes from the 2nd century AD, to give a brilliant picture of the home comforts of 1800 years ago.

A comparison with Pompeii seems valid. Look across to the other hillsides of Ephesus, which must also contain similar treasures. Each year, through steady digging by the Austrian Archaeological Institute, more and more of Ephesus is being revealed and reconstructed. Give it another ten years, and Ephesus will outstrip Pompeii for its solid reconstruction of life during the Roman Empire.

The rebuilding of Ephesus is a constant process. An added pleasure is to watch the Turkish labourers at their careful digging, supervised by the expert eyes of Austrian and Turkish archaeologists. The most recent Austrian project is to restore the South Gate of the Agora alongside the Celsus Library. This impressive monument was funded in the 3rd and 4th centuries BC by two emancipated slaves, Mazaeus and Mithridates.

Finally, the great highlight: the Theatre. From a seat in the gods one gets a superb view of the magnificent Arcadian Way which led for one third of a mile from the ancient harbour. Imagine the scene when Cleopatra landed there 2000 years ago, to make a spectacular grand entrance to meet her lover, Mark Antony.

The Theatre itself provides a good chance for anyone who wants to sing, recite poetry or tell jokes: just to test the acoustics from the spot where St. Paul preached against Diana.In the first week of May, Ephesus organises an international festival, with a number of shows in the Theatre. In addition, every summer sees a variety of special events - ranging from pop concerts to the Moscow Symphony Orchestra, or even a display by the Whirling Dervishes of Konya. Shortly before a performance is due, two dozen peasant women are employed to weed between the seats.

Further down the Arcadian Way is the Harbour Gymnasium and Baths. By then, however, most visitors are worn out: so they turn right to the parking area, where the 20th century awaits with WC's, coke stands, picture post-cards, souvenir stores and transport.

Aphrodisias and Pamukkale

The Greco-Roman site of Aphrodisias is usually linked with a same-day visit to the petrified waters of Pamukkale - a natural wonder created by the lime content of hot mineral waters that have cascaded down a terraced cliff.

TRAVEL These two sightseeing high-lights are normally approached along the Menderes Valley via Selçuk from Kuşadası or Izmir. As a one-day excursion, it's an extremely long circuit - a 520-km round trip from Kuşadası, with limited time to absorb the full potential of Pamukkale. Some tours save time and distance by skipping Aphrodisias. But that seems a pity, when relatively so close to a first-division classical site.

More preferable is to stay overnight at Pamukkale. The first day's driving is then around 300 kms, which permits morning departure at a more reasonable hour; a leisured inspection of Aphrodisias; and an evening and part of the following morning at Pamukkale itself, with time to look closer at the Greco-Roman remains of Hierapolis.

Likewise, as a two-day swing, an excursion is feasible from southern resorts like Marmaris or Antalya.

By public transport, Pamukkale is easy to reach by direct bus or train to Denizli and thence 17 kms north by dolmuş. There is a daily direct bus, very cheap, from Selçuk. Numerous pensions are scattered in the village below Pamukkale, with several pricey motels along the ridge. To reach Aphrodisias is more complicated and time-consuming: bus to Nazilli on the main E24 highway; then by dolmuş to Geyre village via Karacasu.

The road to Aphrodisias from Kuşadası follows the E24 highway due east along the Menderes valley, through supremely fertile countryside bounded by hills each side of the plain. Farmers cultivate olive trees, all kinds of fruit, vegetables and grain. It is a supremely beautiful journey of about 160 kms. At harvest times, peasant families sell fruit to passing travellers from wayside stalls. In mid-June, there are peaches everywhere.

A popular lunch-stop on coach tours, some 5 kms before reaching Karacasu, is an open-air restaurant called Zihni, operated by two mildly eccentric brothers. Their fixed-price menu comprises unlimited wine, a couple of pides - one sausage, one of cheese - a taster of omelette, şiş kebab with rice, salad and seasonal fruit. All for less than £2! The brothers even give an impromptu music performance, luring guests to join in and dance, so that a simple lunch is also a big laugh. In the pine-tree woodland alongside are pitched two nomad tents - black, woven from goat-hair.

Aphrodisias

The Greco-Roman site of Aphrodisias - dedicated to Aphrodite, the highly popular goddess of love, nature and fertility - is now well established on tourist itineraries. Dating from 4000 BC, Aphrodisias flourished from the 1st century BC to the 5th century AD, when it was an important art centre specialising in bulk export of marble Roman statues. Limited excavations were made in the first half of the 20th century. The full potential of the site was revealed after an earthquake in 1958, which led to rehousing of the inhabitants of Geyre village. The whole area could thus be cleared for excavation under the direction of Turkish-American Professor Kenan Erim, backed by a National Geographic Society grant.

Over the past 30 years a complete entertainment centre has been uncovered and restored, including a theatre, concert hall and Roman baths, with marble heads by the dozen.

Visits start with the museum. A complete line in Roman emperors is exhibited. Curiously, for a city devoted to worship of Aphrodite, none of the female statues could be X-rated as aphrodisiac. Photographs of the finds were published in National Geographic magazine, not Playboy. Aphrodite is chaste, rather than erotic. Most of the figures are entirely draped. Others are a little more daring, revealing a coy shoulder.

The recommended route around the site crosses what formerly was the main square of Geyre village, and then leads to the Theatre. Tour groups often are guided round in the reverse direction to that suggested by the Museum arrows. Along the path are blocks of stone neatly labelled, all ready for when new funds may permit more reconstruction. Several other areas are blocked off, pending future excavation.

A dazzling surprise awaits at the

Theatre, which is in wonderful shape. The tiers of white stone seats look as though they date from only 200 years ago, instead of 2000. Below, you can explore the adjoining theatre baths. A path above the theatre offers a panoramic view of the Agora, and then leads down again to the massive Baths of Hadrian. In the Temple of Aphrodite, stones with carved crosses testify to later conversion of the pagan Temple to a Christian church.

Another surprise awaits at the Stadium, in perfect condition for Festivals and Sports Days cheered on by 30,000 fans. A dusty path emerges onto the top tier of the Stadium: 22 rows of seats, and everything marked out for track events. Magnificent! Then look around at the slopes of Babadağ - a Daddy of a Mountain. It's like being in the central bowl of the universe. Theatre, music, a workout in the gymnasium, gossip and massage at the Baths, shopping in the agora, athletic events at the stadium, boxing and wrestling matches, and worship of the goddess of love - those Greeks and Romans knew how to enjoy themselves in a glorious setting.

TRAVEL Back to the E24 main highway, continuing up the Menderes Valley, with the countryside becoming more parched as the road climbs above the 2000-ft level.

Grain and tobacco give way to fig trees, their green leaves covering large parts of the otherwise bare landscape. Deep-rooted, they demand very little moisture for survival. This area grows most of Turkey's figs, exported from Izmir in time for Christmas. In several dried-up locations erosion control work is in progress, particularly where rubble-strewn tributaries are just fierce torrents a few times a year. All the washed-out soil meandered

downstream over the centuries, and finally silted up Ephesus, over a hundred miles away.

Then the cultivated areas become still more narrow, and it's barren almost to the road itself. Through busy but dusty Denizli, a side-road turns up to Pamukkale, passing a turn-off to Laodicea: a classical city which was a great trading and banking centre, and locale for one of the Seven Churches of the Apocalypse. Today a hippodrome built by Emperor Titus survives, though most of the stones were carted off last century to build a railway. This site can safely be skipped, unless you're dead keen. Much greater things await, further along.

At first view of Pamukkale, it looks like a chalk quarry: a huge white scar in the face of a 400-foot cliff. Closer, it ranks as one of Turkey's great natural wonders. The calcium cascade - terraces of snow-white stalactites, formed by the deposits from mineral-rich volcanic springs - draws thousands of sightseers every year. The tourist influx is not just a 20th-century business. Two thousand years ago, the classical city of Hierapolis on the clifftop thrived from long-stay visitors. Hierapolis could afford enough temples to justify its Greek name of 'Holy City', and traces of its wealth remain.

Pamukkale (Turkish for 'Cotton Castle') has been millennia in the making. Water gushes to the surface at 95° F and is so charged with minerals that a twig immersed for a few days will emerge with a brilliantly white stone-hard skin.

These waters explain the prosperity of Hierapolis, which in Greek and Roman days was a great centre of healing. The sick, after prayer and ritual purification, were led to the "Passage of Whispering Ghosts", from which they emerged half-drugged due to carbon dioxide fumes in the waters. They were then dunked in a pool in which tourists can still wallow today at the Pamukkale Motel. Non-residents can bathe for 40p: an idyllic experience, swimming in a pool littered with Roman columns, shaken down by earthquakes. Brilliant flowers lean over the water's edge. A notice said: "No eating, drinking or spitting in the swimming pool."

Other motels along the cliff edge have similar bathing arrangements. From these clifftop pools, the hot-spring waters ripple into a series of natural basins that are terraced on ledges down the cliff face. Reflecting the blue sky, in a setting of dazzling white, each basin becomes a joyous paddling pool.

An outstanding impression at Pamukkale is that the Roman constructions were on much greater scale than anything the 20th century has to offer - limited to the few motels along the ridge. The modern establishments have their swimming pools, fed by hot spring water - but nothing so ambitious as the Roman buildings. The city baths and gymnasium of 2nd century AD are truly enormous. Part of this massive structure houses the museum. There were more baths elsewhere in town.

Halfway up the hillside is a well-preserved Roman theatre seating 10,000. Contrast that with the present-day lack of entertainment, except perhaps some canned music and a tea-garden. Obviously the Romans made a big thing of taking the waters. They came here in their thousands, to take a cure; to work out in the gymnasium on the side; to feast and go to a play. A considerable lifestyle was developed.

Scattered over the hillsides are hundreds of stone bases and parts of columns. If archaeologists had the time, money and the work-force, they could bring another whole Roman city to life again. Further along the ridge, out of Pamukkale's main centre, is a mile or two of burial grounds - a necropolis lined with over a thousand stone sarcophagi, and chamber tombs built like houses with massive stone walls. It's a great open-air coffin museum, quite fantastic. Maybe Hierapolis was not so good on cures, after all.

Past the necropolis is a village called Karahayıt Kuyu where numerous pensions offer room with mineral-water baths. At a camp-site in the village, there is steaming hot water - temperature 135° F compared with 95° F at Pamukkale - rippling down over a ledge, and then channelled into a large natural style swimming pond. The mineral content gives a red deposit to the rocks, in contrast to the brilliant white cotton of Pamukkale. A dip costs 40p, all very informal. Low hills surround the location.

This could be a pleasant stopover for self-drive travellers: pull in at a low-cost pension, and then return to Pamukkale for more detailed sightseeing. Most of the houses have bathrooms fed by the hot mineral water. Guests can cure their rheumatism all-inclusive in the pension price.

Also included is enjoyment of the village atmosphere, sitting on a terrace to view the local activity. Little wisps of steam come from odd corners, as the water flows through leaky pipes from one house to another. It's a world apart from commercialized tourism.

Priene, Miletus and Didyma

TRAVEL: Three classical sites in one day - Priene, Miletus and Didyma. It sounds like pushing too hard. But these three are so close together that a one-day excursion south from Kuşadası or north from Bodrum can be tackled quite comfortably. Guided coach trips or a self-drive car are the best bet, as connections are very time-consuming by public transport. Kuşadası to Didyma is 85 kms.

On the road south from Kuşadası to Söke, the scenery is of great beauty - hills, trees and greenery, with occasional sightings of the sea. It is like something out of Italy, a Tuscany in Turkey. Olive groves are spread up the terraced hillsides, with cypress trees along boundary lines. The hills have interesting shapes, all ready for an artist to start painting. There are scattered farm houses, odd hay fields, outcrops of rocks and occasional groups of bee-hives.

Located roughly half way between two equally historic cities - Ephesus and Halicarnassus (Bodrum) - Priene and Miletus were both settled in the 10th century BC by Ionians. Both shared the same fate: as the meandering Meander River (Turkish Menderes) silted up their respective ports, they lost their function and died. Just like Ephesus.

This geography can best be surveyed from the hill slopes of Priene, overlooking the flood plain. Tour groups usually visit Priene first, so that the steep climb to the hilltop site is done before the sun becomes too sweltering. A 9 a.m. arrival is perfect. The other two sites of the trio - Miletus and Didyma - require little climbing, so are tolerable in midday or afternoon heat.

Of the two cities, Miletus was the richer and more important. Originally situated on a gulf, near the mouth of the Meander, it had four harbours, a flourishing wool export trade, a powerful navy and an itch to colonize. Its seafaring people set up no fewer than 80 colonies or trading posts, extending from the Black Sea and all around the Mediterranean.

Priene

Priene, on the opposite 'bank' of the Meander plain, was quite different from its bigger brother: devoted less to commerce and war than to the arts of living - religion, sport and culture. This small city-state, sitting on the lower slope of Mt. Mycale, is Hellenistic in style. Modest in scale, it had elegance.

Its cosy little theatre - only eight rows of seats - was designed for the intimate style of early Greek drama, as opposed to the more spectacular productions favoured by later Greeks and the Romans. The council chamber, gymnasium and compact market square were all on the same modest scale. Priene was among the earliest Greek cities to have proper town planning, with streets laid out on a chessboard pattern. Six main streets, long and wide and paved with marble, were crossed by fifteen narrower streets with marble steps. Houses were light and airy with a central courtyard, and had running water in every room. Priene offered gracious living.

Five splendid columns in the Temple give photographers their big chance. That vantage point offers a superb view across what formerly was a broad gulf: open sea, twenty miles across. Today it's all good fertile farmland. The swings and curves of the river bed can be traced by a strip of brighter green. When the Menderes finally reaches the present-day coastline, it is down to a trickle: all gone for irrigation.

Miletus

The remains of Miletus today are at least five miles inland, with the coastline still marching out to sea at a steady 20 feet per year. Considering the original power and size of Miletus, there's not much standing. Some of the best bits were lifted last century to other countries. The monumental Market Gate of Miletus, for instance, found a new home in Berlin. But the major highlight is certainly worth the trip: the largest theatre in Asia Minor, 54 rows high and built largely of marble. Vaulted corridors to the upper tiers were constructed by the Romans on a monumental scale.

From the Byzantine fortress above the theatre, the basic ground plan of Miletus shows up: another city-block grid of spacious streets that were lined by sumptuous buildings - town hall, customs house, baths, gymnasia - befitting a city that was the Athens of Asia Minor. Solid Roman quays border fields where the harbour entrance was guarded by two stone lions that are still in place. It seems incredible that ships once sailed into this harbour, across what is now five miles of ploughed land. Eastwards, several miles along the road towards Bodrum, is the freshwater Lake Bafa which formerly was part of that same inlet of the Aegean Sea.

Didyma

Linked to Miletus by a 20-mile sacred way, Didyma was the Delphi of Asia Minor: a centre of prophesy that ranked second in importance to the Delphic oracle. Funded by the citizens of Miletus, a monumental Temple of Apollo was planned around 330 BC on so vast a scale - over double the size of the Parthenon - that they never finished the job, though they worked on it for 150 years. Then work lapsed for a century. It was resumed by Roman Emperor Caligula, but broken off by Hadrian. The temple was finally wrecked by earthquake in late 15th century.

Substantially reconstructed, the Temple is enormous. Broad steps lead into an outer hall of columns, some of which had capitals adorned with busts of gods. Lying on the ground near the site entrance is the head of a winged Medusa, a survivor of the frieze above. This vestibule is merely one fourth of the temple ground plan, but it was all that most pilgrims saw. The rest was sacred, hidden behind a great wall, still standing.

To consult the oracle, favoured pilgrims went down one of the two narrow corridors, still intact. Meanwhile, priests came chanting down a majestic stairway, fifty feet wide, into the main hall of the temple. There stood a giant cult-statue of Apollo, and the tripod where the oracle was seated in a state of self-imposed delirium. There was high drama as powerful rulers asked advice on private and public affairs, War and Peace, getting ambiguous answers that needed interpretation by the priests. Hollywood couldn't have done it better.

Chapter Five
The Turkish Riviera

Formerly, the biggest single obstacle to tourism along the southern coast - from Bodrum eastwards - was the appalling condition of the roads: OK for camels, but ruinous for cars.

During the past ten or twenty years, a major effort has gone into highway construction, so that the entire southern coastline is now opened up. The leading resorts of the south-western corner of Anatolia are Bodrum and Marmaris, with more modest facilities in the Fethiye direction.

Opening of Dalaman airport to international charter and scheduled-service traffic (and also domestic flights from Istanbul and Ankara) has likewise boosted the region's tourism potential. Formerly the minimum transfer time of five hours by road from Izmir airport deterred many tour operators from packaging these resorts. Today, arrival at Dalaman airport gives the visitor a favourable first impression of Turkey, followed by travel along good roads through fertile countryside and forested hills, with glorious views of blue sea. It is the idyllic setting for which so many people are looking. The journey to the chosen resort is itself an enjoyable part of the holiday.

Marmaris

Travel: 100 km from Dalaman Airport, two hours by bus.
270 km from Izmir, six hours by bus.

120 km from Fethiye, three hours by bus.
160 km from Bodrum, three hours by bus.
15 hours by bus from either Istanbul or Ankara.
There are daily ferries to Rhodes.
Information Bureau (Turizm Danişma Büro) - İskele Meydanı 39 - next to the Customs Office at the harbour landing-stage. Tel: 1035.

The approaches to Marmaris can lift you into a good holiday mood, gateway to a scenic paradise. The road from Gökova is of superlative beauty, with hillsides of lush pine forests. An occasional wayside restaurant advertises fresh trout, which most people don't expect in Turkey. Along the final stretch before reaching Marmaris, a two-mile wall of eucalyptus trees, both sides of the road, provides total shade.

Marmaris is the up-market St. Tropez of Turkey, jutting into a magnificent bay almost totally land-locked in a fjord-like setting. Called Physkos in ancient times, Marmaris flourished as a port on the trade route between Anatolia and Egypt via Rhodes. Curiously there are few remains from that period, though some remnants of smaller cities around the bay can be reached by boat.

Closer to modern times, 1798, Nelson's entire Mediterranean fleet anchored in the superb natural harbour before sailing off to defeat the

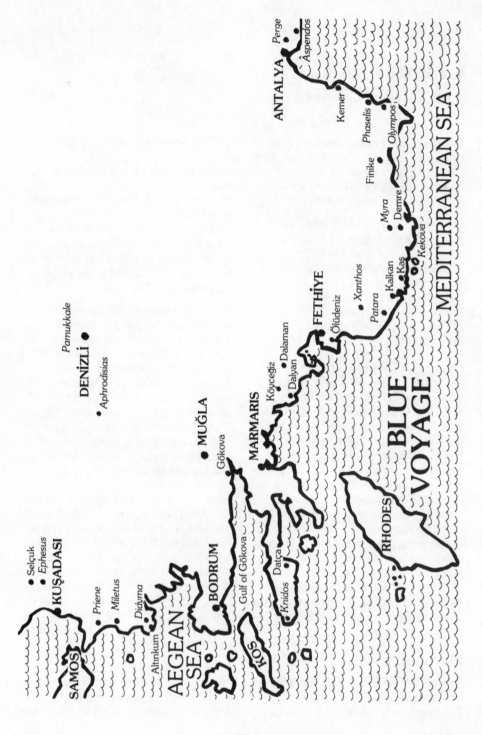

French at the Battle of the Nile. Today, Marmaris has diversified from fishing to tourism. The waterfront now serves Turkey's largest marina, packed with graceful yachts, from international mega-luxury through to Bodrum gulets and racy flotilla boats. They fly all West European flags, but mainly German, British, French and Italian.

No problem if you come to Marmaris without your own yacht. For Marmaris is one of the headquarters of the boat charter business, a popular starting-point for yacht-holiday packages wrapped around the idea of a Blue Voyage. There's choice of flotilla sailing, bareboat hire, or just reserving a cabin aboard an eight-passenger gulet.

Otherwise, just stroll mid-morning along the promenade, and take your pick of day trips around the Bay - either to a single destination or to a circuit of islands, beaches and coves for idyllic swimming. When the summer temperature hits ninety and your feet burn on the sands, it's a perfect way to cool off with a sea breeze blowing in your face and a plunge overboard at each stop.

A typical £3 boat journey starts 11 a.m. from Marmaris, visits several islands, beaches and a phosphorescent cave, finally returning at 6 p.m. A similar journey includes a 3-hour stop at the small resort of Turunç Bay for sand, sea and lunch. A 50-minute boat journey reaches the site of ancient Amos, with its acropolis, temple and Roman theatre. You can even go on a midnight cruise, Marmaris by Night, with on-board discothèque and a pianist-singer: starts at 10.30, returns 2 a.m., first drink free.

There's plenty doing at Marmaris. All along the lively promenade are restaurants, cafés and bars, where holiday crowds pass the time after their sunset stroll, reviewing the fleet. Prices are quite reasonable, considering the jet-set location. The Palmiye Restaurant and the Yarasa Tavern have their own orchestras, and Kemal's Place is renowned for fish. Try the red mullet, sea bass, prawns and octopus. When a leisured evening meal is finished, the taverns and discos warm up as landlubbers and boat people fraternise in a linguistic Babel. Open air cinemas operate during summer, and there are occasional folk shows of Western Anatolian dances. Every June the Marmaris Festival offers a mixture of music, art and culture.

The marina promenade is backed by a labyrinth of small streets and alleys. Traditional whitewashed houses with red rooves are stepped up the terraced hillside. Severely hit by earthquake in 1958, Marmaris has made total recovery, helped by the growth of tourism.

Inside the old town, a former Ottoman Caravanserai has taken on new life as a tourist shopping centre. A plaque at the entrance gate records that ". . . it was built by Süleyman the Magnificent who was conqueror of continents and oceans, and the boss of Arabian and Persian kingdoms. 1545 AD."

On the hilltop above, overlooking the port, is another of Süleyman's constructions: a fortress built in 1522 when he was preparing to conquer the neighbouring island of Rhodes, stronghold of the Knights of St. John. That was a costly trip - 90,000 men lost out of an army of 200,000. The journey comes much cheaper today, on a two- or three-hour excursion aboard the regular ferries.

Marmaris Bay is short on natural sandy beaches. Outside of the big hotels, which supply their own sand, beaches are pebble or shingle. The nearest stretch of natural sand is at Turunç Bay, a popular stopping-point for boat trips or half an hour by dolmuş. However, the beach at Marmaris itself is really quite reasonable: fairly wide, with sand and some shingle, but very crowded during the season. To the east of Marmaris are the beaches of Günnücek (noted for a grove of frankincense trees); and Aktaş and Adaköy, backed by pine trees.

Two thousand years ago, another regular visitor to the coastline of southwestern Anatolia noted the lack of really good sand. The solution can be enjoyed at Kedrai, an ancient site on Şehir Adası - Castle Island, popularly known as Cleopatra's Island - located near the head of the Gulf of Gökova. According to legend, Cleopatra transported ship-loads of finest quality white sand from Egypt, to make a suitable beach for herself and Anthony. This thoughtful gesture is appreciated by today's visitors - either yachtsmen on their Blue Voyage, or by tourists from Marmaris on a coach-and-boat day trip. Maybe Cleopatra's idea was not so extravagant as it sounds. With a thriving export trade from the Marmaris area to Egypt, the returning ships probably brought the sand as ballast.

A parallel idea is followed by the major hotel and holiday village developments. If there's not enough good sand in what otherwise is an excellent location, a man-made beach is created.

The hotel accommodation of Marmaris is scattered low profile for several miles around the bay. The main construction sites are on the western side of Marmaris. More central are numerous pensions and smaller hotels which are particularly attractive to those who like being close to the night-life and belly-dancers. Transport to the scattering of hotels is no problem. Besides the usual low-cost dolmuş services, the municipality of Marmaris carts passengers even cheaper aboard tractor-hauled wagons which ply along the sea front.

Southwest along the coast are three top-grade holiday villages or resort hotels: Turban, Altın Yunus and Martı. The Turban is one of the Tourism Bank's original developments - a 600-bed bungalow vacation village backed by the pine-woods which are typical of the whole bay. The complex merges unobtrusively into the hillside, with a cool sea breeze to moderate the summer heat. Non-residents can pay for entrance to the beach.

Further along, Altın Yunus (Golden Dolphin) is the most recent development, with de luxe hotel bedrooms, villas, Time-share properties and a full complement of sport facilities including a 2-mile jogging track. Then comes the village of Içmeler with thermal springs, a small yacht harbour and the Martı Holiday complex. The location is superb, with views across to the island of Keçiada.

Anywhere in Marmaris Bay, windsurfers can usually expect a very calm sea in morning and evening, with the wind rising in early afternoon to provide good conditions for the experts. Prevailing winds are into the coves, giving added safety for beginners.

The Datça Peninsula

Starting from Marmaris and running due west is the road to Datça (76 kms) and thence another 38 kms to the remains of the ancient city of Knidos. Dedicated archaeologists may disagree, but the journey itself is far more rewarding than the ruins. This very narrow 50-mile finger of land points the official boundary between Aegean Sea to the north and Mediterranean to the south and east. The drive is supremely beautiful - winding up and down along the hog's back of the peninsula, bending through woodlands, with hundreds of bee-hives sited on terraced hillsides of aromatic scrub.

Historians claim that six or seven hundred years BC the peninsula had a 100,000 population, living in some fifty villages. Today it's a mere 8,000, mostly concentrated at Datça itself, with just a few other tiny settlements along the 100-odd miles of coastline.

That shoreline is a yachtsmen's paradise, with at least a hundred peaceful coves where vessels can anchor (counting both sides together - Gökova Bay on the north, and Bay of Isar on the south). It's one of the highlight areas of the Blue Voyage.

Along the heights you get an occasional glimpse of the Gulf of Gökova towards Bodrum, with views spread like a relief map. Then the road swings again and the viewpoint changes, back to the southward panorama over the Bay of Isar.

From time to time the road drops down to the blue water's edge, facing across the bay to more islands. It's a perfect location for camping and other variations on the simple life. There, sure enough, is a typical mocamp established along a shingle beach on a dreamlike bay. A couple of puff-up boats are moored to a jetty, which a few bronzed sun-worshippers are using as a diving platform. There's room for everyone in the shade of pine trees. Campers can use their own tent or caravan, or rent a tent or bungalow.

Further along is the much larger holiday village of Aktur Mocamp, 50 kms from Marmaris. It can accommodate around 10,000 people in holiday apartments, bungalows and camp-site, with all the necessary restaurant and shop facilities, and a resident diving school. The houses are pleasantly shaded, with little gardens. The shoreline of good, fine sand covers two bays. One is usually windy, which is fine for the surfers; the other is usually protected from the wind. Occasionally the wind switches round, and it's "all change".

Datça

Information Bureau (Turizm Danışma Büro) - by the harbour and bus station. Tel: 1703.
76 kms from Marmaris, with numerous buses.
Direct daily buses from Izmir in 6 hours; during the season from Istanbul or Ankara in 16 hours.
Daily ferries during summer link Datça with Bodrum, a 2-hour journey.
Marmaris-Datça-Bodrum would make an interesting routing between the two major resorts, with Datça as a halfway stopover.

Datça offers total contrast compared with the big resorts. A small resort, it's an inexpensive stopover point, with many pensions, a few small hotels and the Club Datça holiday village. The Marina has moorings for 30 yachts, and space for another ten at the holiday village. Offshore is a popular cruising ground for dolphins.

There is a coarse-sand beach just past the marina. Adjoining that beach is what looks like a lagoon or a very large pond, fed by a fresh-water spring that is slightly warmer than sea temperature. This spring is reputed to be good for rheumatism. If you have no ills to cure, you can still enjoy a swim.

Datça functions specially as a staging-point for visiting the ruins at Knidos, 38 kms further along.

Knidos

There are several ways of reaching Knidos. The organised method is by day-trip coach or minibus tour from Marmaris, or boat excursion from Bodrum. Go-it-alone, the key staging point is Datça. A dolmuş service operates to the nearest village, followed by a 5-km walk to reach the site at the extreme tip of the peninsula. A taxi from Datça costs £11 return, with the driver waiting a couple of hours at the site. The best alternative is a whole-day circuit by boat from Datça, costing £4. Starting-time is 9 a.m., return 7 p.m., with swimming-stops at several bays, and adequate time to visit Knidos.

The present site of Knidos was a major commercial centre from 4th century BC onwards, exporting wine. Knidos today is a peaceful location, with animals nibbling the herbage amid the ruins of the ancient city. This trading city had the advantage of two good harbours: one on the Aegean Sea; the other on the Mediterranean - a most useful facility, when winds were awkward. Formerly linked by a canal, their entrances could be closed by a system of chains, as protection from enemies.

The first excavations at Knidos were made in 1856 to 1859 by the British archaeologist Sir Charles Newton. He removed everything worth having - several hundred cases, packed with sculptures - to the British Museum, including a seated statue of Demeter. The plunder continued during the 19th century, when blocks of marble were shipped to Egypt for construction of the palace of Mehmet Pasha. Other remaining blocks of marble helped towards the construction of Dolmabahçe Palace in Istanbul.

The site was famous for a very naked statue of Aphrodite, goddess of love, carved by Praxiteles, greatest of the master sculptors. Originally commissioned by the people of Kos, it was rejected as being too immodest. The statue was then bought by the city of Knidos, and housed in a purpose-built temple. Renowned throughout the ancient world, the work has gone missing, but there's a copy in the Vatican Museum.

Since 1974, American archaeologists have reopened the excavations, and discovered the ruins of a town: especially a large and small amphitheatre, an odeon, remains of statues, and the grid-pattern avenues which split up the town. North-east of the town, at an altitude of 288 metres, is the Acropolis.

The Dalyan Delta and Caunos

Köyceğiz Information Bureau (Turizm Danışma Büro) - Kordon Gölpark 1 - central, by the waterfront. Tel: 1703. TRAVEL: 30 minutes from Dalaman airport, 31 kms. Marmaris 63 kms; Fethiye 80 kms.

A rewarding excursion from Marmaris or Fethiye - by road or boat - has the classical site of Caunos as the main objective. Even if you've had enough ruins, the trip is worth taking, to enjoy the superb scenery and wildlife of the Dalyan Delta.

Arriving by road, the approach is via a little lakeside town called Köyceğiz, which has big tourism ambitions for the area. The region has five aces in its hand: a large freshwater lake that specialises in fish farming; hot sulphur springs for thermal tourism; a reed-filled lagoon like the Norfolk Broads, but with mountains each side, and hot sun; a three-mile beach of powder-fine sand, anything from 50 to 150 yards wide (but totally devoid of shade); ancient rock-cut tombs like a stage set overlooking a river, and the ruins of Caunos.

The lake covers an area of 20 square miles, formed by the silting up of a bay. A narrow 6-mile channel like a river connects lake and lagoons to the Mediterranean, with the outflow almost blocked by a sand-bar. The name Dalyan in Turkish means a fishing weir, and the waterside villagers earn their living from fish netting and cultivation, just like the inhabitants of Caunos 2000 years ago. Local restaurants serve bream, bass or mullet.

Tourism is the new business. At Dalyan's river quayside, boatmen wait for passengers who want transport through the meandering waterway amid a wilderness of reeds, to the sandy beach or the remains of Caunos. Quite apart from the ruins, it makes a memorable boat journey through a wildlife paradise. A keen bird-watcher can spot forty bird varieties in one hour, including green-headed ducks, wild geese, herons, kingfishers, egrets and cranes.

The alternative approach is aboard a

Blue Voyage yacht or day-boat from Marmaris, anchoring at Ekincik Bay. There, the local fishermen's cooperative takes visitors by motor launch through the narrow entrance into the lagoon, and thence to the classic site which is two miles from the sea.

Starting from virtually zero baseline, a number of major tourism developments were planned for the next few years: a small marina at Ekincik Bay, with an 800-bed holiday village on the pine-covered slopes, and various hotels totalling 1400 beds; at the mouth of the estuary, which would be bridged, berthing facilities for pleasure boats and a 550-bed first class hotel; by the lagoon behind İztuzu Beach, developments totalling 3600 beds; at the Sultaniye Thermal Baths, a spa centre for 2,400 persons.

All that - only half an hour from Dalaman airport. Somehow, the Dalyan Delta wouldn't be quite the same. In particular, an agonised debate broke out, Turtles versus Tourism. Formerly, marine turtles were widespread throughout the Mediterranean. However, because of pollution and the exploitation of beaches for tourist use in Italy, Greece and Israel, they have become almost extinct in those countries during the past 40 years. The turtles need quiet sandy beaches for their egg-laying, and are disturbed by noise and bright lights. Today, the long, natural beaches of Turkey and some Greek islands are the turtles' last refuge. In Turkey, their best known breeding-sites are Akyatan in the Adana region, Belek in the Antalya region, and Dalyan Beach. The green turtle (Chelonia mydas) prefers the eastern parts of the Mediterranean coast; while the loggerhead turtle (Caretta caretta) prefers the western area -

111

particularly Dalyan Beach, scheduled for mammoth tourism development.

All good conservationists will cheer the final decision. The İztuzu lagoon development has been reduced to a single hotel of 634 beds, sited well back from the beach, instead of the massive 3600-bed complex of bungalows and holiday village. All beach huts, tents, caravans and buffets have been removed. Construction of a beach road, and a bridge over the estuary, has been abandoned. Likewise, berthing facilities and a hotel at the estuary mouth have been cancelled. The beach and its surroundings have been declared a natural conservation area.

The turtle has won.

Lycia

Draw a straight line across the map of southern Turkey, between Fethiye and Antalya. Jutting south of that line is the Teke Peninsula (Teke means billy-goat). It is a region of high limestone mountains that cuts off the Elmalı Plain from the Mediterranean. Here was the ancient territory of the Lycians - basically a tough sea tribe who built small settlements around the coast and along the river valleys. They formed a Lycian League, which operated as a federal republic.

Ever since the dawn of history, Lycia was isolated, and stayed independent longer against powerful outsiders like Persians or Romans. Even into the early 19th century, Lycia and its history was little known. For similar reasons of geography, this area has been the last in south-western coastal Turkey to yield to tourism. Today the surrender to the sun-worshippers of north-western Europe is complete. Each little resort is witnessing a construction boom in guest-houses, small hotels, restaurants, bars and carpet shops.

When I first toured the region by ship, in 1950, there was no way of travelling round this coast by road unless by amphibious camel. The weekly coast-hugging journeys by Turkish Maritime Lines included stops at the isolated harbours of Finike, Kaş and Kalkan, where the vessel was the villagers' main means of transport to the outside world.

Roads from one coastal village to another were alarming affairs, dusty old camel trails, up one horrible gradient and down the next, with hairpin bends so acute that intrepid lorries had to reverse to get round them. A journey by road from Finike or Kaş to Antalya could take two days: northwards over the mountain passes to Elmalı and via Korkuteli through a dramatic gorge to Antalya. No wonder the region stayed independent so long!

Today that's all changed, thanks to building of a scenic coastal highway that runs south from Antalya to Kemer and Finike, and thence along the southern shore of the peninsula through Demre, Kaş and Kalkan; and finally north, past the major classical site of Xanthos, to Fethiye. Much of this coastal highway goes against the grain of the mountains, and side roads remain ferocious - the official word is "unimproved". The Teke Peninsula is still one of the last homes of the working camel. Elsewhere, camels are just part of the tourist industry, posing on beaches for holidaymaker snaps.

Six torrential rivers carve down from the horseshoe-shaped belt of mountains that rear up to 3,000 metres. Winter and spring torrents water the valleys and coastal plains, with bone-dry summers helped by irrigation to bring crops to maturity. The warm wet winters are also ideal for vegetable and greenhouse crops, giving potential for three harvests a year. Citrus plantations convert the plains to year-round greenery. Mountain slopes are covered with the usual Mediterranean bush and scrub, grazed by herds of black goats; and superb forests of red and yellow pines, larch, oak trees and cedar.

In sum, Lycia is a region of fabulous natural beauty with a superb coastline for yachtsmen. Indeed, most of the gorgeous little bays and coves are still quite inaccessible by road, so that boat trips are the ideal form of sightseeing.

Ashore, you can potter around what's left of the Lycian civilization. Especially between 8th and 4th centuries BC, they built tombs better than houses. More extensive Greek and Roman remains have survived, but have not been fully excavated. They are certainly worth visiting, though mostly they are in the second division compared with Ephesus, Perge and Side. Curiously, the region is also the authentic home of Santa Claus - read the full story when you come to Demre. If you like your tourism natural and uncommercialized, Lycia's the place to go before the rush starts. After-dinner gossip in a waterfront bar is the height of evening entertainment, though an occasional disco is now surfacing.

Most holidaymakers arrive by charter flight to Dalaman, and catch a bus for the 50-kilometre ride to Fethiye. The alternative and more dramatic approach is by air to Antalya, landing right on the doorstep of Lycia. Antalya offers a direct view of the great range of Bey Mountains that plunge from

their 2376-metre peak steeply to the sea. You can understand how the precipitous cliffs have kept the region isolated so long. Soon after leaving Antalya - past the 4-mile Konyaaltı Beach and the out-of-town commercial harbour - the road enters the Olympus-Bey Dağları Coastal National Park. This begins the South Antalya development area, covering almost 50 miles of coastline, with project finance supplied partly by the World Bank.

The scenic highway can rate among the most beautiful in Turkey, swinging around the irregular coastline. Delightful little coves offer sand or shingle, quite undeveloped. Passing motorists just pull off the road, park beneath the shade of trees, and soak in the simple life. Even the ultimate simple-lifers - Stone Age man - had a similar idea. At Beldibi Beach (just after a road tunnel near the start of the drive) is the Beldibi Cave where prehistoric man lived and painted pictures on the walls.

At a few small camp-sites, motorists can pitch a tent, with a modest snack bar or restaurant for those who don't bring picnic supplies. The Kındıl Çeşme site is operated by the National Parks Administration. Tatty ribbon development has been firmly blocked. All the way through the superb hills, woodlands stretch far up the mountainside, thick and luxuriant - larch and cluster pine on the lower levels, with cedar higher up.

Tourism in the Lycian Peninsula is wrapped around all the K's - Kalkan, Kaş, Kekova and Kemer. So let's take them in that west-east order, starting from Fethiye, with a pause for the principal classical sites en route - Xanthos, Myra and Phaselis.

Fethiye and Ölü Deniz

Fethiye

Information Bureau (Turizm Danışma Büro) - İskele Meydanı 1 - by the marina. Tel: 1527.
TRAVEL, and SITES to visit: Dalaman airport 55 kms; Marmaris 120 kms; Antalya 225 kms; Ölü Deniz 15 kms; Dalyan and Caunos 80 Kms; Xanthos 70 kms; Kaş 108 kms.

As a lively market centre, Fethiye has switched painlessly into tourism, with small hotels, a pleasing marina and development of purpose-built guest-houses. Most of the town is new, following a bad earthquake in 1957. Lycian rock tombs from around 4th century BC, built like small temples or private houses, survived unscathed and shouldn't be missed. They are easily visible from the main highway: an uphill walk, or take a taxi. Otherwise, very little remains from the original town called Telmessos, which flourished 2400 years ago.

There is good choice of boat trips, mainly based on circuits of twelve idyllic islands scattered in Fethiye Bay. Şövalye island has a small restaurant and beach. Opposite, on the mainland 5 kms from Fethiye, is the long Çalış Bay beach with restaurants, camp-sites and discos - a good spot for sunset viewing. Other picnic and camping beaches are at Katrancı Bay, 17 kms north from Fethiye; at Günlük Bay (Kücük Kargı) in a stand of liquid amber trees; and Değimenbaşı, 7 kms from Fethiye amid a magnificent pine forest. Regular whole-day coach excursions operate to Xanthos, or to Caunos and the Dalyan Delta. The Xanthos trip is quite feasible by low-cost public bus, with a mile to walk from the drop-off point.

Much of the weight of holiday development has shifted to Ölü Deniz - 'Dead Sea' - thanks to building of a good highway. Ölü Deniz is something unique: a lagoon of superlative beauty, with the surrounding hills protected as a Nature Reserve. The narrow entrance channel into the lagoon is now barred to pleasure boats, to avoid pollution problems. Any further development is blocked. The existing Hotel Meri is a group of bungalows stepped up a very steep hillside, with a waterside restaurant open to non-residents. Its small sandy beach is perfect for small children.

Outside the lagoon - that is, before the road reaches Ölü Deniz itself - is a very long and wide sandy beach, backed by a random growth of pensions, camp-sites, restaurants and discos. Some of the erections look tatty, but all prices are cheap, including boat trips galore, scuba diving and water-sports. During the season, dolmuş vehicles stream in with loads of sun-worshippers from Fethiye. It's a world apart from the peace of Ölü Deniz itself.

There is yet a third aspect to the area. Until 1923, several villages around were part of a Greek-speaking enclave. Following an exchange of populations, the Greek villages were totally abandoned and have remained deserted ever since. More recently an Englishwoman and her Turkish husband, Captain Bob, have converted a group of these traditional houses for use as self-catering holiday villas. Called Ocak Köy, the development is marketed through UK travel agencies. Morning call is by the braying of donkeys, who are the transport division of a Donkey Safari into the hills.

114

Xanthos

En route from Fethiye, the road climbs over a range of hills, wriggling up and down and around bends like a snake demented with toothache. It winds through beautiful pine forests with broad fire-breaks and distant views of the sea.

From several centuries BC, the principal city of Lycia was Xanthos. Its remains are still the most impressive in the region. The main highway between Fethiye and Kalkan passes within a mile of the site, which is the most rewarding in the Lycian peninsula - though it's not in the Ephesus class. Lycian rulers preferred to be buried above-ground, in monuments perched on pillars or podiums, with a decorative marble frieze. In 1838, archaeologist Sir Charles Fellows explored the site, was deeply impressed, and published journals which aroused great public interest. Until then, very little was known of the Lycian civilization.

Four years later, the British navy lent a hand. Sailors from HMS Beacon went ashore and, during a 2-months' operation, stripped the site of everything worth lifting. They shipped 78 packing cases of marble sculptures and reliefs from the big funerary monuments, and presented them to the British Museum. This episode is variously described by Turkish publications as "loot", "ruthless plunder" or "rape". Since then, in a spirit of atonement, Britain has given Turkey a plaster cast of some of the reliefs. Deeply impressive is the Tomb of the Harpies, roosting on a monolith overlooking a Roman Theatre, like a seat in the gods. Other remains that still survive are the acropolis, defensive walls, the city gate and buildings from the Byzantine age.

Patara

The road from Fethiye to Kalkan goes inland all the way, with virtually nil access to the coast. A dirt road leads off the main highway for six kms to Patara, where an ancient city and its harbour are buried beneath sand-dunes. Ruins are scattered over a very large area. Patara was formerly a major commercial port, but was also famed for the cult of Apollo the sun god. Today, modern man still comes to Patara for sun-worship, attracted by the enormously long and wide beach of clean yellow sand. Patara is a popular whole-day trip from Kalkan or Kaş, by sea or road. Shade is non-existent. You can rent shade - a sheet tied to four upright poles - or bring your own.

Kalkan

Kalkan is a tiny resort, quite charming, located 3 hours from Dalaman airport. It features a typical small marina where Blue Voyage yachtsmen pull in for the night, or to replenish their supplies of bread, wine, ice and rakı. Hemming in the harbour are the usual carpet and kilim shops, café-bars and the like. In the background is a gleaming-white mosque behind a waterfront restaurant. Above the steep pie-dish of the village are dramatic mountain slopes.

Many of the bars are on rooftop terraces, all with sea view and a breeze. Extremely attractive is a waterfront pension called Balıkçı Han, converted from a 19th-century Turkish inn. It is beautifully modernised with ten double rooms, including a honeymoon suite. Worth remembering, if marriage is on your mind.

There is no sand in town - just a tiny

pebble beach to the left of the marina. You must go elsewhere for sand-worship: to Kaputaş or Patara, for instance. At the top level of the village are low-cost dolmuş and taxi services, and the bus stop to Fethiye and other distant locations.

A free boat service operates across from Kalkan harbour to The Platform, which offers bathing from rock-cut terraces. There is similar access to Kalamar Beach Club, which likewise offers free boat transport to their bathing terraces, bar and restaurant in a small cove a mile from Kalkan centre.

Near Kalkan and around the coast is favourite dolphin territory. Five a.m. is reputed to be a good time for dolphin-spotting, but often they escort boats along the coast at a more sensible hour.

A popular excursion is a 3-caves boat trip, eastwards towards Kaş, combined with time on the sandy beach of Kapıtaş. The Blue Grotto is the largest and most attractive with a phosphorescent colour scheme and a resident population of seals. A morning visit is best, before the noonday breeze makes entry more difficult. Dove Cave - close back to Kalkan - is better in late afternoon when the sun's rays highlight the brilliant colours. When the boat captain honks his horn, hundreds of rock-doves come fluttering out in protest at having their siesta disturbed. This cave can be entered only by swimming through a very narrow entrance, which can be quite spooky. Opposite is the wide-mouthed Güvercinlik Cave, with waters fed by a cold freshwater stream - 55° F compared with upwards of 77° F in the sea. Be prepared for the shock.

For sea-caving enthusiasts, this limestone region is a good hunting-ground. In Kaş, contact Dr. Temuçin Aygen, a geologist who is president of the Turkish Speleological Society. You'll find him at the Pamfilya Travel Agency.

Kapıtaş Beach

The coast road between Kalkan and Kaş has been hacked from the limestone cliffs - a superb drive. Partway along, there's a bridge called Kapıtaş, crossing a savage-looking cleft in the rocks. It's very easy to drive past, without noticing that there's a golden beach way down below. 180 concrete steps lead to the cove, where sun-worshippers roast like barbecued sheep. The beach shelves very rapidly, so be cautious with children. The sands are utterly perfect, but there are no facilities like ice cream salesmen, or peddlers selling postcards. Take a picnic and your own shade.

Kaş

Information Bureau (Turizm Danışma Büro) - Cumhuriyet Meydanı 6 - on main square by the harbour. Tel: 1238-3226. TRAVEL, and SITES to visit: Dalaman Airport 158 km, 4 hours by bus; Kalkan 26 km; Blue Grotto 19 km; Xanthos 44 km; Demre 48 km; Antalya 198 km.

From a hilltop along the main road, there's a fantastic view over the Kaş area and across to the Greek island of Kastelorizo just outside the Bay. It's a little corner of blue paradise, with pleasure boats cruising away on their individual Odysseys. If you have never been a yachting enthusiast, ask yourself: "What have I been doing, all these years?" During a stay in Kaş, you can make up for lost time, with a boat trip every day along the Mediterranean's most idyllic coastline.

Until quite recently, Kaş was a dozey little fishing village and market centre. Now, quite suddenly, tourism has arrived, and Kaş has become the "in" place for a Turkish holiday. The expansion has come rapidly, and the main town square can no longer be described as "sleepy". In high season, visitors easily outnumber the four thousand residents. Construction workers are rocketing Kaş into the future, with a fivefold increase in tourist numbers planned for the five-year period of 1987 to 1992. With yachting so important, the marina capacity is being enlarged to shelter 250 vessels.

Even so, simplicity is still the keynote. Accommodation is unsophisticated, at least until several top-grade hotels are built around the bay. There is good supply of village rooms and pensions, clean and comfortable, with a shaded garden or rooftop terrace for leisure hours. Many of the establishments operate on a room-only basis. Just like in other resorts, you can easily get a friendly breakfast at an open-air café or tea-garden for about 60p: the standard offering of bread, butter, cheese, olives, jam and tea.

In what is now a thriving holiday resort, many aspects of local life continue quite unchanged. Take an evening stroll, and watch housewives rounding up their goats, or driving free-range chickens, squawking and protesting, into their night quarters. An old woman spins wool with a traditional spindle, but resolutely shakes her head when a passing tourist asks if he may take a photo.

Among the attractions of Kaş is a fine collection of Lycian tombs, mostly dating from around 4th century BC

when the town's name was Antiphellos. Rock tombs were designed like temples or houses, with Greek-style Ionic columns, triangular pediments and front doors. In the necropolis on the outskirts of Kaş is a splendid rock-cut house tomb with seats, and a relief depicting two dozen girls holding hands and dancing, with their skirts lifted by the wind. Another fine monumental sarcophagus stands by the harbour quayside. But everyone's favourite tomb is handily located in one of the main streets, standing on a podium opposite a souvenir store. Many of the other stone coffins have long since been dismantled, and recycled into village house-building.

Close to the necropolis is a well-preserved Hellenistic theatre, with 26 rows of seats that look straight out from the hillside to the sea. If the ancients were bored with the play, they could always admire the scenery. Annual 'greased wrestling' tournaments, festivals and folklore displays are held at this site.

Kaş does not have sand within easy walking distance. But the whole area abounds in little coves where you can enjoy solitude on a pebbly beach. Dolmuş boats shuttle back and forth; or friendly boat kaptans on the waterfront offer wide choice of all-day trips with swimming and sun-bathing stops, sea-cave visits or excursions to Kekova. They offer a three days and three nights' Blue Voyage, including breakfast and dinner each day, with a maximum of eight passengers. Quoted price was £40, but that could change. There are day trips across to the Greek island of Kastelorizo, but no staying overnight. The Greek islanders do their shopping in Kaş.

Jutting out from Kaş is a narrow

117

peninsula, fitted with a most beautiful scenic road - a five-mile circuit. The views are fabulous - sometimes on the spine of the peninsula with scenery both sides, or down to the waterside for dreamy little coves. On the western side the sea is almost completely enclosed, with the water sparkling like a blue mirror. At the tip of the pensinsula, Greece is only two miles away.

If a five-mile walk doesn't make you shudder, consider a late afternoon stroll. On the outward walk, keep to the eastern side of the peninsula (with some shade as the sun sinks below the hill crest). Then return along the westward side, to enjoy the sunset. There is very little habitation - just a few herds of black goats, grazing amid the sage and the olive trees. The sage is used for herbal tea. Try some at a tea-house, asking for adaçayı.

Kekova

The prime boat trip from Kalkan or Kaş is to the long, thin island of Kekova, famous for its sunken city. On a typical cruise, a boat leaves Kaş at 9.30, sailing for about two hours past uninhabited islands to a ruined village called Aperlae, where the outline of ruins can be seen below the water. There's time to swim and snorkel, using on-board equipment. A dinghy gives access to the shore, which is scented like a herb garden with origano, thyme, mint and sage. Tortoises live amid the remains. Other boat captains have alternative stopping places for a morning swim.

Then the boat sails to Tersane Bay on Kekova Island. The crew prepares a lunch of fish - caught that morning - with bread, salad and wine. There is another chance to snorkel and swim,

viewing the plentiful underwater life. Beware of sea urchins!

After lunch the boat continues along the northern shore of Kekova Island, towards Kale on the mainland, where part of an ancient city sank into the sea, probably through earthquake. The remains are graded as an underwater archaeological site, and swimming or snorkelling is not permitted. But, with imagination, you can pick out the harbour, jetty and quayside, with houses, staircases going up, and even the holes in the stonework where joists ran across. A tomb is perched above the water level.

Landing at Kale, which means Castle, visitors climb a steep path to a Byzantine fortress, with breath-taking views of the area. Numerous sarcophagi are scattered around. The village below is a popular stopping place for Blue Voyage yachts, and several restaurants and boarding houses now line the waterfront. A newly-surfaced road is opening up Üçağız Bay and Kale to landlubbers, but the beautiful boat journey remains the preferred means of access. There are several sea caves in the vicinity. On the island of Kekova itself are more Lycian tombs, and the remnants of a Byzantine church.

Demre and Myra

After 48 kms of snaking highway from Kaş, the road finally winds down to the Kasaba valley, which is almost totally filled with citrus plantations, and greenhouses for early vegetables and tomatoes.

Father Christmas is the only reason for stopping in the dusty market town of Demre which adjoins the ancient city of Myra. The story is that St. Nicholas was born about 300 AD in

Kabak kızartması	: Fried zucchini slices served with yogurt
Patlıcan kızartması	: Fried aubergine slices served with yogurt
Zeytinyağlı fasulye	: Green beans with chopped tomatoes

* Savoury pastries, "börekler"

Sigara böreği	: Fried filo pastry filled with cheese
Su böreği	: Layers of filo pastry baked with cheese or meat filling
Talaş böreği	: Puff pastry filled with meat

* Salads, "salatalar"

Cacık	: Chopped cucumber in garlic flavoured yogurt
Çoban salatası	: Mixed tomato, pepper, cucumber, and onion salad
Patlıcan salatası	: Pureed aubergine salad
Piyaz	: Haricot bean salad

* Desserts, "tatlılar"

Baklava	: Flaky pastry stuffed with nuts in syrup
Tel Kadayıf	: Shredded wheat with nuts and syrup
Sütlaç	: Creamy cold rice pudding
Komposto	: Cold stewed fruit
Dondurma	: Ice cream

* Fruits, "meyvalar"

Grapes	: Üzüm
Honeydew melon	: Kavun
Peaches	: Şeftali
Watermelon	: Karpuz
Plums	: Erik
Apples	: Elma
Apricots	: Kayısı
...rs	: Armut
...ries	: Kiraz
...as	: Muz
	: İncir

MINI-CONVERSATION GUIDE

c = "j" (cami = Jami)
ç = "ch" (Foça = Focha)
ğ = lengthener (Dağ = Daa)
ı = non-English vowel sound closer to short i than to long e (e.g. Topkapı)
ö = ö as in German "böse" (e.g. Göreme)
ş = "sh" (Kuşadası = Kushadası)
ü = as in French "tu" (e.g. Ürgüp)
(**Note**: In Turkish, every letter is pronounced)

Everyday phrases and polite expressions:
To the words "Hoş geldiniz" ("Welcome"), you reply "Hoş bulduk."

Hello	: Merhaba
Goodbye	: Allahaısmarladık (said by the person leaving)
	Güle güle (said by the person seeing his friend off)
Good morning	: Günaydın
Good evening	: İyi Akşamlar
Good night	: İyi Geceler
How are you?	: Nasılsınız?
I'm fine, thank you.	: İyiyim, teşekkür ederim
Please	: Lütfen
Thank you	: Teşekkür ederim, or, mersi
Yes	: Evet
No	: Hayır
There is	: Var (used to express the availability
There is not	: Yok or unavailability of something, respectively)
I want	: İstiyorum

Numbers

1 : Bir	20 : Yirmi	200 : İkiyüz
2 : İki	25 : Yirmibeş	300 : Üçyüz
3 : Üç	30 : Otuz	1000 : Bin
4 : Dört	40 : Kırk	2000 : İkibin
5 : Beş	50 : Elli	
6 : Altı	60 : Altmış	
7 : Yedi	70 : Yetmiş	
8 : Sekiz	80 : Seksen	
9 : Dokuz	90 : Doksan	
10 : On	100 : Yüz	
11 : Onbir	101 : Yüzbir	

The Time

When?	: Ne zaman?
Yesterday/today	: Dün/bugün
Tomorrow	: Yarın
Morning/afternoon	: Sabah/öğleden sonra
Evening/night	: Akşam/gece
One hour	: Bir saat
What is the time?	: Saat kaç?
At what time?	: Saat kaçta?

Days of the week

Sunday	: Pazar
Monday	: Pazartesi
Tuesday	: Salı
Wednesday	: Çarşamba
Thursday	: Perşembe
Friday	: Cuma
Saturday	: Cumartesi

While travelling

Airport	: Havaalanı
Port	: Liman
Town center	: Şehir merkezi
Where is it ?	: Nerede?
Is it far?	: Uzak mı?
Tourism bureau	: Turizm bürosu
Repair garage	: Araba tamircisi
A good hotel	: İyi bir otel
A restaurant	: Bir lokanta
Attention	: Dikkat

In the garage

Petrol	: Benzin
Petrol station	: Benzin istasyonu
Oil	: Motor yağı
Change of oil	: Yağ değiştirme
Diesel	: Mazot, Motorin, Dizel
Tire	: Lastik

Brakes	: Frenler
Spark plugs	: Bujiler
It does not work.	: Çalışmıyor

In the restaurant

Bread	: Ekmek
Meat	: Et
Water	: Su
Mutton	: Kuzu eti
Mineral water	: Maden suyu
Lamb	: Koyun eti
Fruit juice	: Meyva Suyu
Beef	: Sığır eti
Wine	: Şarap
Veal	: Dana eti
Beer	: Bira
Chicken	: Piliç / Tavuk
Ice	: Buz
Fish	: Balık

Several Turkish dishes

* **Hors-d'oeuvres "mezeler"**

Arnavut ciğeri	: Spicy fried liver with onions
Çerkes tavuğu	: Cold chicken in walnut puree with garlic
Çiğ Köfte	: Spicy raw meatballs
Midye dolması	: Stuffed mussels
Yaprak dolması	: Stuffed grape leaves

* **Soups, "çorbalar"**

Yayla çorbası	: Yogurt soup
Düğün çorbası	: Meat soup with egg yolks stirred in
İşkembe çorbası	: Tripe soup

* **Pilafs, "pilav"**

Sade pilav	: Plain rice pilaf
İç pilav	: Rice with nuts, curra
Bulgur pilavı	: Cracked wheat pi

* **Cold vegetables in olive oil, "zeytinyağ**

İmam bayıldı	: Split aubergine w

the now-vanished coastal town of Patara, and was educated at Xanthos. He became the bishop of Myra, and was renowned for his generosity and good deeds. In due time, he was canonized. St. Nicholas was known as the protector of sailors and children, and was adopted as the patron saint of Russia until they changed him for Lenin. He is also the patron saint of thieves, lawyers and pawnbrokers.

Basis of the Santa Claus legend is that three local maidens went to the bishop, saying that unless they could find dowries for marriage, they would be sold into prostitution. During the night, the warm-hearted bishop tossed a bag of gold through each of their open windows.

There are variations on this story, depending who tells it. But essentially there is a clear tradition of anonymous present-giving, linked to the feast day of St. Nicholas - December 6. Hence, by roundabout route, we arrive at the modern Santa Claus - the kindly whiskered character known to the Turks as Noel Baba.

In Demre stands the restored version of the church and burial chapel built in Saint Nicholas's honour immediately after his death in mid-4th century. In 1087, some merchants from the Italian city of Bari stole most of Santa's bones, and took them triumphantly back home to their Basilica of San Nicola, where they are now enshrined in the crypt. Fortunately some spare bones were left over, and these are today treasured in Antalya Museum.

The Turkish tourism authorities do their best to sustain the legend, which is good for business, judging by the number of tour coaches which pull up during the season. A pleasing statue of Father Christmas has been erected in

a little park garden adjoining the church. He carries his traditional sack, and children cluster around him. A Demre Festival is held 3-6 December every year, to commemorate the world's favourite saint.

A mile outside Demre is the historic site of Myra, where rock tombs rise dramatically on a hillside behind the well-preserved Roman theatre - still used for cultural events. Hard scrambling is needed to reach most of the tombs, but it's worth the effort. Chunks of sculpture and columns are scattered in the undergrowth. Around the site, irrigation channels ripple with water to supply an enormous acreage of greenhouse tomatoes. In the long term, Demre may start catering more actively for overnight visitors. Quite apart from Myra and Father Christmas, Demre has close access to lengthy stretches of sandy beach. Likewise, Finike - 30 kms further along - has an open 15-km stretch of sand and pebbles, virtually unexploited, except for the simplest possible bathing huts and cabins. Meanwhile, the local townships seem much more interested in tomato business.

Phaselis

Along the final stretch to Kemer - only 10 miles to go - is a turn-off to the ancient trade centre of Phaselis. The city was founded in 690 BC by colonists from Rhodes. It was the last city on the borders of Lycia and the region of Pamphyllia (which stretches along the coast to Alanya).

The highspot in its history came in 333 BC, when Alexander the Great entered the city and wintered there. He was delighted by the waterside location of Phaselis, with its harbours, avenues and temples. Mid-winter, he liked to see the roses in full bloom, and enjoyed the scent of lilies.

During Roman times, particularly during 2nd century AD, the city attained peak prosperity - followed by gradual decline through turmoil, looting and piracy. When the Turks took over, greater importance was given to Antalya and Alanya. Phaselis was completely abandoned. Today's ruins all date from Roman and Byzantine times. Recent excavations have been partly financed by the World Bank.

Phaselis had three harbours, linked by a splendid avenue 33 feet wide. Today you can easily trace the aqueducts and the market places, a theatre, baths, a Hadrian's Gate and an acropolis. The little theatre is charming, with trees and shrubs that lean over and provide shade. Varied plants grow in the crevices between the stone seats. The aroma of pine trees and the chirrup of cicadas complete the sensual delight. Down at the little harbours - adjoining coves - small boats pull in for bathing on the shingle beaches. The over-all atmosphere is a joy. Don't miss it.

Kemer

TRAVEL: 40 kms from Antalya - one hour
Information Bureau (Turizm Danışma Büro) - Belediye Binası - ground floor of the Town Hall, near the harbour.

Kemer is something different: a completely purpose-built resort which started as a development blueprint in Ankara. Instead of haphazard growth which has characterized most of Turkey's holiday industry, the Ministry of Tourism started by laying out the infrastructure first - roads and services - and then inviting Turkish or foreign

firms to develop their chosen sector along the miles of coastline.

The setting is magnificent. On the outskirts of Kemer are citrus plantations, set against a beautiful backdrop of forested mountains. The coastline itself is a series of little coves with sand and rocks.

Focal point of the town centre is Kemer Marina, completed in 1986 with all modern facilities to handle 150 yachts. The spotless clear water glints with little shoals of fish. In the background are totally new streets of holiday apartments, pensions, a few small hotels and new shops and boutiques. The Municipal Beach stretches round the Bay, across from the Marina - some golden sand, some shingle. The original village of Kemer is set further back from the shoreline.

Closest to the centre is the Club Méditerranée holiday village, with five sandy beaches separated by outcrops of rock that give each one an individual character. Thus, one tiny cove is reserved for classical music. Every afternoon, sun-bathers are stretched out beneath umbrellas on the sand, or sit comfortably on a pathway above. During a typical performance of Verdi's "La Traviata", discrete loudspeakers offer near perfect acoustics for the rich sound of Italian opera.

Club Med has its usual French accent; elsewhere along the Kemer coastline is German-speaking Club Robinson.

Club Salima is more international in character, and is promoted by some UK operators. Villas are attractively set out amid grass, flowers and the shade of trees. The Club operates a scuba diving school, and gives belly-dancing lessons. Some villagers come each week to give a demonstration of local life: eight persons who bake bread, spin, play typical music, and erect a nomad tent in front of the tennis court. They also bring three camels, one horse and a donkey.

The most recent development is the 1000-bed Palmiya Hotel, run by the Spanish group, Iber. Duplex villas are spread in a semi-circle around the main public areas. Rooms are well finished, partly tiled, of attractive design and imaginative architecture.

The next vacation village is aimed to suit the Swedish life-style, planned by the Vingresor firm who have a 1500-bed project in Side. Their stated intention is to construct a chain of similar villages during the coming years.

The Kemer pattern may be the shape of Turkey's future tourism development. But contact with Turkey outside the fence could be minimal.

Chapter Six
The Mediterranean Coast

Antalya

TRAVEL: some direct charter flights from UK; otherwise via scheduled services from Istanbul. By road, 541 kms from Izmir or 292 kms from Denizli (Pamukkale) on highway E24; 70 kms to Side, 135 kms to Alanya. Information Bureau (Turizm Danışma Büro) - Cumhuriyet Caddesi 91 - in main street building opposite the terrace promenade above the harbour. Tel: 11747 or 15271

Antalya is the tourism gateway to the 300-mile sine-wave pattern of Mediterranean coastline, stretching right round to the Syrian border. Until now, only the crescent-shaped coast from Kemer to Antalya, Side and Alanya has seen any major development of the tourism potential. In Greek and Roman times, today's holiday zone from Antalya Province to Alanya was called Pamphylia, and that name is still used in archaeological and tourist literature.

Antalya - the largest town along the Mediterranean coast, except for the port of Mersin - is built atop a range of cliffs in the corner of a bay about 20 miles across. It's a Riviera-type location of fabulous beauty, with splendid mountains that dominate the scenery.

Shielded by the Taurus Mountains from the extreme climate of Anatolia, Pamphylia enjoys 300 days of sunshine a year - including Christmas, when it's still possible (a bracing 66° F) to swim in the blue Mediterranean. The sub-tropical valleys and coastal areas produce Turkey's finest oranges and bananas.

For Turks and tourists alike, Antalya's reconstructed harbour is the honeypot. It's a prize-winning Marina and Leisure Centre which rivals anywhere in the Mediterranean. The best seagulls'-eye view of the harbour is from the terrace tea-garden along the promenade above. Enjoy the view, the sea breeze and a glass of tea, and you still have change from 10p.

Declared a conservation area in 1972, the narrow streets of traditional houses leading down to the harbour are enjoying a new lease of life. Some are converted into charming little bars, restaurants or guest-houses. Others, with courtyards, offer displays of locally-made carpets and kilims.

Typical is the Turban Adalya Hotel, which originally was built in 1869 as the branch office of a bank. Later it was used as a warehouse. The building has been tastefully recycled into a 1st-class 58-bed hotel which harmonises with that corner of the harbour. The rooftop bar and restaurant makes a good viewing platform.

The character of the old port has been preserved, while offering all modern facilities for up to 50 visiting yachts. Bronzed fishermen mend their nets, while their colleagues who have switched to tourism offer boat-rides. Early evening, when pleasure boats are manoeuvring into their berths, is an enjoyable time to inspect the fleet. Open-air cafés fill up with thirsty yachtsmen, landlubber holidaymakers and local residents: a lively, multi-lingual Babel. Then the restaurants and tourist shops awaken into activity, followed by the night-owl bars. The harbour area is still bouncing at midnight, aided by the sound of wassail from yachts in party mood.

By day, sightseeing should include the Yivli Minaret Mosque - the Fluted or Grooved Minaret - built by the Seljuk Turks in early 13th century. The finest monument is Hadrian's Gate, large and decorative, built to commemorate the Emperor's visit in 130 AD. Arches lead through to a street with traditional timber houses, which happily have survived the passion to replace everything with concrete.

Finally, the Archaeological Museum is certainly worth a visit. The layout is delightful. Many exhibits are placed outside in a pleasant garden that looks across Antalya Bay to the mountains of Lycia. Rich in finds from Perge and other regional sites, the Museum offers a good introduction to the ancient cities. The 'Gallery of the Gods' is a line-up of all the deities who were worshipped at Perge. That leads into the Emperors' Gallery, filled with the big names of Roman times. An ethnographic section features a display of the nomads' life, with fully furnished yörük tents, and photographs of camels laden with camping gear and household goods. These mountain yörük people have only recently switched to a settled life. A few still cling to their pastures.

Time to sample the beaches:

particularly as the 4-mile Konyaaltı Plaj starts right there by the Museum. In fact, although Antalya is the gateway to many miles of superb sands that run through to Alanya, the town centre has none. Konyaaltı on the western outskirts is a mess of shingle and pebbles. The beach is lined with grotty shacks and tents, ramshackle restaurants and cafés. Not recommended.

Much better is on the eastern side of town, towards Lara Beach - really a resort in its own right, 12 kms from Antalya centre. Lara Plaj is easily reached by low-cost dolmuş transport that follows the coastal road along a flat cliff-top. Several first-class hotels are spread along this road, with access to coves far below; and more hotels are being built. Luxury is featured at the Club Hotel Sera, which even has its own helicopter landing-pad. The Sera's prices are international rather than Turkish. Otherwise there is a good range of accommodation at Lara Plaj, from camp-sites and pensions and through all hotel grades. There is plentiful restaurant choice.

Antalya is an excellent base for excursions. Day tours abound. Southwest takes you along the coastal road of the Bey Dağları National Park to Kemer and Phaselis. North is the highway to Termessos, the classical site located 3500 feet up in the mountains, with stupendous views. A two-day swing could take you to Pamukkale and back, passing the Insuyu Caverns of stalactite formations and underground lakes; and thence via Burdur across an arid plateau with salt lakes that yield sodium sulphate, heaped in enormous white mounds.

East is a classic trio of Perge, Aspendos and Side which can rival anything on the Aegean coast. They can readily be combined in a one-day trip, with time at Manavgat Falls to cool off.

Termessos

For a breath of mountain air combined with culture, consider a trip due north from Antalya to Termessos, forking left off the main E24 Burdur road. Don't confuse this high mountain site with Telmessos, the ancient name for the present-day harbour of Fethiye! Termessos is perched on an impregnable mountain platform that offers superb grandstand views through gaps in the mountains to the green coastal plain twenty miles away. The remains are mostly Roman - the usual theatre, temples, gymnasium and agora - though the site dates from long before Alexander the Great came marching up the E24. For the finest viewpoint of all, an energetic two-mile uphill hike past hundreds of sarcophagi ends by a firewatch tower. It's well worth the slog.

Further north - along another turn-off from E24 - is the Karain Cave, 27 kms from Antalya. It is the oldest inhabited cave that has yet been found in Turkey, dating from the Paleolithic Age, 50,000 BC. A single entrance leads into three large halls. It is a natural cave, facing the Mediterranean, on the steep slopes of the Çadır peak of the Katran mountain. The early tenants had plentiful water supply, thick vegetation which offered wild fruits and vegetables, and good hunting. Even today, the region is known for wild goat, deer, rabbit, partridge, quail, duck and goose, while streams teem with fish. Human remains go way back to prehistoric times. Skeletons, chipped and polished stone tools, shaped flints and weapons from this site are displayed in Ankara's Museum of Anatolian Cultures, with other items in Antalya's Museum.

Perge

Only ten miles east of Antalya, Perge is an ancient Greek town where St. Paul preached during his first missionary journey. In fact, some historians claim that Paul preached his first-ever sermons here, and made his first converts. In those days, Perge was already a considerable city. It flourished still more during the golden age of Pax Romana, particularly in 2nd and 3rd centuries AD. Public buildings were built, enlarged or embellished with statuary, often donated by wealthy public-mind citizens.

Best overall view of Perge is from the theatre, high up in the gods. You get a complete picture of the 15,000-seat Roman theatre, while looking across to the neighbouring entertainment facility - the stadium - and thence to the acropolis which overlooks the remainder of the city. The stadium is the best preserved in Turkey, after Aphrodisias. It could seat 15,000 people to watch athletic events and gladiator fights.

In the main city are huge entrance gates, monumental Roman baths, a splendid colonnaded street (whence came many of the statues in Antalya's Archaeological Museum), and an agora with mosaic paving on the shop floors. Out of the available sites along the Mediterranean coast, Perge gives the clearest idea of a typical Greco-Roman city layout.

Aspendos

Next along highway E24 is Aspendos, four kms up a side road. You pass an interesting Seljuk bridge on the right,

MINI-CONVERSATION GUIDE

c = "j" (cami = Jami)
ç = "ch" (Foça = Focha)
ğ = lengthener (Dağ = Daa)
ı = non-English vowel sound closer to short i than to long e (e.g. Topkapı)
ö = ö as in German "böse" (e.g. Göreme)
ş = "sh" (Kuşadası = Kushadası)
ü = as in French "tu" (e.g. Ürgüp)
(**Note**: In Turkish, every letter is pronounced)

Everyday phrases and polite expressions:
To the words "Hoş geldiniz" ("Welcome"), you reply "Hoş bulduk."

Hello	: Merhaba
Goodbye	: Allahaısmarladık (said by the person leaving)
	Güle güle (said by the person seeing his friend off)
Good morning	: Günaydın
Good evening	: İyi Akşamlar
Good night	: İyi Geceler
How are you?	: Nasılsınız?
I'm fine, thank you.	: İyiyim, teşekkür ederim
Please	: Lütfen
Thank you	: Teşekkür ederim, or, mersi
Yes	: Evet
No	: Hayır
There is	: Var (used to express the availability
There is not	: Yok or unavailability of something, respectively)
I want	: İstiyorum

Numbers

1 : Bir	20 : Yirmi	200 : İkiyüz
2 : İki	25 : Yirmibeş	300 : Üçyüz
3 : Üç	30 : Otuz	1000 : Bin
4 : Dört	40 : Kırk	2000 : İkibin
5 : Beş	50 : Elli	
6 : Altı	60 : Altmış	
7 : Yedi	70 : Yetmiş	
8 : Sekiz	80 : Seksen	
9 : Dokuz	90 : Doksan	
10 : On	100 : Yüz	
11 : Onbir	101 : Yüzbir	

The Time

When?	: Ne zaman?
Yesterday/today	: Dün/bugün
Tomorrow	: Yarın
Morning/afternoon	: Sabah/öğleden sonra
Evening/night	: Akşam/gece
One hour	: Bir saat
What is the time?	: Saat kaç?
At what time?	: Saat kaçta?

Days of the week

Sunday	: Pazar
Monday	: Pazartesi
Tuesday	: Salı
Wednesday	: Çarşamba
Thursday	: Perşembe
Friday	: Cuma
Saturday	: Cumartesi

While travelling

Airport	: Havaalanı
Port	: Liman
Town center	: Şehir merkezi
Where is it ?	: Nerede?
Is it far?	: Uzak mı?
Tourism bureau	: Turizm bürosu
Repair garage	: Araba tamircisi
A good hotel	: İyi bir otel
A restaurant	: Bir lokanta
Attention	: Dikkat

In the garage

Petrol	: Benzin
Petrol station	: Benzin istasyonu
Oil	: Motor yağı
Change of oil	: Yağ değiştirme
Diesel	: Mazot, Motorin, Dizel
Tire	: Lastik

anything on the Aegean coast. They can readily be combined in a one-day trip, with time at Manavgat Falls to cool off.

Termessos

For a breath of mountain air combined with culture, consider a trip due north from Antalya to Termessos, forking left off the main E24 Burdur road. Don't confuse this high mountain site with Telmessos, the ancient name for the present-day harbour of Fethiye! Termessos is perched on an impregnable mountain platform that offers superb grandstand views through gaps in the mountains to the green coastal plain twenty miles away. The remains are mostly Roman - the usual theatre, temples, gymnasium and agora - though the site dates from long before Alexander the Great came marching up the E24. For the finest viewpoint of all, an energetic two-mile uphill hike past hundreds of sarcophagi ends by a firewatch tower. It's well worth the slog.

Further north - along another turn-off from E24 - is the Karain Cave, 27 kms from Antalya. It is the oldest inhabited cave that has yet been found in Turkey, dating from the Paleolithic Age, 50,000 BC. A single entrance leads into three large halls. It is a natural cave, facing the Mediterranean, on the steep slopes of the Çadır peak of the Katran mountain. The early tenants had plentiful water supply, thick vegetation which offered wild fruits and vegetables, and good hunting. Even today, the region is known for wild goat, deer, rabbit, partridge, quail, duck and goose, while streams teem with fish. Human remains go way back to prehistoric times. Skeletons, chipped and polished stone tools, shaped flints and weapons from this site are displayed in Ankara's Museum of Anatolian Cultures, with other items in Antalya's Museum.

Perge

Only ten miles east of Antalya, Perge is an ancient Greek town where St. Paul preached during his first missionary journey. In fact, some historians claim that Paul preached his first-ever sermons here, and made his first converts. In those days, Perge was already a considerable city. It flourished still more during the golden age of Pax Romana, particularly in 2nd and 3rd centuries AD. Public buildings were built, enlarged or embellished with statuary, often donated by wealthy public-mind citizens.

Best overall view of Perge is from the theatre, high up in the gods. You get a complete picture of the 15,000-seat Roman theatre, while looking across to the neighbouring entertainment facility - the stadium - and thence to the acropolis which overlooks the remainder of the city. The stadium is the best preserved in Turkey, after Aphrodisias. It could seat 15,000 people to watch athletic events and gladiator fights.

In the main city are huge entrance gates, monumental Roman baths, a splendid colonnaded street (whence came many of the statues in Antalya's Archaeological Museum), and an agora with mosaic paving on the shop floors. Out of the available sites along the Mediterranean coast, Perge gives the clearest idea of a typical Greco-Roman city layout.

Aspendos

Next along highway E24 is Aspendos, four kms up a side road. You pass an interesting Seljuk bridge on the right, while their colleagues who have switched to tourism offer boat-rides. Early evening, when pleasure boats are manoeuvring into their berths, is an enjoyable time to inspect the fleet. Open-air cafés fill up with thirsty yachtsmen, landlubber holidaymakers and local residents: a lively, multi-lingual Babel. Then the restaurants and tourist shops awaken into activity, followed by the night-owl bars. The harbour area is still bouncing at midnight, aided by the sound of wassail from yachts in party mood.

By day, sightseeing should include the Yivli Minaret Mosque - the Fluted or Grooved Minaret - built by the Seljuk Turks in early 13th century. The finest monument is Hadrian's Gate, large and decorative, built to commemorate the Emperor's visit in 130 AD. Arches lead through to a street with traditional timber houses, which happily have survived the passion to replace everything with concrete.

Finally, the Archaeological Museum is certainly worth a visit. The layout is delightful. Many exhibits are placed outside in a pleasant garden that looks across Antalya Bay to the mountains of Lycia. Rich in finds from Perge and other regional sites, the Museum offers a good introduction to the ancient cities. The 'Gallery of the Gods' is a line-up of all the deities who were worshipped at Perge. That leads into the Emperors' Gallery, filled with the big names of Roman times. An ethnographic section features a display of the nomads' life, with fully furnished yörük tents, and photographs of camels laden with camping gear and household goods. These mountain yörük people have only recently switched to a settled life. A few still cling to their pastures.

Time to sample the beaches:

particularly as the 4-mile Konyaaltı Plaj starts right there by the Museum. In fact, although Antalya is the gateway to many miles of superb sands that run through to Alanya, the town centre has none. Konyaaltı on the western outskirts is a mess of shingle and pebbles. The beach is lined with grotty shacks and tents, ramshackle restaurants and cafés. Not recommended.

Much better is on the eastern side of town, towards Lara Beach - really a resort in its own right, 12 kms from Antalya centre. Lara Plaj is easily reached by low-cost dolmuş transport that follows the coastal road along a flat cliff-top. Several first-class hotels are spread along this road, with access to coves far below; and more hotels are being built. Luxury is featured at the Club Hotel Sera, which even has its own helicopter landing-pad. The Sera's prices are international rather than Turkish. Otherwise there is a good range of accommodation at Lara Plaj, from camp-sites and pensions and through all hotel grades. There is plentiful restaurant choice.

Antalya is an excellent base for excursions. Day tours abound. Southwest takes you along the coastal road of the Bey Dağları National Park to Kemer and Phaselis. North is the highway to Termessos, the classical site located 3500 feet up in the mountains, with stupendous views. A two-day swing could take you to Pamukkale and back, passing the Insuyu Caverns of stalactite formations and underground lakes; and thence via Burdur across an arid plateau with salt lakes that yield sodium sulphate, heaped in enormous white mounds.

East is a classic trio of Perge, Aspendos and Side which can rival

Chapter Six
The Mediterranean Coast

Antalya

TRAVEL: some direct charter flights from UK; otherwise via scheduled services from Istanbul. By road, 541 kms from Izmir or 292 kms from Denizli (Pamukkale) on highway E24; 70 kms to Side, 135 kms to Alanya. Information Bureau (Turizm Danışma Büro) - Cumhuriyet Caddesi 91 - in main street building opposite the terrace promenade above the harbour. Tel: 11747 or 15271

Antalya is the tourism gateway to the 300-mile sine-wave pattern of Mediterranean coastline, stretching right round to the Syrian border. Until now, only the crescent-shaped coast from Kemer to Antalya, Side and Alanya has seen any major development of the tourism potential. In Greek and Roman times, today's holiday zone from Antalya Province to Alanya was called Pamphylia, and that name is still used in archaeological and tourist literature.

Antalya - the largest town along the Mediterranean coast, except for the port of Mersin - is built atop a range of cliffs in the corner of a bay about 20 miles across. It's a Riviera-type location of fabulous beauty, with splendid mountains that dominate the scenery.

Shielded by the Taurus Mountains from the extreme climate of Anatolia, Pamphylia enjoys 300 days of sunshine a year - including Christmas, when it's still possible (a bracing 66° F) to swim in the blue Mediterranean. The sub-tropical valleys and coastal areas produce Turkey's finest oranges and bananas.

For Turks and tourists alike, Antalya's reconstructed harbour is the honeypot. It's a prize-winning Marina and Leisure Centre which rivals anywhere in the Mediterranean. The best seagulls'-eye view of the harbour is from the terrace tea-garden along the promenade above. Enjoy the view, the sea breeze and a glass of tea, and you still have change from 10p.

Declared a conservation area in 1972, the narrow streets of traditional houses leading down to the harbour are enjoying a new lease of life. Some are converted into charming little bars, restaurants or guest-houses. Others, with courtyards, offer displays of locally-made carpets and kilims.

Typical is the Turban Adalya Hotel, which originally was built in 1869 as the branch office of a bank. Later it was used as a warehouse. The building has been tastefully recycled into a 1st-class 58-bed hotel which harmonises with that corner of the harbour. The rooftop bar and restaurant makes a good viewing platform.

The character of the old port has been preserved, while offering all modern facilities for up to 50 visiting yachts. Bronzed fishermen mend their nets, local life: eight persons who bake bread, spin, play typical music, and erect a nomad tent in front of the tennis court. They also bring three camels, one horse and a donkey.

The most recent development is the 1000-bed Palmiya Hotel, run by the Spanish group, Iber. Duplex villas are spread in a semi-circle around the main public areas. Rooms are well finished, partly tiled, of attractive design and imaginative architecture.

The next vacation village is aimed to suit the Swedish life-style, planned by the Vingresor firm who have a 1500-bed project in Side. Their stated intention is to construct a chain of similar villages during the coming years.

The Kemer pattern may be the shape of Turkey's future tourism development. But contact with Turkey outside the fence could be minimal.

and enjoyed the scent of lilies.

During Roman times, particularly during 2nd century AD, the city attained peak prosperity - followed by gradual decline through turmoil, looting and piracy. When the Turks took over, greater importance was given to Antalya and Alanya. Phaselis was completely abandoned. Today's ruins all date from Roman and Byzantine times. Recent excavations have been partly financed by the World Bank.

Phaselis had three harbours, linked by a splendid avenue 33 feet wide. Today you can easily trace the aqueducts and the market places, a theatre, baths, a Hadrian's Gate and an acropolis. The little theatre is charming, with trees and shrubs that lean over and provide shade. Varied plants grow in the crevices between the stone seats. The aroma of pine trees and the chirrup of cicadas complete the sensual delight. Down at the little harbours - adjoining coves - small boats pull in for bathing on the shingle beaches. The over-all atmosphere is a joy. Don't miss it.

Kemer

TRAVEL: 40 kms from Antalya - one hour
Information Bureau (Turizm Danışma Büro) - Belediye Binası - ground floor of the Town Hall, near the harbour.

Kemer is something different: a completely purpose-built resort which started as a development blueprint in Ankara. Instead of haphazard growth which has characterized most of Turkey's holiday industry, the Ministry of Tourism started by laying out the infrastructure first - roads and services - and then inviting Turkish or foreign

firms to develop their chosen sector along the miles of coastline.

The setting is magnificent. On the outskirts of Kemer are citrus plantations, set against a beautiful backdrop of forested mountains. The coastline itself is a series of little coves with sand and rocks.

Focal point of the town centre is Kemer Marina, completed in 1986 with all modern facilities to handle 150 yachts. The spotless clear water glints with little shoals of fish. In the background are totally new streets of holiday apartments, pensions, a few small hotels and new shops and boutiques. The Municipal Beach stretches round the Bay, across from the Marina - some golden sand, some shingle. The original village of Kemer is set further back from the shoreline.

Closest to the centre is the Club Méditerranée holiday village, with five sandy beaches separated by outcrops of rock that give each one an individual character. Thus, one tiny cove is reserved for classical music. Every afternoon, sun-bathers are stretched out beneath umbrellas on the sand, or sit comfortably on a pathway above. During a typical performance of Verdi's "La Traviata", discrete loudspeakers offer near perfect acoustics for the rich sound of Italian opera.

Club Med has its usual French accent; elsewhere along the Kemer coastline is German-speaking Club Robinson.

Club Salima is more international in character, and is promoted by some UK operators. Villas are attractively set out amid grass, flowers and the shade of trees. The Club operates a scuba diving school, and gives belly-dancing lessons. Some villagers come each week to give a demonstration of the now-vanished coastal town of Patara, and was educated at Xanthos. He became the bishop of Myra, and was renowned for his generosity and good deeds. In due time, he was canonized. St. Nicholas was known as the protector of sailors and children, and was adopted as the patron saint of Russia until they changed him for Lenin. He is also the patron saint of thieves, lawyers and pawnbrokers.

Basis of the Santa Claus legend is that three local maidens went to the bishop, saying that unless they could find dowries for marriage, they would be sold into prostitution. During the night, the warm-hearted bishop tossed a bag of gold through each of their open windows.

There are variations on this story, depending who tells it. But essentially there is a clear tradition of anonymous present-giving, linked to the feast day of St. Nicholas - December 6. Hence, by roundabout route, we arrive at the modern Santa Claus - the kindly whiskered character known to the Turks as Noel Baba.

In Demre stands the restored version of the church and burial chapel built in Saint Nicholas's honour immediately after his death in mid-4th century. In 1087, some merchants from the Italian city of Bari stole most of Santa's bones, and took them triumphantly back home to their Basilica of San Nicola, where they are now enshrined in the crypt. Fortunately some spare bones were left over, and these are today treasured in Antalya Museum.

The Turkish tourism authorities do their best to sustain the legend, which is good for business, judging by the number of tour coaches which pull up during the season. A pleasing statue of Father Christmas has been erected in

a little park garden adjoining the church. He carries his traditional sack, and children cluster around him. A Demre Festival is held 3-6 December every year, to commemorate the world's favourite saint.

A mile outside Demre is the historic site of Myra, where rock tombs rise dramatically on a hillside behind the well-preserved Roman theatre - still used for cultural events. Hard scrambling is needed to reach most of the tombs, but it's worth the effort. Chunks of sculpture and columns are scattered in the undergrowth. Around the site, irrigation channels ripple with water to supply an enormous acreage of greenhouse tomatoes. In the long term, Demre may start catering more actively for overnight visitors. Quite apart from Myra and Father Christmas, Demre has close access to lengthy stretches of sandy beach. Likewise, Finike - 30 kms further along - has an open 15-km stretch of sand and pebbles, virtually unexploited, except for the simplest possible bathing huts and cabins. Meanwhile, the local townships seem much more interested in tomato business.

Phaselis

Along the final stretch to Kemer - only 10 miles to go - is a turn-off to the ancient trade centre of Phaselis. The city was founded in 690 BC by colonists from Rhodes. It was the last city on the borders of Lycia and the region of Pamphyllia (which stretches along the coast to Alanya).

The highspot in its history came in 333 BC, when Alexander the Great entered the city and wintered there. He was delighted by the waterside location of Phaselis, with its harbours, avenues and temples. Mid-winter, he liked to see the roses in full bloom,

Brakes	: Frenler
Spark plugs	: Bujiler
It does not work.	: Çalışmıyor

In the restaurant

Bread	: Ekmek
Meat	: Et
Water	: Su
Mutton	: Kuzu eti
Mineral water	: Maden suyu
Lamb	: Koyun eti
Fruit juice	: Meyva Suyu
Beef	: Sığır eti
Wine	: Şarap
Veal	: Dana eti
Beer	: Bira
Chicken	: Piliç / Tavuk
Ice	: Buz
Fish	: Balık

Several Turkish dishes

* **Hors-d'oeuvres "mezeler"**

Arnavut ciğeri	: Spicy fried liver with onions
Çerkes tavuğu	: Cold chicken in walnut puree with garlic
Çiğ Köfte	: Spicy raw meatballs
Midye dolması	: Stuffed mussels
Yaprak dolması	: Stuffed grape leaves

* **Soups, "çorbalar"**

Yayla çorbası	: Yogurt soup
Düğün çorbası	: Meat soup with egg yolks stirred in
İşkembe çorbası	: Tripe soup

* **Pilafs, "pilav"**

Sade pilav	: Plain rice pilaf
İç pilav	: Rice with nuts, currants, and onions
Bulgur pilavı	: Cracked wheat pilaf

* **Cold vegetables in olive oil, "zeytinyağlılar"**

İmam bayıldı	: Split aubergine with tomatoes and onions

Kabak kızartması	: Fried zucchini slices served with yogurt
Patlıcan kızartması	: Fried aubergine slices served with yogurt
Zeytinyağlı fasulye	: Green beans with chopped tomatoes

* **Savoury pastries, "börekler"**

Sigara böreği	: Fried filo pastry filled with cheese
Su böreği	: Layers of filo pastry baked with cheese or meat filling
Talaş böreği	: Puff pastry filled with meat

* **Salads, "salatalar"**

Cacık	: Chopped cucumber in garlic flavoured yogurt
Çoban salatası	: Mixed tomato, pepper, cucumber, and onion salad
Patlıcan salatası	: Pureed aubergine salad
Piyaz	: Haricot bean salad

* **Desserts, "tatlılar"**

Baklava	: Flaky pastry stuffed with nuts in syrup
Tel Kadayıf	: Shredded wheat with nuts and syrup
Sütlaç	: Creamy cold rice pudding
Komposto	: Cold stewed fruit
Dondurma	: Ice cream

* **Fruits, "meyvalar"**

Grapes	: Üzüm
Honeydew melon	: Kavun
Peaches	: Şeftali
Watermelon	: Karpuz
Plums	: Erik
Apples	: Elma
Apricots	: Kayısı
Pears	: Armut
Cherries	: Kiraz
Bananas	: Muz
Figs	: İncir

with eight pointed arches built on angular piers to safeguard against the force of the stream. It replaced a Roman bridge at this crossing-point of the River Eurymedon, which has now changed its name to Köprüçayı (which means 'bridge-stream'). The river was navigable in ancient times as far as Aspendos, which thrived as a river port, exporting wheat, horses and wine.

The theatre of Aspendos is the best preserved of any in Anatolia - thanks partly to the Seljuks in the 13th century, who kept the building in trim as a caravanserai, a good pull-in for camel-drivers. Certainly it rates as the most magnificent Roman building in Pamphylia province. Built in 2nd century AD, it was a gift to the city by two brothers, who dedicated the theatre to the gods of the country and to the Emperor Marcus Aurelius. Seating 15,000, the theatre stages regular performances during the annual Antalya Festival. Wrestling tournaments are also held: 20th-century gladiators, spilling no blood.

From the top gallery, look out onto the surrounding countryside. A farmer and his tractor ploughs a field, against a dramatic mountain backdrop. Here and there are the scattered remains of former ancient buildings, including segments of a tremendous aqueduct which once brought water to the city from 20 miles away. Most visitors rest content with just viewing the theatre.

Side and Manavgat

TRAVEL - One hour's drive from Antalya airport.
If you are arriving on a through bus which doesn't side-swing into Side, get off at Manavgat, and take a dolmuş for the 3 kms into Side itself.

Information Bureau (Danışma) - Side Yolu Üzeri, Manavgat - at the entrance crossroads into Side, coming from Manavgat. Tel: Side 265.

At the approaches to Side, signs advertise dozens upon dozens of hotels, motels and pensions. There are stretches of Roman aqueduct and scattered remains, and you start getting the feel of a seaside resort built within the walls of a major classical site.

Side in a pre-Greek language meant "pomegranate" - a symbol of the fertility of the coastal plain, watered by rivers fed from the background Taurus Mountains. The city - colonized and developed by Greeks in 7th century BC - flourished in Hellenistic and Roman times, with a respectable paying sideline in piracy and slave trade until Pompey in 65 BC put a stop to the business. Eight hundred years later, the tables were turned and Side itself was harried by Syrian-based Arab pirates from 7th century AD, and was finally abandoned after a 10th-century fire.

For the next nine hundred years, Side was deserted. The ruins crumbled and were covered in drifting sand. In 1838, the British archaelogist Sir Charles Fellows paid a visit, but was unimpressed. In the late 1890's, a new chapter opened. Greek-speaking Moslems moved across from the island of Crete - then in a state of Greek and Turkish turmoil - and built themselves a village on the ancient site. They used the Roman and Byzantine remains as a stone quarry, cannibalizing whatever they needed for a house, a shed, or a wall. Thus Side entered the 20th century: a tiny coastal village that slumbered amid the remnants of a major Roman city.

From 1947, Turkish archaeologists from Istanbul University started digging into the sand drifts, and reconstructing from the devastation of time and earthquakes. Many of their finds were removed to museums. After 20 years, Side could rate as the most systematically excavated of any city along the southern coast.

In more recent years, tourism has reared its head. Villagers found a useful income in letting a room or two to visitors; and then perhaps adding to the accommodation with a simple extension.

The main attraction was the glorious sandy shoreline, both sides of the promontory. Side became popular with Turkish families for bucket-and-spade holidays. Then German and British tour operators saw the potential of a resort where holidaymakers could spread out on the beach, explore the ruins, or take side-trips to the Manavgat waterfalls or to other classic remains up and down the coast. So Side grew: from nothing as a tourist resort, to something which today is really quite extraordinary.

Tourists have to be fed. Coffee-houses, tea-houses, restaurants and ice-cream stands sprang up. Camp-sites were laid out in the shade of Roman walls. Then came motels, offering low-cost accommodation - cheaply built, because the trade was too seasonal to justify spending much capital, but soon mellowed with luxuriant growth of bougainvillea, geraniums and sunflowers. The grounds of a typical family-run hotel are lined with ancient walls on three sides, with entry through a Greco-Roman gateway. Gardens are littered with fallen columns.

At some stage the government took fright. They didn't mind the accommodation in the traditional stone Turkish houses; that was fine. But they didn't want to see multi-storeyed, international-grade hotels dominating the Roman remains. So, essentially, the plan is that all the new major hotels must be spread along the coast. Hence the current wave of new building is well outside of central Side.

All along the coastline are numerous beaches, some small, some long - pebble or sand - miles in both directions. The sea is banded blue and green, brilliant and sparkling. At most of the sandy stretches, holiday villages or club hotels have been set up, often with not another building in sight.

Meanwhile, on the original site of Side, you have this fantastic jumble - Greek, Roman and Byzantine remains, all mixed up with cafés and restaurants, little shops selling carpets and Lacoste shirts, suede jackets, onyx giftware. For Side has gone international. Along the main street is a daily carnival procession of international visitors in their colourful T-shirts and their jeans, and their multi-lingual conversations with German dominant - matched by the equal linguistic fluency of the local traders. Every carpet and leather store is open till midnight. Browsing among the shops is the main evening entertainment in Side.

This whole central area is a pedestrian precinct, gaudy but cheerful, with the main shopping street between entrance gate and harbour following the line of the original High Street of Roman times. When history and culture beckon, you are right there, in the midst of it all.

Imagine a promontory jutting out to sea. At the furthest tip, beside a beach, build two temples, dedicated one to Apollo, the other to Athena.

According to tradition, Side is the place where Mark Anthony had a tryst with Cleopatra, who bathed from the sandy beach, though other resorts make a similar claim. Romantics can speculate whether these temples mark the location - though, in fact, the temples were built later. But it's a great place for watching the sunset. Here's where Hollywood would pitch the big scene.

Further back along this promontory are huge Roman and Greek ruins; a well-preserved theatre to seat at least 13,000 and a black goat or two to keep the weeds down; an agora that had been used as a slave market; a:.d monumental Roman baths which have been solidly rebuilt to house the site museum.

This reconstruction gives visitors a good insight into the clean-living Roman life-style. The normal bath routine started in the Frigidarium - the cold room, which was also for undressing. Next stop was the Calidarium, the hot room, heated by a hypocaust. That is, the floor was supported on brick columns, around which circulated hot air from the furnace. The process continued into the steam or sweating room - the Sudatorium. Then followed another warm room - the Tepidarium - with more underfloor heating. The ordeal then finished back in the Frigidarium. Two thousand years later, all you get in Side is luke-warm showers heated by solar panels.

Manavgat

Close to Side are the cool and shady Manavgat waterfalls.

They are mini-falls, maybe a three-ft cascade. Niagara has nothing to worry about. But a pleasant restaurant and tea-garden is spread out on rocks and terraced platforms which protrude over or alongside the foaming waters. Visitors can cross foot-bridges and be served at table on their own little island. Fresh trout or roast chicken are the specialities. Ducks and ducklings have miniature islands to themselves, and pose in neat formations for family photos.

It's a refreshing change from hot days of clambering among ruins or sweltering on beaches. Low-cost taxis shuttle from Side to the falls; or the journey to Manavgat town can be done by regular dolmuş. Incidentally, Monday is market day, colourful with villagers and their produce: a chance to haggle for craft items.

Below Manavgat's bridge are tranquil tea-gardens on both sides of the river, shaded by trees. Short river cruises take visitors to the Falls.

Alarahan

A side turning off E24 highway, 26 kms before reaching Alanya, leads for nine kms up a fertile river valley to the caravanserai of Alarahan. If you're in command of your own transport, a visit is worth the detour. The local farm scene itself is interesting: bananas and citrus, cotton, peanuts and a great acreage of greenhouses that produce early vegetables and salad crops. Women and girls are dressed in the traditional baggy trousers called şalvar.

The caravanserai, built in 1231, formed part of a chain that led from Alanya through to Konya. Covering half an acre, the building remains in very good condition. Around the cool barrel-vaulted corridors, merchants and camel-drivers could find free overnight shelter as they transported silks, carpets and spices along this medieval trade-route. Fortifications were sited halfway up the hillside to command a defile into the mountains. A smaller caravanserai called Şarapsahan is located on the main road 15 kms from Alanya: a one-day march by camel, between the two stops.

Alanya

TRAVEL: 135 kms along E24 from Antalya, 2 hours by bus; 65 kms from Side; 128 kms to Anamur.
Information Bureau (Turizm Danışma Büro) - opposite the Museum, on corner near Damlataş Cave - Tel: 1240

A tourism map of Alanya is easy to draw: something like the rock of Gibraltar jutting for two miles out to sea, ending with a sheer 800-ft cliff; a straight line 20 miles from the west, sandy beaches all the way; another straight line running east, with more sandy beaches. The E24 highway closely hugs the pine-tree coast, with banana plantations spreading up to the mountain foothills. Alanya town itself is clustered where the fortress rock drives a wedge between the East and West Beaches.

Motoring in from direction of Side, the Alanya holiday district is heralded by major camp-sites, 20 miles out, including a BP Mocamp: the start of low-density ribbon development of the beaches. Every couple of kilometres is another hotel or holiday village, half-hidden among the trees. Along the highway, more banana plantations are being uprooted and replanted with hotels, motels and camp-sites.

In 1987 there were forty holiday hotels in the Alanya area, totalling just over 6000 beds. Another 6000 beds were in pensions. Forty more hotels are planned for 1988 onwards, to add 1000 hotel beds each year to Alanya's capacity. The boom has come entirely since 1980. Before then, only a handful of hotels existed.

Today, Alanya is deeply into the sun-lounger business. Unlike the resorts around the rugged south-west corner of Turkey, the boating potential is not so interesting. The classic sites - Side, Aspendos, Perge - can be ticked off in a one-day excursion. The main sights of Alanya itself wouldn't take more than a day. On a two-week holiday, reckon to spend at least ten days on those gorgeous sandy beaches. Don't worry too much if your Alanya hotel is miles out of town. Low-cost bus and dolmuş transport is always available at the main gate on the highway.

Most of Alanya's hotels are along West Beach. So, for orientation, let's start there: just where the rocky peninsula meets the municipal beach at Atatürk Park. Grouped in that corner are the local museum, the Tourism Information office, Damlataş Cave, and the start of a road leading to Alanya Castle.

Damlataş (means 'Dripping Stones') is a stalactite cavern, still dripping, with 95% humidity which is reputed to be helpful for asthma sufferers. For the tourist there is the usual display of coloured lights that jazz up the stalagmite formations, worth a ten-minute glance unless you want to stay longer to enjoy a nice cool 73-degree escape from the heat outside. Plentiful benches are set around the caves, for benefit of those who come to fix their asthma, staying four hours a day for a three-week cure.

Alanya Museum concentrates on the archaeological story of the region, with displays that cover from Bronze Age

Kalkan
A charming little resort, where
traditional houses have been
converted for the holiday trade.

Kapitaş
A golden beach, easily reached
by boat or road from Kaş or
Kalkan.

Kaş
A delightful fishing village, with great scope for all-day boat trips.

Kemer

The newly built Marina, serving a beautiful stretch of coastline backed by forested mountains.

down to Byzantine times. The prize exhibit is a magnificent bronze statue of Hercules, from 2nd century AD. The ethnographic room contains local items of Seljuk and Ottoman periods.

The road from the Information centre to the Castle is three uphill kilometres. If you cannot capture a passing dolmuş, a one-way taxi is worth while. Afterwards, you have a pleasant stroll down the other side, to East Beach, running the gauntlet of ladies who want to sell you silk scarves.

For many years, Alanya was a pirate stronghold until the Romans cracked down in 65 BC, sinking their fleet. In a fit of generosity, Mark Antony gave the town and surrounding region to Cleopatra, who needed the mountain timber to rebuild her Egyptian navy. So Cleopatra slept here, enjoying the scenery as well as Mark Antony. From any angle, the fortress is deeply impressive: four miles of turreted walls, rising from sea level to the clifftop inner castle. At the furthermost tip of the fortifications is a platform from where condemned prisoners were hurled onto the rocks 800 feet below.

Down at sea level, close to the harbour at East Beach, the Red Tower (Kızıl Kule) is a most unusual building to the European eye: a massive red brick and stone octagonal tower built in 1226 by a Seljuk sultan to protect his naval dockyard alongside (which is still there). The five-storey building is used as a modest museum. An interesting exhibit is a nomad tent of black goat-hair, held together with ropes and wooden pegs. It is fully furnished with cushions, carpets, grind-stone for grain, cooking pots, gourd for drinking water, bells for the animals, and a cradle.

The roof of the Red Tower looks like a stage set around an inner courtyard, with steps at different levels, pointed archways, enormously thick walls, and a view beyond to a mosque minaret, hillside houses and the citadel walls. It's worth the effort of climbing the very steep stairs.

Pirates are 2000 years in the past. But local boatmen keep their memory alive with trips around the promontory, pointing out the Maidens' Cave where pirates kept their stock of female prisoners until released on ransom or sold off as slaves. There's also a Lovers' Cave, a Phosphorescent Cave, and of course the beach where Cleopatra bathed. Along the waterfront facing the harbour, an upgraded promenade has been constructed, offering a new line of shops and restaurants. The next few years will see much expansion.

East of Alanya

Right now, tourism development ends at Alanya. For the next 200 miles the E24 highway hugs the Mediterranean coast through to the port of Mersin. Particularly around the coast from Gazipasa and Anamur through to Silifke, the scenery is spectacular. In many stretches, the road is carved into the cliff face, towering above the sea, not for the nervous. There are beautiful little sandy coves, quite deserted. Several daily buses cover the route, and some coach tour itineraries follow this highway. Travel agencies at Alanya offer day excursions to Anamur, famed for a magnificent Crusader Castle. Give it another ten years, and this coastline will be 'discovered'.

Chapter Seven
Central and Eastern Anatolia

Ankara

Information Bureau (Turizm Danışma Büro) - Gazi Kemal Bulvarı 33 -ground floor of Ministry of Tourism -Tel: 231 7380 (10 lines).
TRAVEL: by air, train or very frequent bus services from Istanbul, 438 kms; Izmir 595 kms; Konya 262 kms. The E5 road from Istanbul is the busiest in Turkey. Mostly a three-lane highway, it will ultimately be improved to motorway standards. Meanwhile, owing to the volume of juggernaut traffic using E5 as the link between Europe and Middle East, driving can be somewhat tense. Massive pile-ups are frequent. Buses normally make a halfway rest-stop near Bolu, in a beautiful green mountain area that looks unbelievably like Austria: an alpine setting with 5,000-ft peaks, access to popular lakes, and skiing in winter.

In 1922, when Kemal Atatürk led the nation to victory against the occupying Greeks, Turkey was in sorry condition. Long years of misgovernment had left the country exhausted and backward. Atatürk, pledged to a programme of modernization, shifted Turkey's capital from Istanbul to Ankara, in the middle of the Anatolian plateau.

Ankara's history reached back to Hittite times, about 3000 BC. The ancient citadel, which crowns the heights overlooking the surrounding plain, had few facilities for modern government. Everything had to be built from the bottom up. Over the past 60-odd years, a boom atmosphere has prevailed. Government ministries, banks, broad boulevards and blocks of modern apartments have spread out below the old town and along each side of Atatürk Bulvarı which marches in a straight line past numerous embassies to the upper-crust Çankaya hill, where the Presidential Palace is located.

To the traveller, nothing is more startling than his first view of modern Ankara. In contrast to the surrounding arid plateau, even Nature has been transformed. Trees - which critics said would never grow in Ankara's climate - line the pavements and provide welcome shade in the neatly-planned parks. There is a European atmosphere of bustling, go-ahead activity. However, for most tourists, a one-day stopover is enough to cover the sightseeing potential.

Atatürk's memory is honoured in the modernistic limestone Mausoleum (Anıt Kabir) which also houses the Atatürk Museum. The oldest and most interesting parts of the city are located near the Ulus intersection (with a large equestrian statue of Atatürk) and up to the Ankara Citadel (Hisar or Kale) perched on the dominating steep hillside.

Within the castle walls - mainly dating from 7th century AD but kept in good condition ever since - is a complete settlement of 17th- and 18th-century wooden houses with courtyards' a-clucking with chickens, children playing, and women hanging out washing to dry. Your photographs could pass for a peasant village anywhere in Anatolia, miles from anywhere: quite unbelievable for the very heart of the Turkish capital. The Citadel hilltop offers a superb view of the Turkish capital, and across to other hillsides where a similar village atmosphere prevails.

To save time and energy, take a cab direct from your hotel to the top of the Citadel. Careful route-planning then gives an easy downhill walk through the Castle village, out of a side gate to the Museum of Anatolian Civilisations and thence downtown (perhaps taking another taxi) to the Hacı Bayram Mosque and Augustus Temple, ending with some Roman Baths close by. The Augustus Temple was built in 2nd century BC, later converted by the Byzantines to a church. Most of the site is now occupied by the tomb and mosque of a dervish saint, Hacı Bayram. The 3rd century AD Roman Baths give an idea of the immense floor area they occupied, but relatively little of the monumental structure remains.

The Museum of Anatolian Civilisations alone is worth the trip to Ankara. Housed in a converted Han (inn) and the adjoining 15th-century Mahmut Paşa Bedesten - a former covered market - the building is popularly known as the Hittite Museum. Although the collection is rich in Stone Age finds, it is the finest in the world for exhibits that cover the entire Hittite period from 1750-700 BC. The layout itself gives great pleasure. Don't miss this museum! Ankara's next best is the Ethnographical Museum, featuring Seljuk and Ottoman art and general folkware, located above Atatürk Bulvarı between two major overpasses.

Ankara is home for three million people, but has no great whirl of nightlife. Most government officials yearn for the fleshpots of Istanbul. Sundays in Ankara are deadly dull. Many international business visitors, stuck in Ankara over the weekend, pass the time with a day's excursion to Boğazkale - the present-day name of Hattusa, capital of the Hittites. The standard tour to the ancient city includes the Lion Gate, the Great Temple of the Storm God, the Citadel, and storerooms where 10,000 cuneiform tablets were found early this century. These archives enabled experts to compile a complete history of the Hittites, who formerly were little known except for a few Biblical mentions. Two miles away from Boğazkale is the open-air sanctuary of Yazılıkaya, where a gallery with low relief carvings portrays 63 gods and goddesses from the Hittite pantheon which ran to a thousand or more.

Cappadocia - Where Christians were Cavemen

Information Bureau (Turizm Danışma Büro)
at Ürgüp - Kayseri Caddesi 37. Tel: 1059.
at Nevşehir - Lale Caddesi 22. Tel: 1137.
at Aksaray - Bankalar Caddesi, Belediye İşhanı Kat 1 - first floor of City Hall. Tel: 12474.
Distances to Nevşehir: Istanbul 722 kms; Ankara 284 kms; Konya 226 kms; Adana 286 kms.

Travel

Where to go, on a spare weekend in Ankara? That's the question that often bugs business travellers, marooned until Monday in the Turkish capital. Best possible excursion is to the incredible Cappadocia region, in the heart of Turkey, about 280 kms from Ankara along the E5 highway. There, an eroded moon landscape of rock pinnacles, giant cones and deep ravines is setting for a fantastic early Christian settlement of underground cities, rock-hewn churches and monasteries. The entire area rates high among Turkey's greatest tourist attractions.

For the same reason, Cappadocia is a major highlight on many coach-tour circuits of central Anatolia. A typical section of the itinerary is routed Konya-Cappadocia-Ankara, or vice versa.

Outwards from Ankara, the route stays with E5 as far as Aksaray. Afforestation is bringing new green areas to the bare hillsides. The road passes through wheat and barley territory - alternate fields lying fallow - with some sheep and cattle herding. The cowboys ride donkeys.

Then a broad spread of blue water makes an appealing contrast to the arid landscape. Tuz Gölü is a widely-sprawling salt lake, 625 square miles in area - the second largest in Turkey after Lake Van. During summer, the water's edge recedes through evaporation, leaving behind a line of salt for processing in dozens of small factories spread around the perimeter. The lake is not recommended for bathing. It's like swimming in olive oil, and salt stings the eyes. It would also be disappointing for anglers: no fish.

Aksaray

Close to Aksaray district, there are numerous plantations of poplars.

These are planted at the birth of a child. By the time the trees mature, they serve as a marriage gift - the capital fund to set up a new household. Aksaray is a handy lunch-stop, at the turn-off junction for Cappadocia - for Nevşehir and Ürgüp. On the horizon are the conical shapes of extinct volcanoes.

The road follows the 13th-century caravan trail that linked Aksaray and Kayseri, with enormous caravanserais spaced at intervals of one-day trek by camel. The Hoca Meşut Caravanserai, built 1231 to 1239, is typical. It has two parts: one open, one covered - respectively for summer and winter use. The construction is more like a castle, with its huge gate and turrets. It is Turkey's third largest caravanserai after those of Aksaray and Kayseri: the size of a cathedral, with a small mosque in the middle of the open courtyard.

Nevşehir

Near Nevşehir, the volcanic nature of the terrain becomes obvious. Rock everywhere is used as a building material, and even for marking field boundaries. In Nevşehir itself, virtually every building is assembled from large stone blocks, apart from the grotesque 11-storey concrete Hotel Göreme, designed to resemble a rock-dwelling. A hill rises steeply to a Castle, with multi-coloured houses set perfectly against a green foreground of slim poplar trees.

At Nevşehir a right turn leads along a valley towards Kaymaklı and Derinkuyu, about 13 and 19 miles south of Nevşehir. Some houses higher up the hillside are built partially into the rock. Others, half abandoned, are used for animal shelters or stores.

Derinkuyu

The valley flattens out, to open up a distant view of snow-capped mountains, due south, with apricot orchards in the foreground. The area is honeycombed with around thirty ancient underground cities, of which two are open to the public. At Kaymaklı is a remarkable 4-storey underground settlement. Even more incredible is Derinkuyu, the largest of the cities built by Byzantine Christians who felt threatened by Arab raiders.

Above ground, present-day Derinkuyu (which means 'Deep Well') offers delightful little vignettes of village life: a group of baggy-trousered women with headscarves and yashmaks, who squat in a circle of gossip; cloth-capped farmers driving their tractors; children pausing in their street games to wave to passing tour buses. At the entrance to the underground city, more bright-eyed children peddle costume dolls.

Derinkuyu is an astonishing eight-storey Christian settlement which formerly housed 10,000 people. They lived like rabbits in a warren, with escape holes everywhere. If danger threatened, they rolled across each entrance a huge circular stone the size and weight of a very large millstone. They could fire arrows through a central loophole.

The city was fully equipped with air vents, water storage, sewage disposal system, a prison, a church, dining halls and wine cellars, storage chambers with six months' supply of food, bedrooms and even a missionary school. Bemused crocodiles of tourists wind their way through honeycombed rocks, up and down tunnels and narrow flights of steps, with caves or rooms or storage-chambers to left or right, ducking low to avoid damaging the roof. It's like a cheese-mite's view when travelling through an Emmenthaler. Maybe it was all designed by a Swiss cheese-maker.

Ortahisar

At the other extreme of lifestyle is the village of Ortahisar, where safe living quarters were built within a honeycombed rock pinnacle that rears like a fortress from the centre of the more modern town. Steps and tunnels lead higher and higher, past rooms that are fitted with fire-places. Every apartment is different. It has the feeling of very sophisticated architecture - perhaps designed by a pre-incarnation of Henry Moore - with balconies and terraces looking out onto the surrounding view.

The rock is so soft that you can almost crumble it with your fingers. When it rains, the tuff stone can be worked as easily as plastic. Even with the most primitive tools, home building was a simple do-it-yourself operation: no need of carpenters, roofing specialists, tilers.

All the sights and sounds of village life come floating up: donkeys braying, carts jingling, cockerels crowing, children playing. You get a pigeon's-eye view of house courtyards where housewives peg out the family wash. Grass grows on flat roofs of storehouses, where chickens forage free-range. In late summer, the roofs are used to dry apricots and red peppers. As a curious speciality, the local villagers store green lemons from the coast in the readymade underground storerooms. Kept in an ideal constant temperature, the fruit slowly turns yellow, and can be sold up to a year later.

From above, much higher than the neighbouring mosque minaret, there is a superb view of the whole erosion basin, with thousands of similar rock pinnacles. Along the road are more store-houses that tunnel into the hillsides. Often, cave and house merge together. Inside rooms are technically caves, while outside rooms have the normal apparatus of windows, front door, and chimneys. The more accessible caves along the main tourist trail are converted to sales outlets for carpets, antiques or handicrafts, like a series of Aladdin's caves. Some of the rock pinnacles - near Göreme, for instance - are converted into restaurants.

Hills in the surrounding district look very scanty of vegetation, but are rich in volcanic minerals. Villagers can support themselves on tiny patches of land planted with apple trees, grain crops and vegetables. The local wine has a good reputation.

Göreme

All the goggling at Derinkuyu and places like Ortahisar and Uçhisar is just a warm-up for the big feature: the Göreme Valley, where the thesaurus runs out of superlatives.

The final approach is dramatic: down a steep hill with hairpin bends; and there, suddenly, is one of the world's most fantastic views. Even though visitors have read about the site, and seen pictures of it, the effect of that first view is stunning. The entire valley is covered with weird rock formations, of which virtually every pinnacle and cliff-face has been converted into church, chapel, monastery or hermit cell.

An information board at the entrance to Göreme Open Air Museum sets the

historic background. In the 4th century, the Roman Empire was divided into two parts with the Eastern half going to the Byzantines. Cappadocia became part of a new Christian world. Early Christians taking refuge from hostile non-believers found suitable shelter in the region's unusual geological formations.

Earlier local populations had established dwelling-places, hewn from the soft rock. The first missionaries soon found the region equally suitable for use as a monastic centre, with churches and monasteries easily carved out of the same rock. Cave churches were painted with scenes from the Old and New Testament. The entire area was a major centre of Christianity during the 6th to 9th century, and contains almost 400 churches. During the 12th century, the Selcuk Turks settled in Anatolia. Then, with the Mongol invasion during the 13th century, Christianity lost its power, and the site was abandoned. Many of the frescoes have been restored, thanks to work done by the Turkish government and UNESCO. But much more remains to be done to preserve this heritage.

Zelve

Another fantastic group of rock formations is located a few miles north of Göreme, at Zelve, which likewise became a considerable monastic retreat. Numerous churches were carved into the valley walls during the Byzantine period. Some are quite high above the valley, and are reached by narrow sequences of staircases. When the Byzantines scattered, Turkish villagers moved in. They left as recently as the 1950's because of the danger of falling rocks. As a reminder of Turkish occupation, a solitary

134

mosque still remains near the approaches to the former monasteries.

This valley contains the best collection in the region of so-called 'fairy chimneys'. Other eyes may see them as circus seals, doing a balancing act. Several groups of pinnacles look like a meeting of the Ku Klux Klan, in their tall conical hoods. There are hundreds of new rock formations in embryo, which probably will convert into pinnacles and fairy chimneys during the next few thousand years, keeping Cappadocia safe for tourism.

Konya

Information Bureau (Turizm Danışma Büro) - Mevlâna Cad. 21 - near Mevlâna Museum. Tel: 11074
TRAVEL: Konya features on many coach-tour itineraries as a sightseeing stopover en route across the wide, bleak Anatolian plateau. Reckon a half-day drive to or from the next main sightseeing highlight - 262 kms north to Ankara; 226 kms northeast to Cappadocia; 218 kms southeast to the coast at Silifke through Taurus Mountains along the splendid Göksu gorge; 300 kms southwards to Side or Alanya; or 440 kms to Pamukkale. No airport, but plenty of buses.

Turkey's 7th largest town - nearly a million population - has prospered as a route and market centre for at least the past 2000 years. In classical times, Konya was an important stage on the route from Ephesus to Tarsus and Antioch: a Greek and Roman road walked by early Christians. Under the Seljuk Turks, Konya was a major stopover for camel caravans that followed the diagonal trading routes across Anatolia. Last century a similar basic line was chosen for the Berlin-Baghdad railway, and today's modern highways follow the same pattern.

Konya's origins go back 5,000 years. According to Greek legend, Perseus - the son of Jupiter and Danae - came to this region, chopped off the head of Medusa (the Gorgon lady with snakes for hair-do), and nailed it on a pillar. Hence the city's classical and Biblical name of Iconium, meaning "city with an image".

Successively conquered by the Hittites, Phrygians, Lydians, Greeks, Persians and Romans, Konya was closely linked with the early Christians.

At Konya, St. Paul and St. Barnabas preached, gathered disciples, stirred up trouble with the authorities, and had to run for it to escape being stoned. The town became one of the earliest centres from which Christianity spread. Among St. Paul's local converts was an 18-year-old girl called Thecla. Breaking off her engagement, she was accused of being a Christian and sentenced to be burned. Then - miracle - the flames of the pyre were put out by sudden rain. Disguised as a boy, St. Thecla followed Paul from Konya to Antioch, preached the Gospel and converted many. Later she returned to Konya, where she died, aged 90.

Konya became capital of the Seljuk Sultanate of Rum in 1097, until it lost that rank in the mid-13th century when it fell to the Mongols, and finally the Ottomans. Konya enjoyed a golden age during the Empire of Rum. The Sultans encouraged the arts and learning, and built fine Seljuk monuments. Konya also became a religious centre, particularly through the teachings of a mystic called Mevlâna Celaleddin, founder of the Whirling Dervish order which spread throughout Islam. Today's city is a modern and prosperous market centre for the surrounding farming region. Tourism is a bonus, wrapped around the remains of that brilliant Seljuk era.

The Alâeddin Mosque, one of the oldest in Turkey, is a fine example of Seljuk architecture, with a huge prayer hall. Opposite is the Karatay Medrese, with a fine carved marble doorway, entrance to a collection of ceramics. Close by, the İnce Minare Medrese - named after its Slender Minaret - is also remarkable for its front door and archway, which gave full rein to Seljuk craftsmanship in stone cutting. The Seljuks specialized in doorways. The monument is now the Museum of Seljuk Stone and Wood Carving.

The Mevlâna Mausoleum - formerly the seminary of the Order of Whirling Dervishes and now a secular museum - centres on the great hall where the ritual dances took place. "Many roads lead to God," said Mevlâna, "I have chosen that of dance and music."

Into the 20th century, the Dervishes wielded considerable power, but had become rigid and dogmatic. Along with other religious orders, they were banned by Atatürk in 1925 as being unsuited to a modern secular republic. However, since the 1950's the dances have been revived as a cultural heritage, rather than strictly religious.

Performances are given every year in mid-December, to commemorate Mevlâna's death on 17 December 1273. These presentations have become a major tourist attraction, but still retain their deep religious meaning for the faithful. The white-robed dervishes in tall cylindrical hats rotate slowly at first, then quicker, to the music of flutes, drums and male choir.

Robes billow out as the dervishes spin like tops into a state of ecstasy. During summer, Konya's dervishes also whirl at Ephesus and other culture-interest locations, and even go on international tour. If you see a performance advertised, it's worth even a long journey - an unforgettable experience.

The museum hall contains Seljuk works of art, including priceless 700-year-old carpets, manuscripts and musical instruments. The founder's tomb is covered with a golden shroud, heavily embroidered. The entire site is virtually a place of pilgrimage, with devout Moslems come to pray. In fact, Konya still keeps its religious traditions and is known for strict observance of Ramadan.

About 45 kms south of Konya is the neolithic site of Çatalhöyük: one of the world's oldest towns, dating from 6800 BC. Entrance to the mud houses was through holes in the roof. There's nothing much to look at. Everything worth seeing - tools, jewellery, mother goddess cult figurines and wall paintings - has been removed to Ankara's Museum of Anatolian Civilizations.

Eastern Provinces

Bend the map of Turkey vertically in half. The fold will probably run through the Cappadocia and Kayseri area - about 764 kms from Istanbul, or 890 kms from Izmir, via Konya. The western half of the map accounts probably for 99% of holiday travel in Turkey. Tourist density is highest in Istanbul; then spreads around the Aegean and south-west coastal fringes, with forays inland to the Anatolian heartland of classic sites and cities. At Cappadocia - dead centre in

Turkey - tourist itineraries currently turn back towards Europe.

The eastern half of Turkey is a harsh land of high mountains and extreme climate, reaching to the borders of Syria, Iraq, Iran and the Soviet Union. Three main highways serve the region, which most Turks themselves have never visited.

E23 from Ankara heads due east through Sivas, Erzincan and Erzurum, the largest town in Eastern Turkey. Further along, E23 forks left for Kars, close to the Soviet border, or continues as E23 through Ağrı into Iran, skirting the lower slopes of Mount Ararat. Quite apart from being the reputed landing-place of Noah's Ark, Mount Ararat centres on the area described by Biblical tradition as the burial-place of Noah's wife, and as the spot where Noah planted the first vineyard. Mountaineering on 16,850-ft Ağrı Dağı (Turkish name for Ararat) is possible only with special permission from the Ministry of Foreign Affairs, and with local guides. Casual hikers looking around for bits of the Ark are not welcomed.

Another axis road runs from the carpet-making town of Kayseri towards Malatya and then onwards to Elaziğ and Van, on Turkey's largest lake. An alternative is to head for Adıyaman - six hours by bus from Kayseri - which is the usual base for reaching the 7000-ft peak of Nemrut Dağı. The tradition is to go up there to meet the dawn; or, alternatively, to stay for sunset. The rising or setting sun is a bonus. The main reason for the trip is to marvel at a group of enormous stone gods, who have been watching the sunrises and sunsets for the past 2000 years.

A third route starts from Adana - a textile town at the centre of Turkey's largest cotton-growing area - and continues as the E24 through Gaziantep (where they grow pistachio nuts) and Mardin to the Iraqi border. Also from Adana, the E5 around the Gulf of Iskenderun reaches Biblical Antioch (Antakya) before continuing a few more kilometres into Syria. As a great Roman and Christian centre, Antioch is remembered as the birthplace of St. Paul and St. Luke; and the city where followers of Christ first called themselves Christians. Outside Antakya is the grotto where St. Peter preached for the first time. The Archaeology Museum contains the world's finest collection of Roman mosaics.

Some time in the 21st century, all these locations in Eastern Turkey will be 'developed' with splendid hotels, smooth service in gourmet restaurants, discos and cocktail bars. Meanwhile, those essentials are missing. Eastern Turkey is reserved for those with a keen interest in mountains, biblical studies or remote archaeological sites - and who are tough enough to shrug their shoulders if the hotel doesn't have a jacuzzi.

Chapter Eight
Black Sea Coast

Climate of the Black Sea coast is totally different from the rest of Turkey, with year-round rainfall and less extreme temperatures: warm and humid. It is a very green mountainous coastline of thick pine forests. The most important cash crop is hazel nuts, of which Turkey is the world's leading exporter. At the eastern end of the Black Sea, around the town of Rize, there is sufficient rainfall to grow Turkey's entire requirement of tea.

The full weight of international tourism has not yet arrived. There are several reasons. Although the coastal cities have a long history starting with settlement by Greek colonists from 7th century BC, followed by the rule of Romans, Byzantines and Ottomans, they do not offer the more dramatic remains that typify the Aegean coast. Today a coastal road runs the whole distance, or parallel with the coast, in reasonable condition most of the way. But tourism developments are somewhat limited. The individual traveller can always find simple hotels and guest-houses; but these are not the stuff of package holidaymaking.

Through proximity to Istanbul, Kilyos and Şile are active sandy-beach locations which particularly are busy during summer weekends. A local industry at Şile is the making of embroidered blouses and nightwear. The inland area around the town of Bolu rates as part of the Black Sea zone, and is easily reached as a halfway point between Istanbul and Ankara along highway E5. Well worth a special effort is Safranbolu, where old timber houses are beautifully preserved.

The most striking part of the coastline is eastwards from Sinop, where a good coastal road hugs the shoreline through tobacco-town Samsun, Ünye (hazel-nut territory) and Giresun, from where Europe's first cherry trees were transplanted by the Roman Emperor Lucullus. The numerous beaches and coves and fishing villages are quite untouched by international tourism. In fact, Trabzon is the only Black Sea town which has been discovered by travel business. The city is well connected, with regular air and bus services from Istanbul and Ankara.

Turkish Maritime Lines also operate a weekly ferry service from Istanbul, taking two full days for the journey, with three grades of cabin on offer. This popular journey in summertime requires advance reservation. Check sailing dates. Typical timings have been: depart Istanbul 5.30 p.m., arriving Samsun 24 hours later, and Trabzon on the second evening at 8.00 p.m.

Trabzon - formerly called Trebizond - was the last stronghold of the Byzantines, until they finally fell to Mehmet the Conqueror in 1461. Several major Byzantine monuments survive - particularly the 13th century church of St. Sophia, with masterpieces of fresco decoration. On a steep cliff 48 kms inland is Sumela Monastery - founded in 385 AD, to become the most important monastic settlement of Anatolia during Byzantine times. Greek monks continued to live there until expulsion in 1923. The monastery is ruined, but the setting is magnificent, overlooking a lush river valley. Minibus and dolmuş services make access easy. Check transport arrangements at Trabzon's Tourism Information Office: 31 Taksim Caddesi - phone 35833 - 35818 - 35830.

Further east of Trabzon is tea-picking terrain, where some 200,000 people are dependent on the Turkish taste for endless glasses of tea throughout the day. Don't forget to pack your brolly!

Chapter Nine
Food & Drink

The Royal Taste of Turkish Cuisine

Turks claim their cuisine rates among the world's top three, along with French and Chinese.

It all started in the imperial kitchens of Topkapı Palace, where the greatest chefs of the Ottoman empire devoted their working lives to creating recipes to delight the palate of the Sultans and their court. The Turkish theory was that when men eat well, they can make love well. Obviously the Sultan needed that kind of a boost, with four wives and numerous concubines as a back-up. In their aim to rival the epicurean foods of ancient Rome, the Palace chefs scoured the empire for ideas, ingredients, spices. It became a two-way flow, with the triumphs of their kitchens colonizing the Ottoman territories. Today the Turkish cuisine still reigns supreme in the Balkans and throughout Middle East and North Africa.

Virtually all Eastern Mediterranean countries share the Turkish taste for kebabs and pilavs, stuffed dolmas, eggplant specialties, feta cheese, sweet pastries, glasses of tea, and Turkish coffee. The Turkish cuisine includes an encyclopaedic variety of recipes for appetisers, soups, meats and fish, vegetables and desserts. Eggplant alone can be prepared in more than 40 different ways. Herbs give an extra lift to even the simplest dishes. Quite modest Turkish kitchens can display at least twenty different spices.

Turkey is among the world's few countries - about six altogether - which are totally self-supporting in food products. That partly explains why meal prices are much lower than anywhere in Europe. Hence, also, the richness and variety of the Turkish cuisine, based on local production of high-quality vegetables and salads, lamb and poultry, yoghurt and a wide range of fruits from cherries and strawberries to oranges, dates and bananas. Even pineapples are now grown under glass. Much of the pleasure in a Turkish holiday comes from sampling that rich choice. If you have an appetite for culinary adventure, cut loose from tourist-hotel dining rooms which offer modified "international" menus. In fact, the best policy is to book bed-and-breakfast accommodation only, leaving you totally free to explore the variety of what the Turkish cuisine has to offer.

Even on the simplest fast-food level, Turkey can tantalise your taste-buds. The food is interesting, even for anyone who is just eating snacks on the hoof.

With a light tray fitted with collapsible legs, a Turkish food vendor is in business. At bus stations and other central locations, youths sell circular bread-rolls called simit, covered in sesame seeds. Try one for flavour, nibbling as you walk along, just like the Turks. Sandwich salesmen make up their product on the spot - slitting a submarine-shaped roll, slicing in hard-boiled egg, tomato and a sliver of gherkin. It's much fresher than anything British Rail could devise!

There are all the fruits, according to season, sold from piled-high barrows or in farmers' markets. Something different: try a juicy cucumber, peeled, and eaten like a banana with a twitch of salt. Down by the waterfront, fresh fish is grilled or fried and served piping hot in a hunk of good bread. Another great specialty is deep-fried mussels - midye tava - which are specially good in Istanbul. Street-corner kiosks do a thriving lunch and evening-snack trade with şiş kebab; or sausages, salami and frankfurters sizzled on a red-hot grill, served in a sliced roll and topped with tomato or a slice of cheese. Other vendors sell corn-on-the-cob, nuts, and a great variety of Turkish pastries. Try the macaroons!

For a sit-down meal, restaurants are specialized. Lowest cost are the busy self-service cafeterias - kafeterya - which can offer a very good choice: soup, salads, rice and bread, maybe a dozen different stewed vegetable and meat dishes, puddings, fruit and soft drinks. Business starts very briskly at 12 noon and tapers off by 1.30 when the local office workers return to their desks. Evening mealtimes are much wider spread. It's worth going early, when all the food has just come through from the kitchens. Later, the hot dishes become tepid.

Offering a similar range at the same low, low prices are unpretentious little eating-places with stews displayed on steam tables at the entrance. Point to what you want, and a waiter delivers, the minute you sit down. Fast food, very tasty.

Yearning for a pizza? Numerous restaurants now offer the full Italian range. Others - called pideci - produce the Turkish style of slightly leavened flat bread called pide, topped with whatever you want - eggs, cheese, meat. Watching the cook's dexterity with a traditional oven is part of the enjoyment.

Another popular mealtime choice are the kebabci restaurants which specialise in grilled meats. Recommended is döner kebab: marinated lamb or mutton, roasted on a vertical spit and served in thin layers - crusty and smoky on one side, tender and pink on the other. Normally the cook works in full view, by a window open to the street. Similar establishments specialise in şiş kebab, lamb chops and cutlets, grilled over charcoal, while the köfteci restaurants concentrate on grilled meat-balls.

In some areas with open-air or garden restaurants, watch for a sign saying "et mangal" - meat barbecue. They are recognizable by the sight or smell of sacrificial smoke. Individual charcoal braziers are brought to your table. You then cook your own cutlets, chops and şiş kebabs to taste, with no cause for complaints about food being cold; or overdone when you wanted rare.

For dessert, or a teatime snack, innumerable pastry-shops sell sticky, sweet pastries like baklava and kadayif. Turkish sweets, "beauty's lip" or "lady's navel", are as tasty as some of their names suggest, though many of the pastries are very heavy on syrup. There are shops that specialise in yoghurt, or cold rice pudding called sütlaç.

The great joy of all these eating-places is that you don't need a word of Turkish to get precisely what you

141

want. Just look and point. Even in restaurants with menus and waiter service, it's quite normal to be invited into the kitchen, where the chef cheerfully opens up his cooking pots for your inspection and choice.

Among the specialty restaurants, be warned about the işkembeci, serving tripe soup which is considered to be a hangover cure. The recipe includes vinegar, crushed garlic, paprika and a dash of cayenne. Many Turks have it for breakfast.

The biggest single problem with Turkish food is the difficulty of having it served really hot. If you order soup, always add 'sıcak' or 'çok sıcak' - hot, or very hot, pronounced "suh-jak" or "chock suh-jak". You can then send it back for re-heating, when it arrives at room temperature. My theory is that "hot" in Turkish means either "not cold", or "it has been hot".

Fish Restaurants

For a fish meal, it's much more fun to visit a waterfront restaurant, where your choice is likely to be that morning's catch. That's in contrast to the poor fish who look as though they have been dead but not buried for several days, encased in the refrigerated glass coffin of a more up-market establishment.

Always ask the price first. In some tourist locations, fish can be a rip-off. Lobster, especially, can be extremely expensive. I once saw a group of eight jovial Germans order lobsters all round, without checking the price, and the waiters were almost dancing in the street. Menus indicate either a price per kilo, so that your selected fish is weighed and then costed; or, rather vaguely, they indicate that it all depends on the day's market price.

The proprietor can even be open to bargaining! If you display shock at the quoted cost, you may find that a lower price is offered.

Find Your Way Around a Turkish Menu

Most restaurants in tourist locations provide bi-lingual menus, Turkish with English or German. But you cannot depend upon it. Faced with a hundred-item Turkish menu, the first impulse is to panic and just say 'Şiş kebab". But it's worth making an effort to master the menu, particularly to try some of the enormous range of specialities. Usually, the lengthier menus are sub-divided into clearly-labelled courses, so that random picking of one item from each section would produce a meal with variety, if not balance. But let's work our way through some of the classic items of Turkish cuisine, omitting the obvious international newcomers like spaghetti. The full list is enormous!

Typical Turkish meals start with a wide range of hors d'oeuvres called meze or mezeler: first a selection of cold meze to keep you busy; then the hot appetizers, which are served as and when ready. Waiters often bring a trayful of cold starters for easier choice. The hundred-odd varieties range from salty white goat's cheese to wedges of sweet melon, slices of smoked sturgeon to green and black olives, mussels stuffed with rice and fried cheese pastries. When several people dine together, they share a number of meze dishes. Cold and hot meze together can make a full meal in themselves, with rakı as the traditional drink. At formal cocktail parties, a good buffet-style 'rakı table" can substitute for dinner.

Soğuk Mezeler – Cold Appetizers

Beyaz peynir ezmesi – a white cheese dip

Çerkes tavuğu – Circassian chicken in walnut purée with garlic or onion

Humus – purée of chick-peas

Midye plakisi – mussels with some vegetables, cooked in olive oil

Tarama – fish roe salad

Yaprak dolması – stuffed grape leaves

Zeytinyağlılar – Cold Vegetables cooked in Olive Oil

İmam bayıldı – 'the priest fainted' – aubergines fried with onion, tomato and some garlic and parsley

Kabak kızartması – slices of fried baby marrow, with yoghurt

Patlıcan kızartması – fried egg-plant slices served with yoghurt

Zeytinyağlı fasulye – green beans in tomato sauce

Sıcak Mezeler – Hot Appetizers

Arnavut ciğeri – spicy fried liver with onions

Kalamar tava – fried squid

Midye tava – fried mussels

Börekler – Savoury Pastries:

little pies of flaky pastry stuffed with meat, vegetables or cheese. Usually served as appetizers, but the meat böreks can also appear as a main course.

Kıymalı börek – börek with minced beef or lamb

Mantarlı börek – mushroom börek

Peynirli börek – cheese börek

Puf böreği – resembles a Cornish pasty, with cheese or meat filling

Sigara böreği – fried pastry filled with cheese

Su böreği – layers of pastry baked with cheese or meat filling

Talaş böreği – baked puff pastry with a filling of meat, onion and tomato

Tavuklu börek – chicken börek

Çorbalar – Soups

There are many excellent thick vegetable soup dishes, with chunks of meat to boost the flavour, popular as a fortifier for a light lunch. The lighter soups are chosen as first course of a more formal dinner.

Domatesli mercimek çorbası – lentil and tomato soup

Düğün çorbası – a thick 'wedding soup' – meat with egg yolks stirred in

İşkembe çorbası – tripe soup, flavoured with garlic, vinegar and red pepper: supposedly good for hangovers – otherwise, ugh!

Mercimek çorbası – lentil soup (very popular)

Şehriyeli Tavuk Suyu – chicken vermicelli soup

Tarhana çorbası – onions, tomatoes and green peppers, with yoghurt and flour

Yayla çorbası – a soup of beef broth, flour, yoghurt and an egg yolk

Dolma

The most characteristic of Turkish dishes are the 'stuffed' dolmas. Tomatoes, eggplant, green and red peppers, grapevine and cabbage leaves can all provide the outer casing for mixtures of rice, minced meat, nuts and spices. When stuffed with rice and cooked with olive oil, they are served cold as an hors-d'œuvre, and are described on menus as zeytinyağlı dolma. When meat is the filler, they are served as a hot appetizer; or several of them as a main course.

Biber dolması – stuffed green peppers

Etli biber dolması – green pepper meat dolma

Etli domates dolması – tomato meat dolma

Etli kabak dolması – zucchini meat dolma

Etli lahana dolması – minced lamb or beef with tomatoes, cooked in cabbage leaves

Etli patlıcan dolması – eggplants stuffed with ground lamb or beef
Etli yaprak dolması – meat dolma of grapevine leaves

Pilav – Pilaf or Rice Dishes
Rice appears in most Turkish meals – as stuffing for dolmas; as a side dish; or as a main course with meat, fish or vegetables; and in a number of soups and desserts. Turkish rice is well cooked and fluffy, not sticky.
Bulgur pilavı – cracked wheat pilav
İç pilav – savoury rice with liver, nuts, currants, tomato and onions
Kebab pilav – pilav with şiş kebab
Nohutlu pilav – pilav with chick-peas
Patlıcanlı pilav – eggplant pilav with tomatoes
Sade pilav – plain rice
Yufkalı pilav – chicken and rice pie

Balıklar – Fish and Seafood
The greatest variety of fish is available in Istanbul, thanks to the rich resources of the Black Sea, and the seasonal migrations of fish along the Bosphorus.
Balık Köftesi – fish balls
Barbunya – red mullet
Dil Balığı – sole
Hamsi – anchovies: enormous quantities are caught December through March in the Black Sea – try them grilled, or fried like whitebait.
Istakoz – lobster, if you can afford it
Kalkan – turbot, but not so good as in England
Karides – shrimp, plentiful year-round
Kerevit – prawn
Kılıç – swordfish: best eaten as grilled steaks; or in small pieces grilled on a skewer (kılıç şişte); or smoked, as a snack.
Levrek – sea bass, usually served baked (levrek fırında)
Lüfer – blue fish, resembles a herring, but the flesh is more delicate.
Mercan – sea bream
Mersin – sturgeon

Midye – mussels – fried as a hot hors-d'œuvre; or served with rice (midye pilavı); or stuffed (midye dolması).
Morina fırında – baked cod
Palamut – bonito
Sardelya – sardines, usually grilled
Taze istiridye – fresh oysters
Uskumru – mackerel

Etler – Meat
Izgaralar – Grills
In Kebabistan, otherwise known as Turkey, dozens of kebab – cooked meat – recipes have been developed over the past thousand years, to include broiled, baked and stewed variations on the basic theme of diced cubes of meat. The Turkish cuisine specialises in cooking meats together with different vegetables and herbs, to enhance the flavours of both.
Bahçıvan kebabı – gardener's kebab – diced lamb or beef, cooked in a pot with garden vegetables such as carrots, tomatoes, onions and peas
Ciğer kızartması – fried calf's or lamb's liver
Çöp şiş – like şiş kebab, but with smaller cubes of lamb
Dana – veal
Döner kebab – grilled lamb or mutton sliced from a vertical spit
Etli bamya – meat with okra
Etli çalı fasulyesi – green bean stew with diced beef or lamb
Etli güveç – casserole of diced beef with vegetables
Etli ıspanak – spinach with meat
Etli kapuska – meat cooked with cabbage
Etli mercimek – lentil stew
Etli nohut – chick-pea stew, lamb or beef
Etli patates – meat with potatoes
Etli sebze – meat stew with seasonal vegetables
Hindi dolması – stuffed turkey
Hünhar Beğendi – Sultan's delight – an

egg-plant purée, with lamb, beef or veal

İçli köfte – stuffed meat balls, boiled

İskender kebab – döner kebab served on pide bread, with yoghurt

Izgara köfte – grilled meat balls with cheese inside

İzmir köftesi – meatballs in tomato sauce

Kabak bastı – meat with zucchini

Kadın budu – 'Lady's thighs': fried meat-balls of ground lamb

Kağıt kebabı – kebab papillote

Karaşık ızgara – mixed grill

Kestaneli hindi – turkey with chestnuts, a traditional dish for New Year's Eve

Köfte – meat balls

Koyun – mutton

Kuru köfte – fried meatballs

Kuzu – lamb

Kuzu budu rostosu – roast leg of lamb

Kuzu pirzola – lamb chops

Nohutlu işkembe – tripe with chick-peas

Oturtma – eggplant casserole

Patlıcan Musakka – eggplant cooked with minced meat

Patlıcanlı Kebab – eggplant kebab, with onions and peppers

Pideli kebab – meat with pide, a kind of flat bread, served with yoghurt

Şiş kebab – grilled lamb on skewers, with chunks of tomato and green pepper

Şiş köfte – meat balls grilled on a skewer

Sosis – sausage

Sovanlı yahni – beef with onions

Tandır kebabı – oven-roasted lamb, with herbs

Tas kebab – small pieces of meat, stewed like a goulash in a thick sauce with rice

Tavuk – chicken – served in numerous ways: beğendi, with eggplant purée; nohutlu, with chick-peas; bamyalı, with okra; piliç kağıtta, en papillote; güveç, casserole with vegetables.

Terbiyeli pirasa – leeks cooked with

diced beef or veal

Yoğurtlu kebab – lamb or beef kebab, with a yoghurt sauce

Salatalar – Salads

When ordering a mixed salad, watch out for lurking peppers, which can lift the roof off your mouth.

Cacık – diced cucumber in garlic flavoured whipped yoghurt – could also rate as a cold soup

Çoban salatası – 'shepherd's salad' of mixed tomato, cucumber, onion and pepper

Domates ve Hiyar salatası – tomato and cucumber salad

Fasulye Ezmesi – mashed bean salad

Kabak salatası – zucchini salad

Karnıbahar salatası – cauliflower salad

Lahana salatası – cabbage salad

Pancar salatası – beetroot salad

Patates salatası – potato salad

Patlıcan salatası – pureed egg-plant salad

Piyaz – haricot bean salad

Sebzeler – Vegetables

Turkey is exceptionally rich in great variety of fresh home-grown vegetables of high quality. Each vegetable can be prepared in many different ways – fried, casseroled with meat, stuffed as a cold rice or hot meat dolma, or cooked in mousaka style with minced meat. The recipe permutations are endless, with varied additions of herbs, olive oil, lemon juice, garlic, condiments and sauces. Cooked with butter, vegetables are served as a side dish to accompany meat, poultry or fish.

Bamya – okra

Bezelye – peas

Borani – stewed spinach with onion

Domates – tomatoes

Enginar – artichoke

Fasulye – beans

Güveç – vegetable stew

Havuç – carrots

Ispanak – spinach

Kabak – zucchini
Karnabahar – cauliflower
Kuşkonmaz – asparagus
Mantar – mushrooms
Patates – potatoes
Patlıcan – aubergine; egg-plant
Pırasa – leeks
Peynirli kabak – zucchini with cheese
Taze fasulye – green beans

Tatlılar – Desserts
Turkish pastrycooks are famed for their
great specialities like baklava and other
richly sweet pastries. Milk and rice
puddings are also popular, normally
served cold.
Aşüre – a Noah's Pudding of 20
ingredients – basic wheat, rice, beans
and chick peas, boiled with milk and
sugar, and decorated with nuts and
varied dried fruits. Delicious!
Bademli muhallebi – milk pudding with
ground almonds
Baklava – flaky pastry stuffed with nuts,
and soaked in syrup
Bülbül yuvası – 'nightingale's nest'
Dondurma – ice cream
Hanım göbeği – 'lady's navel' – fried
pastries, covered in lemon-flavoured
syrup
Helva – a buttery semolina with nuts
Kabak tatlısı – sliced pumpkin cooked
with sugar, and served with a sprinkle
of ground-up nuts
Kadın göbeği – 'lady's navel'
Keşkül – ground almonds and
pistachios, boiled with milk, sugar,
beaten eggs and potato starch until
creamy
Komposto – cold stewed fruit
Lokma – sweet doughnuts, served with
whipped cream
Lokum – Turkish Delight
Mahallebi – sweet pudding made from
milk and rice flour, usually flavoured
with cinnamon
Sarığı burma – 'twisted turban' pastry
with ground walnuts, soaked in syrup

Sütlaç – creamy rice pudding, served
cold
Tavuk göğsü – a non-vegetarian dessert
of shredded boiled chicken added to a
boiled-up mixture of milk, sugar and
rice flour; served with a sprinkle of
cinnamon
Tel kadayıf – baked shredded wheat
stuffed with ground hazel nuts, with
syrup added
Un helvası – boiled milk, sugar, butter
and flour – shaped when cool, and
sometimes sprinkled with sliced
almonds
Zerde – boiled rice with added sugar,
saffron and rose-water, decorated with
nuts, currants and pomegranates

Meyveleri – Fruits
Armut – pear
Çilek – strawberries
Elma – apple
Erik – plums
İncir – figs
Karpuz – water melon
Kavun – sweet melon
Kayısı – apricots
Kiraz – cherries
Muz – bananas
Şeftali – peaches
Üzüm – grapes

How described, cooked, served or prepared?
az pişmiş – rare
buğulama – steamed
çiğ – raw
dolma – stuffed
fırında – baked
füme – smoked
günlük – 'of the day...' (for fish, etc)
güveç – stew
ızgara – grilled
haşlama – poached or boiled
iyi pişmiş – well done
kağıtta – papillote, cooked in oiled
paper
kremalı – creamed

mevsim – seasonal (salad or fruit)
orta pişmiş – medium rare
pilâki – braised
pure – mashed; purée
salamura – marinated
sıcak – hot
soğuk – cold
şiş – cooked on a spit or skewer
yoğurtlu – with yoghurt
tava – fried
taze – fresh
tencerede pişmiş – casserole
yahni – stewed
zeytinyağlı – cooked with olive oil and
served cold

All The Drinks

Coffee

Considering the world fame of Turkish coffee, it's ironic that the coffee bean is about the only crop which Turkey cannot grow herself. Around 1980 Turkey ran into near bankruptcy, when the oil crisis soaked up Turkey's entire export earnings just to pay the fuel bill. As a supreme belt-tightening gesture, Turkey stopped all coffee imports. Howls from tourists, who couldn't understand why they couldn't get Turkish coffee in Turkey! Since then, Turkey's finances have strengthened. Coffee is freely imported, and Turks can once again enjoy their famous beverage.

No visit to Turkey is complete without coffee - thick, black and sweet. From early morning till late night, coffeehouse waiters hurry back and forth with trays of the diminutive coffee-cups and glasses of water. Connoisseurs insist that coffee must be sweet as love, hot as hell, and with a surface froth so thick that a man in jackboots can walk across it. The water is drunk first, to cleanse the palate.

Depending on your taste for sugar, order Turkish coffee "şekerli" (sugary), "orta" (medium sugar), "az" (little sugar, or "sade" (plain, no sugar). As a first-timer, order "orta" and decide for future drinks whether to move up or down the scale.

Outside the higher-grade hotels, the standard breakfast drink is tea. If you insist on coffee, it will usually be served as instant powder, with a jug of warm water.

Coffee-Houses

Turkish men spend much of their leisure in coffeeshops and tea-houses, playing cards, backgammon or dominoes, talking, looking at TV, or just sitting. Some smoke a reflective nargile - hubble-bubble pipe. Others pass the time with a string of 33 worry-beads - three times round for the 99 names of Allah. Over all floats the insinuating sound of Turkish pop music. Most of the all-male, cloth-capped clientele are regulars. In smoke-filled town coffeeshops, a tourist can feel like an intruder. In village or resort coffeeshops, where there is outdoor seating, a tourist (or even a female of the species) can feel more comfortable.

Land of Tea-Drinkers

Despite the linkage of Turkey with coffee, the average Turk drinks far more tea - maybe a dozen glasses a day at half the price.

Compared with a strong English brew, Turkish tea is much lighter coloured, drunk neat in small glasses without milk, and sugared to taste. Formerly, Turkey used to import tea from India. But since 1945 the Turks have grown their own in a heavy-rainfall area of the

YEMEK ÇEŞİTLERİ	BEHER PORSİYON GRAMI	3. nci SINIFLAR - ' - A
Et suyu, mercimek, sebze ve düğün çorbaları (terbiyeli istendiğinde 1 yumurta bedeli ilave edilir.)	250	230
İşkembe ve paça çorbaları (terbiyeli istendiğinde bir yumurta bedeli ilave edilir.)	250	280
T u z l a m a	250	330
Tavuk, kuzu, koyun, beyin, dana, sığır etlerinden haşlama ve kızartma ile rosta, dana şehriyeli, et kuzu ciğer, sarma, sote, hünkar beğendi, taskebabı, çömlek kebabı, sade beğendi, patatesli talaş kebabı, macar kebabı, piliçli toros kebabı, et ve börek soteleri	150	700
Kokareç, elbasan tava, buhara köftesi, saray kebabı	200	700
Piliç söğüş 1/4	250	750
Piliç çevirme1/2	500	1280
Şehriyeli piliç	150	680
Beyinli kuzu başı	Tam	930
Izgara köfte	150	680
Bonfile, pirzola, şiş kebabı, koç yumurtası, şiş ızgara köfte böbrek ızgara, ciğer ızgara, kuzu çevirme, kaşarlı köfte, büftek, sade döner kebap garnitürlü	150	830
Yoğurtlu ve pideli döner kebabı	200	730
Karışık ızgaralar garnitürlü	200	900
Pideli köfte	200	680
Etli sarma dolmalar, etli yaş ve kuru sebzeler zeytinyağlı enginar sahanda yumurta çılbır	150	350
Etli enginar, karnıyarık, imambayıldı, etli ve kebaplı pilav, içli fırında yumurta, (tek yumurtalı)	150	430
Patlıcanlı kızartmalar, kabak, havuç tavaları, (yoğurtlu olarak) her türlü böreklerde patlıcanlı herse salata	150	380
Midye dolması	1 Adet	180
Zeytinyağlı dolmalar, sebzeler	150	350
Sade püre	100	180
Sade pilav, bulgur pilavı ve makarna	150	330
Cacık, marul salata, turşu, domates salata, fasulye piyazı (Yumurtalı arzu edildiğinde 1 yumurta bedeli eklenir.)	200	230
Amerikan ve Rus salataları trama	150	380
Beyin salatası	Yarım	430
Tuzlu sardalye	7 Adet	330
Beyaz peynir, (tam yağlı garnitürlü)	100	230
Yoğurt	200	180
Mevsim meyvaları	250	280
Dilimlenmiş ekmek (Rayiç bedel üzerinden satış yapılacaktır.)	Rayiç bedelden	
Tatlılar	150	330
Şişe suyu	1 şişe	50

Balık Yemekleri Özel siparişle yapılır «Pazarlığa tabidir» Pazarlık siparişten önce yapılır.

ALKOLLÜ İÇKİLERE (SOĞUK OLMAK ŞARTIYLA) ETİKET DEĞERİNE SINIFLARDA % 10 ZAMLI FİAT UYGULANIR.

N O T : YUKARIDA BELİRLENEN FİATLARA KATMA DEĞER VERGİSİ (KDV) DAHİL EDİLMİŞTİR. MÜŞTERİDEN BU NAM ALTINDA VEYA HERHANGİ BİR NEDENLE FAZLA FİAT TALEP EDİLEMEZ.

1— İşbu tarifede yazılı fiyatlar müşterilere kesilecek hesap pusulası iki nüsha olarak düzenlenir ve bir nüshası müşterilerinin masasında bulundurulacaktır.

2— İşbu tarife büyük punto harflerle herkesin görebileceği bir yer ile kapı girişine asılacak ve her masada küçük boyda basılmış bir adedi Türkçe, bir adedi İngilizce tarife bulunacaktır.

3— Asılan tarifelerin üzerine kapatacak şekilde herhangi bir şey asılması ve kamufle edilmesi yasaktır.

4— Gerek asılacak ve gerekse masada bulundurulacak tarifeler Zabıta Amirliğince tasdik edildikten sonra yerlerinde bulundurulacaktır.

5— Belediye Encümeninin 4/11/1986 Tarih ve 667 Sayılı kararı ile kabul edilen işbu tarife tebliğ tarihinden itibaren uygulanacaktır.

6— Her Lokantada porsiyonların tartılması için terazi bulundurulacaktır.

7— İşbu tarifeye aykırı harekette bulunulduğu takdirde tutulacak zabıt üzerine 1500.- TL. den 4500.- TL.'ye kadar para cezası üç günden 15 güne kadar da işyeri kapatılmak suretiyle icrayı sanattan men cezası uygulanır.

D İ S H E S	GRAMMES PER SERVİNG	3. Class TL.
Meat Bröth, Lentil Soup, Vegetable Soup, Wedding Soup, When special marinade vith eggs and lemon juice requested, the price, of one egg is to be abded	250	230
Tripe and lamb kunuckles soups When special marinade vith eggs and lemon juice requested, price of one egg is to be abded	250	280
Pickled tripe	250	330
Poultry, lamb, mutton, mutton's, brains, veal and beef; stewed, fried or roasted : Hungar Beğendi, saute, veal witth lamb's liver stuffiug, stew served in bowl, Kebab en cocette, chipped meat stew with potatoes, Goulash, Tros Kebap with chicken, sauteed kidneys and meat	150	700
Grilled Lamb's intestines, Meat Stew with yoğurt sauce, "Buhara,, meat balls, Place Kebab	200	700
Quarter chicken, cold 1 / 4	250	750
Grilled chicken 1 / 2	500	1280
Chicken with noodles	150	680
Lamb's head with braıns	Tam	930
Grilled meat ball	150	680
Grilled filet, Lamb chops, "Shısh,, Kebab, Grilled ram testicles, Grilled meat on skewer, Grilled meat balls. Grilled kidneys, Grilled liver, Grilled whole lamb's meat. Grilled meat bals, beef steak plain "Döner Kebab,, on flad bread	150	830
Plain "Döner Kebab,, on flat bread, servet with yoğurt	200	730
Mixed grilled meats, witth side dish	200	900
Meat bals served on fıat bread	200	680
Stuffed vegetables, served vith hot sauce, fresh or canned vegetables cooked with meat, artıchokes in oil, poached eggs with yoğurt	150	350
Artichokes cooked with maat, egglanst stuffed with minced meat ubergines cooked with oil and garlic. served cold, Rice cooked with liver and grapes, Broiled eggs	150	430
Fried sliced eggpland, sliced squash carrats fried in oil, all kirds of puff pastes or bouches, eçgland salad	150	380
Stuffed mussels	1 Adet	180
Stuffed vegetables in oil, served cold	150	350
Puerre - mashed potatoes	100	180
Plain rıce, Pilav from bolied pounded wheat noodles	150	330
"Cacik" (Beaten yogurt ond grated cucumbers) lettuce salad, pıckled cucumbers peppers etc, tomato salad, lima beans salad	200	230
Russian salad-boiled minced vegetables, pickled in mayannoıse, caviar beaten in mayonnaise	150	380
1/2 cold brain in olive oil and lemon Juice	Yarım	400
Pickled sardines	7 Adet	330
Garnitür (Fetta Chesse)	100	230
Yogurt	200	180
Fruits of the season	250	280
Bread, at local official cost	Rayiç bedelden	
Turkish dessarts	150	330
Bott'ed Water	1 Şise	50

FISH DISHES ARE PREPARED UPAN SPECIAL ORDER - PRICES TOBE DETERMINED BY BARGAININK

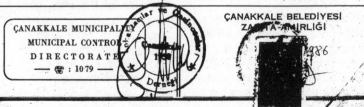

ÇANAKKALE MUNICIPALITY
MUNICIPAL CONTROL
DIRECTORATE
— ☎ : 1079 —

ÇANAKKALE BELEDİYESİ
ZABITA AMIRLIĞI

149

Black Sea coast, centred on Rize, and are totally self-sufficient.

For the holidaymaker, Turkish tea-gardens are a delight - usually in a pleasant setting, with awnings or vines to give shade. Just the price of a glass of tea is enough entrance for sitting as long as you want. Other light drinks are served. Try elma çayı - diluted apple juice, drunk warm or cold; or even ada çayı - sage tea with the flavour boosted with a slice of lemon.

Most tea-gardens cater for family trade, in contrast to the male-oriented town coffeeshops. Likewise, the continental style of café is frequented by young people, families and holiday visitors. It is noticeable that Turks, both men and women, are much heavier smokers than is now customary in Britain. On the other hand, alcohol consumption is much lower.

In cafés, Turks prefer glasses of traditional tea, or soft drinks of the cola type, while only a few order beer. An extremely popular summertime thirst-quencher is ayran - a cool mixture of yoghurt, water and a pinch of salt. Try it!

Also popular are the fruit-juice stands, where manually-operated presses make orange juice, or grapefruit, carrot or cherry according to season. Five or six oranges go into a tall glass. You can also buy juice in cans, useful for picnics. In a bar, try cherry juice - Vişne Suyu - with soda water.

Beer

Another male preserve are the beer halls and beer taverns, mostly selling draught only: fıçı bira. Usually they have a selection of snacks on offer, like fried mussels. Restaurants and cafés mostly stock bottled beers only: Efes Pilsen or Tuborg.

Rakı

This characteristic national hard liquor is double distilled from grape residues, flavoured with aniseed, and burns with a blue flame. It is similar to the French pastis, Arab arrak, or Greek ouzo.

The Turkish way of drinking rakı is in flat cylindrical glasses, and cold. Mostly the Turks mix it half-and-half with water, when it turns milky - in colour, not alcohol content! Hence its popular name: "Lion's Milk". It can also be drunk straight, or with soda or mineral water.

Rakı goes best with meze - all kinds of appetizers or hors d'oeuvres. Most Turks then stay with a bottle or half-bottle of rakı for the remainder of the meal - şiş kebab, grilled meats or fish, and finally fruit. Melon and feta cheese combine specially well with rakı.

Wines

The alternative of wine-drinking has a long history in Turkey. Wine containers dating back to 4000 BC have been found during excavations in Central Anatolia, where vineyards still flourish. Homer described the Phrygian vineyards of 900 years BC.

However, because of the traditional Islamic prohibition of wine-drinking, consumption in Turkey is very low compared with France, Italy or Spain. Although Turkey rates fifth in the world for grape production, the fruit is mainly converted into raisins and sultanas. Only 3% of the crop goes into wine-making. In Ottoman times, wine production was handled by non-Moslems. The average working Turk drinks tea, then beer; rakı if he can afford it. Wine is for the sophisticated middle and upper class. Quality is good. Despite proximity to Greece, there is no equivalent of retsina. In the 20th century, Turkish wines have won gold and silver medals at international wine fairs. The visitor can greatly enjoy judging for himself, with store prices that range from 50p to just over £1 a bottle. Just ask for şarap.

Wine-lists are dominated by a handful of names: Doluca, Kavaklıdere and Kulüp. Virtually all the available wines are dry (sek); a few medium (dömisek); very few sweet (tatlı). The same names are repeated as red (kırmızı) or white (beyaz), and even rosé. The year of origin is not mentioned on labels or wine-lists. All years are equal: no year is more vintage than another.

Among the red wines, try Villa Doluca (top of the range, a little more expensive), Doluca (somewhat heavier, to go with a strongly flavoured dish), Kulüp (full bodied), Dikmen (one of the Kavaklıdere wines from Central Anatolia) and Buzbağ (a prize-winning Burgundy type).

For white wines, again choose from Villa Doluca, Doluca Riesling, Kulüp or Kavaklıdere Kavak. They all go happily with fish, or with a table of meze appetizers.

Imported wines and liquors are much more costly. If you cannot live without your favourite Scotch, you may bring in five bottles duty-free. The Turkish Monopoly produces gin and vodka (spelt cin and votka) and a range of sweet liqueurs. Portakal - which means 'orange' - resembles Curaçao; Beyendik is somewhat like Benedictine; Kanyak is a distant relative of brandy.

Chapter Ten
What to Buy

Shopping is part of a holiday. Whether it's for souvenirs, giftware or even items that will actually be useful, Turkey has much to offer. In the beach resorts, tourist shops stay open till midnight, seven days a week throughout the season. Shop-gazing becomes part of the night-life. In major cities, however, shops keep more regular hours - closed by 7 p.m., and closed on Sundays.

Best policy, particularly for major items, is to start looking during the early days of a holiday - just getting a feel of the price levels, qualities available, and sussing out whether haggling is appropriate or not. Don't rush into buying! When shop-keepers see that you are comparison shopping, you will find their price-quotes become more flexible. Don't buy on the run - during a one-day coach tour, or during time ashore on a cruise - unless you already know the prices.

To haggle, or not to haggle? You'll soon get the message, when bargaining is expected. Main city stores operate European-style fixed prices, but tourist shops are part of the Orient. Show some mild interest in an item - then a sense of shock at the price - begin to walk out, saying you'll try elsewhere... If the price is negotiable, it will start crumbling. After a few times, you'll master the art. For any serious purchase, play it the Turkish way, shopping around. During the last days of the holiday, you can then finalize the larger deals.

Meanwhile, here are background comments on what's worth buying.

Textiles

Whether it's cotton goods or knitwear, the Turkish textile industry has made enormous strides in recent years. Recently, Europe was flooded with Turkish T-shirts until the Common Market countries had to put them on quota. Likewise, many high fashion items in Europe and USA are of Turkish origin. Prices in Turkish boutiques are much lower than in Britain. It's worth travelling out light on clothing, and buying things to wear on arrival.

During the main summer season in Istanbul, Arabs from the Gulf States are the big spenders. Shopkeepers along İstiklâl Caddesi convert their window displays to conform to Arabic taste. However, if you go into any garment store, you will find European styling, tucked away on the back shelves.

For anyone who wants to look like a real ripe lemon of a tourist, buy a maroon fez, curly-toed slippers and the Anatolian peasant's baggy pants called the şalvar. The Covered Bazaar is lined with these products for the tourist trade, which no Turk would dream of wearing. These items can be useful for your next fancy dress party. But they are not for wearing in the street, except to give the Turks a laugh. For casual wear, style-conscious Turkish men and girls prefer T-shirt, blue jeans and trainers - all made in Turkey, despite any fancy labels that have been sewn on.

In the T-shirt department, don't believe the Lacoste labels even though they say "Made in Paris". Wrapped in the authentic style, the short-sleeved two-button product costs a fairly standard £2.50, whether you buy from a street barrow or a shop. Who's to know, when you get home? In Istanbul's Covered Bazaar, you can buy all the rag-trade accessories. They have long rolls of green crocodiles, all ready to snip off and sew onto any garment that trend-setters wish to upgrade into genuine Lacoste.

If you want stylish knitwear, look for the local brand names of Yargıcı or Zeki Triko, who do a substantial export business. For a Moslem country, it's remarkable that Turkey produces some of Europe's sexiest swimming gear: hot designs like Pierre Cardin, for instance.

Leather

Leather goods come in enormous variety, and suede is big business. Take time over purchases, examining workmanship with great care. Styling of leather clothing for men and women is modern and sophisticated. Just like the textiles, Turkish designer leather and suede is sold in the world's most prestigious fashion centres. Boutiques are stacked with readymade garments, but custom made is worth debating if you're not in a tremendous rush. "Delivery in 24 hours" may result in slap-happy workmanship to meet the deadline.

Carpets

Hand-woven carpet-making is Turkey's biggest cottage industry. The most expensive are made from silk. But many Turkish carpets today are machine made. The distinguishing characteristic of handmade Turkish carpets is the method of knotting. When buying, fold a carpet in half; then look at the exposed roots of the pile. A factory-made carpet will show perfect lines of knots, whereas the handmade version will be less regular, though the knots will resist a hard tug.

If you are thinking of buying a carpet, do some really serious pricing before leaving home. It's not unknown for visitors to buy a carpet in Turkey, and then find they could have bought it cheaper back home.

Bargaining is essential. Read the comments in this book's Istanbul chapter, relating to carpet-buying in the Covered Bazaar and elsewhere. To help understand the product better, several excellent English-language booklets are published in Turkey, describing materials, techniques, colours and patterns from the different carpet weaving regions. For two or three pounds, you can become much more knowledgeable - and better equipped in the haggling game.

Antiques

Around some of the classical sites, small boys, or even adults, will approach you with a Roman coin or a figurine, and tell you they have just found it in the ruins. What will you offer? The manufacture of ancient coins, figurines and oil-lamps is now one of Turkey's boom industries. In the unlikely event that the artifact is genuine, it's quite legal to buy and sell in Turkey, but not to export without permission.

For the usual flea-market style of antiques, Istanbul's Covered Bazaar can be a happy hunting-ground.

Arts and Crafts

The traditions of hand workmanship still survive vigorously in Turkey. Although many souvenirs are specially produced for the tourist market on a production line, shoppers can find wide choice of decorative craft giftware. There is gleaming copper everywhere. How about a set of the little Turkish pots for making coffee?

For a present that a dedicated pipe-smoker would cherish, consider buying a carved Meerschaum pipe. Prices range from £5 to £11; or up to double that price for more elaborate pipes, particularly if the entire stem is carved.

Many craft shops are crammed with alabaster, turned or carved in every possible shape: vases, egg cups, bowls, ash trays, chess sets. Onyx is another favoured material, with pieces that can be bought direct from workshops handily located in tourist resorts.

Ceramics are always a popular purchase - particularly tiles and plates, decorated in traditional patterns and colours.

Jewellery

Turkey has an advantage in the relatively low cost of skilled craftsmanship. In the bazaars of Istanbul and Izmir, entire sections are glistening with gold.

If you're into higher mathematics, most jewellers display the day's gold price in Turkish liras - that is, separate figures for one gramme of 22 carat gold, 18 carat and 14 carat. Take your pocket calculator when you go gold-shopping. The jeweller will weigh the piece you are considering; and hopefully you can then split his price into the cost of the metal, and the cost of workmanship.

Special Local Products

Natural sponges are very cheap, particularly in the Bodrum area which is a traditional centre for the industry. Reckon to pay £1 for small sponges, up to £3 for larger specimens. Sandal-making is another Bodrum speciality - ready-to-wear or custom made. In Bursa, look at silk; and Turkish towels.

As a final souvenir of Turkey, why not take home some tasters for your friends: hazel nuts, helva, Turkish Delight, comb honey, candied fruits? On the way out, at the Duty-Free, buy a bottle or two of Buzbağ wine. Everyone just loves the label.

Chapter Eleven
Looking at the Past

Centuries before Christ, Anatolia was sandwiched between two great empires - Greek and Persian. From early times the Greeks colonised the coastal regions, leaving undisturbed the pastoral tribes of the interior - Hittites, Phrygians and the like. Then for 200 years Anatolia was ruled by the Persians, until they were driven out by Alexander the Great. From that date - 333 BC - the region came completely under Greek and, later, Roman domination.

That explains why Turkey is so rich in Greco-Roman remains. North of present-day Izmir - ancient Smyrna, the natural nerve-centre of the Aegean coast - are a dozen major classical sites, including legendary Troy and Pergamum, the medical centre of antiquity. Southwards are another dozen, including Ephesus (a Hellenistic metropolis, capital of Roman Asia), Miletus (rated as a second Athens), Didyma and Priene.

Inheritors of the Greco-Roman tradition were the Byzantines, for whom Christianity was the state religion. They converted pagan temples and basilicas into Christian sites, and built churches lavishly decorated with frescoes and mozaics. Their mastery of dome architecture culminated in the magnificent church of St. Sophia - completed AD 537, and still one of the world's great buildings. The Byzantine style of mural decoration and of dome construction spread later to Russia and the Balkans, where it is still characteristic of church architecture.

The first Turks on the Anatolian scene were the Seljuks, who introduced Islam and new-type buildings: mosques, medrese (seminaries) and caravanserais. Their capital, Konya, still preserves the finest group of major Seljuk public buildings.

When the 15th-century Turks finally overthrew the Byzantine Empire, they brought no building traditions with them, but sought to imitate the Arab and the Byzantine. With Eastern - especially Persian - influence predominating, they created an architecture which stands witness to the Ottoman genius.

The Ottomans poured wealth into the city which, in the latter stages of Byzantine rule, had been allowed to crumble. They built mosques and palaces, schools, hospitals, libraries, baths and public fountains. Of all their architects, the most famous was Sinan. During mid-16th century, he built some of Turkey's finest mosques, rivalling the artistry of St. Sophia. Basing his work mainly on Byzantine themes, Sinan brought the Persian style of tile decoration to perfection.

These tiles were imported from many regions. Konya, in central Turkey, contributed tiles of peacock-blue and sea-green. Iznik was specially famed for its tiles with floral patterns. From Jerusalem came tiles inscribed with Arabic calligraphy; and from

Damascus more of the floral designs which were Sinan's particular delight. Among his finest works in Istanbul was the Mosque of Rüstem Paşa, and the Süleymaniye Mosque. The Selimiye Mosque in Edirne, near the Bulgarian border, is regarded as his greatest achievement.

Time Chart of the Anatolian Civilizations

600,000 to 8,000 BC - Paleolithic and Mezzolithic Ages:
Nomads began to appear in Anatolia, living in caves and rock shelters. They were hunters and gatherers - consumers, not producers. Tools were of stone, bone and wood. Remains have been found in the Antalya region: at the Karain Cave, and in rock shelters of Beldibe and Belbaşi.

8,000 to 5,500 BC - Neolithic Age:
Anatolian civilization became possibly the most prosperous in the world, with a stabilized life-style in settled villages. Hunters became farmers, growing wheat, barley, lentil and similar grain crops. They domesticated dogs, sheep and goats.

Building materials were mud-brick, wood and stone. Colourful murals decorated house walls. People began to work metals, weave textiles and make earthenware vessels. Mirrors were made from obsidian.

6500 to 5650 BC - establishment of Anatolia's first town, Çatalhöyük near present-day Konya.

5500 to 3200 BC - Chalcolithic Age:
A somewhat stagnant period. Writing, for instance, only came to Anatolia a thousand years after its

development in Mesopotamia. However, Anatolian pottery advanced to a very high level. Houses were built with flat roofs, and mud-brick walls rested on stone foundations. For the first time, settlements were fortified by city walls. Copper and other mixtures of metal were used.

3200 to 1800 BC - Early Bronze Age:
Formation of cultures based on metal-working, and development of the earliest city states, including the first settlement of Troy.

1800 to 1500 BC - Middle Bronze Age:
The zenith of the Bronze Age in Anatolia, with production of works of art in gold and silver.

2000 to 1200 BC - Hittite Period:
The Hittites - their origins somewhat mysterious - established a capital at Hattusa (Boğazköy, 90 miles east of Ankara), and built an empire over most of Asia Minor and Syria. The Hittites were the first in Anatolia to use writing (hieroglyphic and cuneiform script). This was the big step forward.

1900 to 1750 BC - small Hittite principalities established

1750 to 1450 BC - foundation of the Old Hittite Kingdom, which captured Aleppo and then Babylon between 1620 and 1590 BC.

1450 to 1200 BC - Hittite Empire reached from the Aegean to the Euphrates, making it the chief rival of Egypt.

1180-750 BC - Dark Age of Anatolia:
Invasion by Balkan tribes brought sudden end to the Hittite empire, and opened a Dark Age. Along the coast of Asia Minor, cities were destroyed and nomads roamed the country until finally they began to

settle. The Hittite capital, Hattusa, was captured by Thracians. Despite this, some Hittite city states continued to flourish in south-eastern Anatolia and in Northern Syria, well removed from the Dark-Age area. However - thanks to excavations carried out since 1948 in Old Smyrna, Miletus, Erythrai, Phocaea and Iasos - archaeologists now limit the Dark Age of Western Anatolia to no more than 150 years (1200 to 1050 BC), though these first Greek-Anatolian settlements were poor and primitive. By 800 BC, virtually the whole Aegean coast had been colonised by Greeks. In the following centuries the Greek settlements reached to the coastlines of Marmara, Black Sea and Mediterranean; and, from the Aegean coast, new settlements penetrated inland up the broad river valleys of Western Anatolia.

900-600 BC - The Urartu:
A civilization of Eastern Anatolia in the Lake Van area, their art influenced by the Assyrians.

750-300 BC - The Phrygians:
The Phrygians - descendants of the Thracian tribes who had destroyed Troy V11 and Hattusa - succeeded the Hittites in central and partly in south-eastern Anatolia, with their capital at Gordion (named after Gordius of 'Gordion Knot' fame, and father of King Midas).

1050-350 BC - Civilizations of Lydia, Caria and Lycia:
Developed simultaneously in western and south-western Anatolia. Although these people had already existed in the third millennium BC, their cultural remains do not go back further than around 700 BC.

The Lydian capital was wealthy Sardis (near present-day Izmir), where coins were first minted and where Croesus ruled until defeated by the Persians in 546 BC. Then followed two centuries of Persian rule throughout Anatolia, mainly through the appointment of local Greek governors called satraps.

The Lycian capital was at Xanthos on the south coast, and their territory reached round from Fethiye to Antalya. In between was Caria, on the south-western coast.

Excavations have unveiled detailed history of these East Greek civilizations of Western Asia Minor, where science, philosophy and literature flourished.

334-30 BC - Hellenistic Age:
Alexander the Great crossed the Dardanelles in 334 BC, drove out the Persians, and opened a new era in Anatolian history. Although split between several kingdoms after Alexander's death, Anatolia's economy boomed. New roads linked rich and populous cities such as Pergamum, Ephesus, Priene and Miletus. Art and culture reached great heights in this prosperous urban environment.

Cities were adorned with majestic public monuments: temples, theatres, sport centres. Site reconstructions help the modern-day visitor get a clear picture of this affluent life-style of 2000 years ago. During this period, Greek was the dominant and official language of Asia Minor.

30 BC to 395 AD - The Roman Age:
Peace and prosperity under Roman rule. Asia Minor became a province of the Roman Empire, with Ephesus as capital. Public buildings and

housing became more opulent than ever before, particularly during a golden age in the 1st and 2nd centuries AD. New wealth was added to the existing cities of the Aegean coast. Cities of the southern coast witnessed rapid development - Patara, Phaselis, Antiphellus, Antalya, Side, Antioch. Emperors were worshipped as gods, alongside the traditional deities.

During the 4th century AD, the Roman Empire weakened.

395 to 1453 AD - The Byzantine Age: In 330 AD Emperor Constantine moved his capital from Rome to the site of ancient Byzantium - renamed Constantinople - with Christianity named as the state religion. In 395 AD the Roman Empire split into western and eastern halves. The Byzantine Empire peaked in the 6th century, during the reign of Emperor Justinian. Then, with the rise of Islam, the Empire went into steady decline until the final fall in 1453, when Mehmet the Conqueror entered Istanbul.

1071-1243 - The Seljuks
The Seljuks from central Asia were the first Turkish dynasty to establish itself in Anatolia, when Sultan Alpaslan won the battle of Malazgirt in 1071. The conquest was followed by large-scale migration of Turkish tribes who settled in different areas of Anatolia.

The Seljuk golden age was in the first half of the 13th century, when great efforts were made to develop Anatolia as a trading centre by attracting land traffic from Asia, as far as China. Caravanserais were built along the main routes, and the Seljuks even developed the concept of insurance. Seljuk rule ended abruptly with defeat by the Mongols in the battle of Kosedağ in 1243.

1299-1923 - The Ottoman Empire
After collapse of the Seljuks, another Turkish principality rose to power in western Anatolia, ruled by Ertuğrul Gazi. The frontiers were greatly extended by his son Osman, who gave his name to the Osmanlı dynasty, called Ottoman by Europeans. Later generations saw dramatic extensions of their Empire, with the final overthrow of the Byzantines in 1453 as their greatest triumph.

The 16th and 17th centuries were the great era of Ottoman expansion, particularly during the 46-year reign of Süleyman the Magnificent. The Ottoman Empire was a major world power that covered the entire Balkans, the Crimea, the Middle East and most of North Africa. Istanbul was neatly placed at the geographic heart of it all.

Later centuries saw gradual stagnation and decline, as various territories gained independence, and Turkey became "the sick man of Europe." Ottoman rule ended in 1923 when Turkey became a Republic, shorn of all foreign possessions, and firmly resolved to abstain from all territorial ambitions.

Chapter Twelve
Dates in Turkish History

1240-1200	Approximate period of seige and destruction of Troy
660	Byantium founded
595	Smyrna sacked by the Lydians
550	Invasion of Anatolia by Cyrus the Great of Persia
546	Persians over-run the Greek coastal cities; King Croesus defeated
484-425	Herodotus - the Greek "Father of History" was born in Halicarnassus (Bodrum), travelled widely and compiled the first grand overview of history
353	Death of Mausolus and building of Mausoleum at Halicarnassus
334-333	Alexander the Great crosses the Dardanelles with an army of 40,000 Greeks and Macedonians, invades Asia Minor, liberates the Greek coastal cities, cuts the Gordion knot and drives out the Persians
133	Pergamum bequeathed to Rome
129	Formation of Roman Province of Asia
67	Roman navy under Pompey cleans up the Mediterranean of pirates based at Alanya and Side
41	Antony meets Cleopatra at Tarsus
31	Anthony and Cleopatra defeated by Octavian

AD	
50-58	St. Paul tours Asia Minor
90	St. John dies at Ephesus, and is buried at Selçuk
325	First Ecumenical Council at Nicaea (Iznik)
330	Constantine the Great moves capital of the Roman Empire to Byzantium - re-named Constantinople - with Christianity adopted as the state religion
395	Division of Roman Empire into western and eastern empires, with the eastern empire based at Constantinople
476	Fall of Rome, with the historic Roman Empire reduced just to its eastern half. Greek language again becomes the dominant tongue of Anatolia, with Latin fading.
527-63	Peak period of the Byzantine age, under rule of Justinian
537	Building completed of St. Sophia
570	Mohammed born
1054	Disputes over church dogma lead to final split between Eastern and Western Christianity - between Greek Orthodox and the Latins
1071	Seljuk Turks invade, defeat Byzantines at Malazgirt, north of Lake Van

1077	Seljuk kingdom established - the Sultanate of Rum
1096	Launch of First Crusade
1147	Second Crusade
1190	Third Crusade led by Frederick Barbarossa, ends in his death by drowning near Silifke; the last Christian army to invade Anatolia until 1920.
1204	Constantinople plundered by the Fourth Crusaders
1326	Bursa captured by the Ottoman Turks
1354	Ottoman Turks cross the Dardanelles - their first entry into Europe
1361	Turks capture Adrianople (Edirne) and subdue Bulgaria
1453	Capture of Constantinople (Istanbul) by Mehmet the Conqueror, marking the final Fall of the Roman Empire
1459	Serbia incorporated into the Empire
1460	Greece occupied
1475	Crimea becomes a protectorate
1516-7	Syria, Palestine, Arabia and Egypt fall to the Ottomans
1517	Sultan Selim the Ferocious takes the title of Caliph (Successor of Mohammed) - a title retained by the Ottoman dynasty until its fall
1520-66	Reign of Süleyman the Magnificent. The Ottoman Empire was extended throughout the Balkan countries to Hungary and Moldavia; around the North African coast - Tripolitania and Algeria; and Iraq.
1522	Capture of Rhodes
1529	The first seige of Vienna
1565	Turks fail to capture Malta, after a long seige
1571	Cyprus captured; Catholic fleets defeat Turkish navy at Lepanto
1669	Crete conquered
1683	The high tide of Ottoman expansion, when the Turks reached the gates of Vienna. From then onwards, the Ottoman Empire stagnated and declined.
1717	Austrians capture Belgrade
1770	Russians destroy an Ottoman fleet at Çeşme
1826	Janissaries abolished
1827	Naval battle of Navarino, with Turks defeated by combined fleet of British, French and Russians
1829	Independence of Greece
1853	Russian army occupies portion of Turkey north of the Danube, and a Russian fleet sinks Turkish warships in Black Sea.
1854-56	Russian moves towards Istanbul bring France and Britain into alliance with Turkey, leading to the Crimean War.
1861-76	Reign of Abdül Aziz. Balkan provinces in constant turmoil.
1877-78	Bulgarian and Bosnian uprising, backed by Russia. Treaty of San Stefano followed by Congress and Treaty of Berlin give independence to Romania and Serbia, autonomy to Bulgaria, while Bosnia and Herzegovina becomes an Austrian protectorate. Cyprus comes under British rule.
1881	Birth of Kemal Atatürk
1882	Britain occupies Egypt

Side

The Roman theatre, with seating capacity for 13,000.

Alanya
Looking down on East Beach,
from the fortress walls.

1908	Young Turks from Salonika revolt, and force the Sultan to restore the 1876 Constitution and recall Parliament.
1911	Italians invade Libya, which is ceded to Italy in 1912
1912-13	Balkan Wars, in which Greece, Bulgaria, Serbia and Montenegro force Turkey to surrender all European possessions except Eastern Thrace
1914	World War 1, Turkey joins Germany. Britain occupies Iraq.
1915	British, French and Anzac forces make landings at Gallipoli, fail to seize the Dardanelles after heavy losses, and finally evacuate the bridgeheads. Arabia proclaims independence.
1918	Turks lose Palestine and Syria. Armistice signed, and Allied fleet anchors off Istanbul. British, French and Italians occupy different sectors of Anatolia.
1919	Greek forces land at Izmir. Kemal Atatürk heads a Nationalist Congress, independent of the government in Istanbul.
1920-22	Bitter struggle between Greece and Turkey, ending in victory for the revitalized Turkish Army under Kemal Atatürk
1923	Treaty of Lausanne establishes River Evros as Turkey's border in Europe, with exchange of Greek and Turkish minorities except for the Greek community of Istanbul. Allied troops withdraw from Istanbul. Proclamation of Turkish Republic, with capital moved to Ankara.
1924	Abolition of religious courts
1925	Wearing of the fez prohibited; western calendar adopted
1926	Introduction of Swiss civil code
1928	Link severed between State and religion. Modified Latin alphabet introduced.
1933	Metric system adopted
1934	Launch of Five Year Plan of industrial development. All Turks required to take a surname. Women get the vote, and can become MP's.
1937	According to an amended constitution, Turkey is "Republican, Nationalist, Populist, Etatist, Secular and Reformist" - the basic guidelines set by Kemal Atatürk.
1938	Death of Atatürk. Ismet İnönü becomes President.
1939	Turkey, Britain and France sign Treaty of Ankara, providing mutual help
1945	Turkey stays neutral until 28 February, then declares war on Germany and Japan
1949	Turkey joins the Council of Europe
1950	Turkish troops sent to Korea
1952	Becomes member of NATO
1959	Applies to become associate member of European Economic Community
1963	Associate EEC application accepted
1967	Second Five Year Plan launched. Pope Paul visits Ephesus.
1972	Third Five Year Plan adopted
1973	Bosphorous Bridge opened, linking Europe and Asia
1974	Turkish forces intervene in Cyprus

1980   Army takes over administration, to end wave of political violence. Parliament dissolved.
1983   New elections held, giving power to Motherland Party, led by Turgut Özal.
1987   Application for full membership of EEC. A referendum permits former banned politicians to return to active political life. A new election again returns the Motherland Party to power with a large working majority.

Chapter Thirteen
Architecture - Looking at Cities - Ancient, Medieval and Modern

Part of Turkey's fascination is to see first-hand how successive civilizations have left their mark on architecture, the layout of cities, or even the design of houses today.

Look, for instance, at the older farm buildings as you travel across the Anatolian Plain. Many have an outdoor staircase to the floor above: animals below, humans overhead. These buildings still follow the elemental construction techniques of the Hittites of 4000 years ago: base walls of stone; then courses of mud bricks; timber supports for the roof. It helps explain why all that survives from original Hittite buildings is that stone base: the rest must be filled in by the imagination.

Most of the classic sites on the tourist circuit are Greek, but modified by the Romans. The difference shows, for instance, in theatre building. The original Greek concept was a circular dancing-floor - 'orchestra' - at the foot of a concave hillside where the spectators stood or sat. Tiers of wooden or stone seats were then added to the shaped hillside, extending around some two-thirds of the orchestra. Later, the open sector was partly closed by a low scene-building where the performers could retire, or change costume.

That simplicity was greatly elaborated in later centuries, when the Romans built up the scene-building to great height, richly decorated with statues

and ornamentation. The auditorium and the orchestra were sliced back to half-circles. With that change in basic construction, the Romans were able to accommodate their more degraded taste for blood sports and animal combats. This change-over can be seen quite vividly in the great theatre of Ephesus.

Much of the interest in the Turkish scene comes from seeing the total switch from the Greco-Roman city plan, with its civic centre for law, trade and politics, its city-grid streets, baths that were monumental social and gymnastic centres, and its theatres and temples - to the completely different style evolved by the Seljuk and Ottoman Turks.

The Islamic City

Certainly, the Islamic Turkish city represents a total break from Hellenistic, Roman and Byzantine traditions. Consider the contrasting points. The Turks, coming from the hot and arid lands of the East, preferred cool and narrow streets, covered or shaded bazaars and the ripple of water.

Focal-point of a city district was the Friday mosque, with all its ancillary buildings: a medrese - theological school - comprising student cells and a classroom that opened onto a four-sided courtyard; a hospital for the sick; soup kitchen and alms houses for the poor; free lodgings for travellers and their servants. With the Islamic zeal for ritual cleanliness before prayer, the Turkish bath - hamam - was in close proximity to the mosque precincts. A typical example of this complete nucleus, unchanged from the 15th century, is the Fatih Mosque complex in Istanbul.

The foundation of a major mosque, or of a hermitage - often financed by state funds derived from poll-taxing the Christians - was also a method of populating a new town or city quarter. Nomadic building workers and their families would arrive, with an economic multiplier effect. Sometimes entire communities, tribes or clans were moved in, governed by a sheikh, and with tax exemptions as a sweetener for giving up the roaming life. Thus nomads became city dwellers. Housing, stables, workshops and covered bazaars would develop haphazard around the mosque area, like a permanent encampment, in a maze of winding streets and dead ends.

Another contrast: the Greeks were a maritime people, and founded their first settlements beside the sea. When the harbours of Ephesus and Miletus silted up, the cities died. Quite the opposite, the Turks from the steppes of Central Asia were a land-locked people who built their transport around horses and camel caravans, not ships.

Hence, when the Seljuk Turks settled in Anatolia from the 11th century, some of their first buildings were of safe havens for caravans - a network of caravanserais, staging points which were the medieval equivalent of a coaching inn, a good pull-up for camels. They were built by sultans or statesmen to protect caravans and their merchandise from plunderers and bandits.

Unlike the commercial inns set up in towns, they were endowed premises wherein travellers were treated as guests of the founders for three days. There were no charges for board, lodging, shoe repairs or the shoeing of horses. They were spaced along the roads leading from east to west, or north to south, at distances of 25 miles, or nine hours a day at a camel's walking pace.

The most common architectural layout of a caravanserai consisted of a quadrangle courtyard with a single heavily-gated entry large enough for the passage of laden camels. The courtyard was surrounded by galleries, comprising fair-sized rooms. Access to the upper floor was by one or more flights of stairs. Travellers who stayed at the inn were mostly merchants, who were sure of finding protected shelter for themselves and their animals; or, in cities, a place to install and sell their merchandise.

Heyday of their construction was the 13th century under the Seljuk Turks who imported the basic blueprint from Central Asia. Solidly built like fortresses, good examples have survived well into the 20th century: at Çeşme and Kuşadası, converted into elegant hotels; at Bodrum, used for tourist shops and boutiques; two good specimens near Alanya; and several along roads leading to Kayseri in Central Anatolia.

Modern

In the secular and republican state that is modern Turkey, the emphasis is no longer on the building of mosques and palaces. Instead, their place is taken by multistorey office blocks of steel and concrete, cloverleaf motorway junctions and massive dams that transform the economy of whole regions.

In domestic architecture, however, the impact of the West has been smaller. Apart from modern blocks of flats in the principal cities, much of domestic building continues to follow traditional themes. In the north, and in forest areas, they are still building half-timbered houses with balconies screened by lattice work. In the central plateau are flat-roofed dwellings of stone. Even mud-brick still has its devotees.

Meanwhile, the 19th and 20th centuries have seen the gradual conversion of the haphazard Ottoman town layout into something closer to the European style. The traditional wooden balconied houses, jostled close together, were always a fire hazard. Entire city sections would be swept clear, to be replaced by more durable streets of brick and stone housing. A historic example is Izmir, mostly destroyed by fire in 1922. The sections that survived around the bazaar still keep their original confusion of winding streets, alleys and dead ends. The rest of the city was laid out with broad, straight boulevards, looking as though planned overnight with ruler and compass.

The process continues today in Istanbul, where a massive exercise in urban renewal is sweeping away great swathes of the more tumbledown areas, to be replaced by modern highways, tidy parks and concrete buildings. The conservationists are out-numbered.

Chapter Fourteen
Who's Who in Anatolia

Mythical

Aphrodite - otherwise known as Venus - goddess of love and beauty; the Marilyn Monroe of classical times. Sometimes appears with a sea-horse or dolphin.

Apollo - or Phoebus, the sun god; the god of prophesy, music, song and the arts. Protector of flocks and herds.

Artemis - otherwise known as Diana - deity of the chase; goddess of the moon, protectress of the young.

Asklepios - the god of medicine and healing, usually depicted with a staff and snake.

Athena - or Minerva; goddess of wisdom; patroness of agriculture, industry and the arts.

Dionysos - Bacchus - god of vegetation, and the fruits of the trees, especially wine.

Hermes - Mercury - messenger of the gods - usually wore a travelling hat, golden sandals, and a purse. Hermes was patron of merchants, thieves, artists, orators and travellers.

Hygieia - the goddess of health; hygiene. Usually holding a serpent in her arms.

Medusa - one of the three Gorgon sisters - lost her head to Perseus, blood everywhere.

Nemesis - the fatal divinity, measuring out happiness and unhappiness.

Poseidon - Neptune - god of the sea, and responsible for earthquakes.

Tyche - or Fortuna - personifying fortune, usually depicted holding a rudder, or with a globe or cornucopia.

Zeus - Jupiter - greatest of the Olympian Gods; father of both gods and men.

Historical

Alexander the Great (356-323 BC) had an early schooling in warfare, in command of troops at age 16. In 334 AD, age 22, he led an army of 35,000 across the Hellespont (Dardanelles), defeated a Persian army and freed Greek cities from Persian rule during an 18-month campaign. He then marched on, to conquer the entire Persian empire.

Cleopatra, born 69 BC, queen of Egypt at age 17, became the ally and mistress of Mark Antony whom she met 41 BC at Tarsus. The affair continued at various coastal resorts of southern Asia Minor, and at Antioch and Ephesus. Died of asp-bite 30 BC.

Constantine the Great (288-337 AD) was the Roman Emperor who decided to move the seat of empire from Rome to the East. In 330 AD he chose Byzantium, renamed Constantinople, as his capital, setting off a feverish burst of construction activity. As a friend of the Christians, he had presided at the Council of Nicaea (325 AD, in present-day Iznik) - an event of the highest importance in church history for its proclamation of the Nicene Creed. By adopting Christianity as the official religion, and enacting a long series of legal reforms, Constantine laid the foundations of Church and state in the Byzantine Empire.

Fellows, Sir Charles (1799-1860) - British archaeologist who explored the Turkish coast areas from 1838 onwards, made numerous discoveries of classic sites - particularly Xanthus, Patara, Myra and Olympus in the Province of Lycia - and shipped large consignments of statuary and monuments back to the British Museum.

Herodotus (484-425 BC) -the "Father of History" was born at Halicarnassos (Bodrum) and travelled widely in his studies of the background to Greek history.

Homer - seven cities claim to be Homer's birthplace, but Old Smyrna (present-day Izmir) gets most of the votes, particularly in Turkey; though the neighbouring island of Chios also has a strong claim. Homer's epic poems narrated the seige of Troy in such detail that it finally led to discovery of the lost site.

Justinian (483-565 AD) - reigned from 527: 38 years of the Byzantine Empire at its brilliant peak. Justinian's law reforms involved a major re-writing of the legal code. A man of considerable ability, he was decisive in government. He spent great sums on building, particularly churches, of which St. Sophia was the supreme achievement.

Kemal Atatürk (1881-1938) - founder of the Turkish Republic. As a young army officer he was deeply involved in politics from his base at Salonica. During World War 1 he inspired the successful Turkish defence of the Dardanelles, at Gallipoli, against the landings of British, French and Anzac forces. After the Armistice, Mustafa Kemal opposed the policy of complete surrender. He then led a campaign of national resistance, particularly against the Greeks who invaded Turkey. Victory in 1922 led to proclamation of a Republic in 1923, with Mustafa Kemal as the first President.

Under benevolent dictatorship of one-party government, he then inspired a long series of reforms, aimed at transforming Turkey into a secular state based on modernization of industry, law and government. "We come from the East," he said, "We go towards the West." Women were emancipated, a modified Latin alphabet was adopted, and illiteracy was vigorously attacked. He assumed the name of Atatürk, which means "Father of the Turks". His guiding principles remain as the foundation stones of Turkey today, and the Army is still regarded as the ultimate protector of those principles.

Mark Antony, born in Rome 83 BC, related to Julius Caesar and gained great power. During his rule over the Eastern provinces of the Roman Empire, he irritated the senate by giving provinces of Asia Minor to his mistress, Cleopatra. Defeated at the battle of Actium, he committed suicide 30 BC.

King Mausolus - famous for his enormous tomb at Halicarnassos (present-day Bodrum) - one of the seven wonders of the ancient world, which gave us the word "mausoleum".

Mehmet the Conqueror took that title from his conquest of Constantinople in 1453 after a long seige which marked the final collapse of the Byzantines. He transformed Istanbul into the thriving capital of the Ottoman Empire during his reign which lasted thirty years.

Pompey - a highly successful and popular Roman general (108-48 BC), exterminated piracy along the southern coast of Anatolia in 67 BC.

Sinan - was born 1482, served in the Janissary Corps, and became chief architect of the Corps of Royal Architects. This organisation, attached to the sultan's court, was responsible for design and control of all public construction works. Through this centralized direction, projects which might take a hundred years to complete in Europe could easily be finished in one-tenth the time.

During a brilliant and prolific 50-year career, Sinan is credited with design of some 360 buildings - mosques, universities, primary schools, hospitals, public kitchens, bridges, baths, aqueducts, palaces, caravanserais and storehouses. He left his mark mainly on Istanbul, with some 290 buildings to his name. He laid the foundations of the classical period of Ottoman-Turkish architecture, which became the official style throughout the Empire.

Süleyman the Magnificent (1494-1566) - greatest of the Ottoman Sultans, ruled 46 years from 1520 over an ever-expanding Empire which reached its peak during his reign. Known in Turkey as Süleyman the Lawmaker, he also had great gifts as a poet and patron of the arts. Under his direction, many of Istanbul's finest monuments were built by Sinan (q.v.).

St. Nicolas was born 4th century AD in the coastal town of Patara, and became bishop of Myra; later known as a generous friend of children with a flair for anonymous gift-making, leading to his legendary role as Santa Claus.

St. Paul, born in Tarsus, made several long missionary journeys throughout Asia Minor. On his third great journey, he preached for over two years at Ephesus.

Schliemann, Heinrich (1822-1890) - German archaeologist, initially made a large fortune from trading activities; then devoted his life to a search for classic Greek sites. His discovery of Troy was one of his greatest triumphs.

Chapter Fifteen
Turkey - The Facts and Figures

Population	53 million - 50/50 urban and rural
Geography	Has land borders with six countries - Greece, Bulgaria, USSR, Iran, Iraq, Syria. Roughly rectangular in shape, 1000 miles E-W, 400 miles N-S. 97% in Asia, 3% in Europe; split by the Bosphorous, Sea of Marmara and the Dardanelles. Bounded north by Black Sea, west by the Aegean, south by Mediterranean.
Religion	99% Moslem, mainly Sunni. A few remaining Greek and Armenian Orthodox, and a 20,000 Sephardic Jewish community, in Istanbul.
Cities	Istanbul 6.5 million; Ankara 3m; Izmir 2m; Bursa 1.4m; Adana 1.3m.
Agriculture	Two-thirds of the workforce engaged in agriculture. Main export crops are cotton, tobacco, fruit, nuts. Sheep - for meat and wool - are Turkey's most important livestock.
Natural resources	Lignite, coal, chromium (a major export), iron, copper, bauxite, sulphur. Local oil resources are very limited, but direct pipelines operate from Iran and Iraq, and natural gas lines from Soviet Union.
Industry	Has developed rapidly in recent decades as Turkey moved from import substitution to export oriented manufacture. Textiles and leather goods are a considerable export, and trade in manufactured food products is expanding.
Administration	Turkey is divided into 67 provinces and municipalities with a centrally appointed governor and locally elected mayor.

Chapter Sixteen
Modern Turkey

The pattern set by the Decline and Fall of the Roman Empire was followed several centuries later by the stagnation of the Ottoman Empire. The impetus from the East slackened, and became sterile. Turkey relapsed into being 'the sick man of Europe'.

In the Capitulations that took place during the 19th century, Turkey was forced by the Great Powers to grant special concessions to foreign residents and traders. In the process, Turkey was opened up to Western - mainly French - cultural influence.

It wasn't till after World War 1, however, that the corruption and stagnation of the sultans was finally shaken off. Under the leadership of Kemal Atatürk, a sustained attempt was made to transform Turkey from an Asian backwater into a modern European industrial state. Anything Eastern was discouraged or abolished - wearing of the fez, Arabic script, Islamic government. Anything Western was adopted enthusiastically: cloth caps, Latin alphabet, a secular constitution. In his campaign against tradition, Atatürk's aim was "to turn the people's face towards the future, by shutting out the past."

Even so, by 1950 Turkey still seemed remote from Europe and from the 20th century. Most of the population worked on the land. Turkey balanced her trade with export of raw cotton, tobacco, hazel-nuts, dried fruits, and a few minerals like chrome. Industry was at infant level. Basic industries were State Economic Enterprises: cement, iron and steel, sugar, chemicals, beer and spirits. Prices were higher than in the outside world. But, in a closed economy protected by high tariffs, inefficient industries did not feel competition. Private-sector factories were encouraged to set up, in a policy of import substitution, and likewise protected by tariffs.

In some ways, the policy worked. Forty years ago, virtually all manufactured consumer goods were imported - even down to simple things like needles. It seemed an impossible dream that Turkey could ever manufacture the goods to supply her own domestic market. But that target was achieved, and import of manufactured consumer goods virtually ended. Cars, refrigerators, TV sets are all made in Turkey.

Typical was the textile industry. Instead of exporting raw cotton, Turkey began making her own cloth - which initially was sent to Italy and Germany for dyeing and printing, and then brought back. In the next phase, Turkey carried out the complete line of textile processes, using foreign technology under license agreements.

Meanwhile, just like everywhere else in the lesser-developed world, there was an accelerating drift from the land. Many village Turks moved to the towns, to seek factory jobs. Others found work abroad, particularly in

Germany, where two million Turks became Gastarbeiter - guest workers with their families.

Then came the oil crisis, which knocked Turkey hard. All farm exports went solely to meet the oil bill. Inflation began to climb, sharply. To restore the trade balance, Turkey pitched hard for export earnings. Good markets were found for manufactured goods in the newly-rich oil countries, which were handily located on Turkey's doorstep. Turkish textiles and white goods, for instance, began selling in large quantities throughout the Middle East. Civil engineers, who had learned their business in building highways and factories in Turkey, landed big construction contracts particularly in Libya and Saudi Arabia. They had the advantage of a hard-working Muslim labour force, accustomed to the climate.

Likewise, Turkey found a new role in transport business, as an overland bridge between Europe and the Middle East. Throughout the long war between Iran and Iraq, Turkey has maintained good relations with both these neighbours - supplying them with everything they need, except weapons. Iraq exports oil by pipeline across 400 miles of Eastern Turkey to the port of Iskenderun. Turkey is likewise connected by pipeline to Iran. Natural gas comes from the Soviet Union.

When the Middle East boom subsided, new export markets were developed from a country which had sharpened its trading skills. Today, Turkish textiles for instance are selling abroad so successfully that nervous European and American governments have sought to impose quotas. Even high-technology steel pipes are now exported to USA.

Meanwhile, sparked by rocketing inflation which severely cut real wages, social problems increased during the 70's. The political divide between left and right turned to violence. Martial law was proclaimed, against a background of up to 20 deaths a day from terrorism. During 1980, soldiers were posted at every street corner in central Istanbul, and outside all banks (which were a favourite target for terrorists who moon-lighted as holdup men). But professional politicians still seemed unable to solve the problems. Finally, in September 1980, for the third time in twenty years, the Army intervened to restore public order. Political and trade union activity was suspended, extremists arrested, fire-arms impounded. Firm government was re-established, and economic measures taken to bring back stability. Virtually overnight, Turkey became among the safest countries in Europe.

Since then, democratic government has resumed again, with the Motherland Party firmly in power. Government policies are closely akin to Thatcher's: privatization of state enterprises; liberalization of tariffs; 'let the market decide'. Runaway inflation has been reduced, but not so drastically as to cut the high growth rate.

Sore points remain. The long-standing feud with Greece finds no solution, particularly since Turkey's 1974 intervention in Cyprus, when the two countries came to the brink of war. Unemployment is a major problem. Guest-workers in Germany are no longer welcomed. Inflation stays high, even though most Turks have found ways of living with it.

But Turkey today is a much more

171

dynamic country than the sleepy land of 40 years ago. Big projects are under way, to exploit more of Turkey's rich natural resources. Hydro-electric potential is over 30,000 megawatts - equal to thirty very large nuclear reactors. Linked with that prospect for energy development, the irrigation potential of these hydro-electric projects is enormous. In South-East Anatolia, a current scheme will irrigate 4.5 million acres in a climate that can grow even avocados and bananas.

With further mechanization and irrigation, Turkey is destined to become the bread basket of the Middle East.

Turkey sees herself today as a bridge between East and West - between the world of Islam, and Europe. With membership of the Common Market as the target, Turkey looks to greater expansion of her industrial capacity. It all makes for a lively and hopeful future.

Chapter Seventeen
Travel Tips and Information

Addresses in Britain

Turkish Tourism and Information
Office, 170-173 Piccadilly, First Floor,
London W1V 9DD.
Tel: 01-734-8681
Telex: 8954905
Prestel: 344208

Turkish Consulate General,
Rutland Lodge, Rutland Gardens,
London, SW7
Tel: 589-0360/0949

Turkish Embassy,
43 Belgrave Square, London SW1
Tel: 235-5252

Turkish Airlines,
11 Hanover Street, London W1.
Tel: 01-499-9247

Addresses in USA

Turkish Consulate General,
1990 Post Oak Blvd., Suite 1300, New
York.
Tel: 622-5849/0324

Turkish Embassy,
1606 23rd St., NW, Washington, DC
20008
Tel: 387-3200

Turkish Tourism and Information
Office,
821 United Nations Plaza, New York,
NY 10017
Tel: 687-2194

Turkish Tourism and Information
Office,
2010 Massachusetts Avenue, N.W.,

Washington, DC 20036
Tel: 833-8411

Addresses in Turkey

American Consulate,
Meşrutiyet Cad. 104, Tepebaşı,
Istanbul
Tel: 151-3602

American Consulate,
Atatürk Cad. 92/3, Izmir
Tel: 132135

American Embassy,
Atatürk Bulvarı 110, Ankara
Tel: 126-5470

American Hospital,
Güzelbahçe Sokak, Nisantasi, Istanbul
Tel: 1314050

British Airways,
Cumhuriyet Caddesi 10,
Elmadağ, Istanbul
Tel: 1484235

British Airways,
Şehit Fethibey Caddesi 120, Izmir
Tel: 141788

British Airways,
Selancik Caddesi 17/1, Ankara
Tel: 1342418

British Consulate,
Meşrutiyet Cad. 34, Tepebaşı, Istanbul
Tel: 1447540

British Consulate,
Mahmut Esat Bozkurt Cad. 49, Izmir
Tel: 211795

British Embassy,
Şehit Ersan Cad. 46/A,

Çankaya, Ankara
Tel: 1274310

Tourism Police - Turizm Polisi,
Alemdar Karakolu, Sultanahmet,
Istanbul
Tel: 5274503

Turkish Maritime Lines,
Türkiye Denizcilik Kurumu T.A.O.,
Rıhtım Caddesi, Karaköy, Istanbul
Tel: 1440207 (Information); 1499222
(Reservations)

Turkish Maritime Lines,
Türkiye Denizcilik Kurumu T.A.O.,
Yeni Liman Alsancak, Izmir
Tel: 210077; 210094

Turkish Touring & Automobile
Association (TTOK),
Türkiye Turing ve Otomobil Kurumu,
Halaskârgazi Caddesi 364, Şişli,
Istanbul
Tel: 1314631 (6 lines)

Turkish Touring & Automobile
Association (TTOK),
Atatürk Bulvarı 370, Alsancak, Izmir
Tel: 217149

(TTOK offices are also located at the
Greek and Bulgarian frontier
crossings; and on the main entrance
road to Istanbul at Topkapı by the city
walls - Tel: 5216588; and at Ankara,
Iskenderun, Mersin and Trabzon).

Getting There

Apart from tour-operator charter
flights - mainly to Izmir, Dalaman,
Istanbul and possibly Antalya - direct
scheduled service flights are operated
by Turkish Airlines (THY) and British
Airways, from Heathrow daily to
Istanbul; less frequently by THY direct
to Izmir or Antalya. Many travel
agencies can arrange lower-cost air
tickets, with return dates that cannot
be changed. THY offers major

reductions for students. Check the
latest discounts and conditions.

Pan Am and virtually all major
continental airlines have connecting
services via western Europe to
Istanbul and Ankara.

By rail - daily from London Victoria to
Venice, and thence by the Istanbul
Express via Trieste, Belgrade and
Sofia; or go via Munich, Salzburg,
Zagreb, Belgrade, Sofia. Forget all
those romantic dreams about the
Orient Express. From Yugoslavia
onwards, it's a gruesome journey.

By coach to Istanbul is a long, long
haul; much better to split the journey
into stages.

By sea, Turkish Maritime Lines
operate a summertime car ferry
service from Ancona in Italy to
Izmir.

Ferry Links with Greece

During summer, regular ferries
connect Turkish ports with
neighbouring Greek islands. They are:
Çeşme-Chios in one hour
Kuşadası-Samos in two hours
Bodrum-Kos in one hour 30 minutes
Marmaris-Rhodes in 3 hours 30
minutes

Local travel agencies operate day
excursions; or you can buy single or
return tickets if you wish to stay
longer in Greece.

From the Greek side, there is a
potential problem. Supposing you
have arrived in Greece on a direct
charter flight - to the island of Rhodes,
for instance. You decide to pop across
to Turkey for a few days, using the
ferry to Marmaris. Afterwards, when
you arrive at Rhodes airport for the
homeward charter flight, your return
ticket may be declared invalid. A one-

day excursion to Turkey is OK. Stay longer, and you could be in deep trouble.

It may sound unfriendly, but it's part of the basic rules of charter flights that strictly they cannot be used as a springboard to other countries. The situation could change. But check this point carefully. To repeat: this hurdle arises only on charter flights to Greece. The rule is not enforced on the Turkish side. You can charter-fly to Turkey and have no problems however long you stay on a Greek side-trip.

Customs

On arrival at any of Turkey's international airports and most border points and ports of entry, visitors can buy well-known brands of liquor, cigarettes and perfume at Turkish duty-free shops before passing through Customs. Prices are generally lower than at Britain's duty-free outlets. At airports, it's a productive way of passing the time while waiting for luggage.

Customs procedures are normal for anywhere in Europe, but with more generous allowances: 400 cigarettes or 200 grammes of tobacco or 50 cigars; 1 kg of coffee and 500 g of instant coffee; five bottles of 0.7-litres of spirits. In addition, another three cartons of cigarettes can be brought in, provided they have just been purchased at the Turkish duty-free shop. Gifts up to about £170 in value, and not intended for trading purposes, may enter Turkey duty free. High-value personal items should be noted in one's passport, for control on exit.

Import of marijuana and other narcotics is strictly forbidden, and subject to heavy punishment.

On exit, the export of antiques is forbidden. Valuable goods and personal items can be taken out providing they have been registered on entry in the owner's passport; or providing they have been purchased with legally exchanged currency. There are no problems for taking out souvenirs.

Passports

No visas are required for stays up to three months. British visitors are welcome to enter Turkey regardless of whatever other foreign stamps are shown in their passport. The same rules apply to nationals from other EEC countries, USA, Canada, Australia and New Zealand.

No vaccination certificates are needed, except for cholera and yellow fever if arriving from an infected area.

Time Change

Except for short periods in spring and autumn, when changeovers of Daylight Saving Time are not synchronised, Turkey is two hours' ahead of UK time; seven hours' ahead of US Eastern Standard Time.

Electricity

220-volt AC everywhere in Turkey, using continental style 2-pin plugs. Pack an appropriate plug adaptor for any appliances you take.

Information

Turkish Tourism and Information Offices are the prime source for well-produced brochures on all the holiday regions and for the principal individual resorts. A hotel guide lists accommodation graded by the

Tourism Ministry. A very useful annual publication gives details of all UK tour operators who offer package holidays in Turkey, winter breaks, coach and overland tours, yachting and cruising in Turkish waters. Individual operators can then be contacted direct, or through local travel agents. Check the Tourism Office for up-dated information on dates of festivals and special events.

Most Turkish resorts and tourist cities have a local information office, which is always the best starting-point for travellers wanting any grade of accommodation, town plans, leaflets or regional information.

Maps

Adequate road and city maps are available in Turkey, but one cannot feel enthusiastic about any of them. Often they are out-dated on highway improvements. The free maps from the Turkish Information Office are good enough for most purposes.

Books

If you want any British books on Turkish subjects, buy them in UK. They are 60% more expensive in Turkey. Several excellent books focus in great detail on archaeological sites. Most of them owe something to four classics written by George Bean, a Greek scholar who lived for years in Turkey. Published by Ernest Benn, their titles are "Aegean Turkey", "Turkey's Southern Shore", "Turkey Beyond the Maeander" and "Lycia". For the political basis to the Turkish Republic, read "Atatürk: the Rebirth of a Nation" by Lord Kinross.

At all major sites and monuments, colourful tourist books are available, published in Turkey. Sometimes the

translation into English is painful, but prices are very reasonable. These site books with their plans are often worth buying for their colour reproductions, which make a good reminder of details which otherwise would be forgotten. For Istanbul, several excellent publications are produced by Çelik Gülersoy, the General Director of the Turkish Touring and Automobile Club.

Also available in Turkey are some good English-language translations of local books on special interests such as Cuisine or Carpets.

Public Holidays

Jan 1 - New Year's Day
Apr 23 - National Independence and Children's Day, with children's parades and festivities
May 19 - Atatürk's Commemmoration, and Youth and Sports Day
Aug 30 - Victory Day, celebrating rout of invading forces in 1922, with military parades
Oct 28 (half day) and Oct 29 - Republic Day, celebrating declaration of the Turkish Republic, with military parades in principal cities

Muslim Holidays

These vary according to the Hegira religious calendar, and move forward by 10 or 11 days each year. For 1988 the dates are:

May 17-19 - Feast of Ramazan, also known as Şeker (Sugar) Bayram, when all children get handouts of candy, and visits are made to friends and relatives.

July 24-27 - Kurban Bayram - Sacrifice Feast. This is the nearest Muslim equivalent to Christmas, with great slaughter of sheep (not turkeys), generosity to the poor, and postal services clogged with greeting cards.

On both these holidays, Turkey closes down on the previous afternoon, with banks and offices shut for the duration. The business visitor to Turkey will be wasting his time, while the tourist will find transport clogged, hotels packed and money exchange difficult. Just imagine it's like Christmas in midsummer!

Ramazan itself is a month of daytime fasting for the faithful - no food, drink or cigarette smoking between dawn and sunset - from April 18, 1988 until May 18, 1988. Observance is limited in the sophisticated cities and principal resorts. Even so, restaurants are half empty until the müezzin, TV and radio proclaim the official moment of sunset. Then, instantly, restaurants are suddenly crowded, bursting into cheerful life.

In more conservative country districts, observance of the fast can be total. However, nothing to worry about: tourists are excused, and can always get a daytime meal and refreshment.

Local Festivals and Tourist Calendar

Traditional festivals - rich in folklore - take place throughout the year, and are colourful events that are highly popular with the local population. Many are wrapped around local harvests - cherry festivals in June, wine harvest in late summer, even apple festivals. Tourists are always welcomed. Here is a selection, with approximate dates:

Late April, early May - Istanbul Tulip Festival, at Emirgân up the Bosphorus
May 1-8 - International Ephesus Festival

May 20-26 - Silifke Festival of Music and Folk Dancing
Last week of May - Bergama Festival, including folk dancing in the Asklepieion theatre
June 8-17 - Marmaris Tourism and Culture Festival
Last week of June - Bodrum Culture and Arts Festival
Mid June and all July - Istanbul Art & Culture Festival
June 30-July 6 - Traditional Grease Wrestling championships in Kırkpınar outside Edirne
July 7-12 - International Bursa Festival
Last week of July - Foça Festival
August 1-31 - Samsun International Folk Dancing Festival
August 10-18 - "Trojan Horse" Festival, Çanakkale
August 15 - Mass for the Virgin Mary, Ephesus
August 15-18 - Ayvalık Festival
August 20 - September 20 - Izmir International Trade Fair
September 15 - 18 - "Cappadocia" Nevşehir Festival - grape harvest and folklore
October 1-9 - Antalya Golden Orange Film and Arts Festival, with some performances in the Roman theatre at Aspendos
December 9-17 - Mevlâna anniversary week, Konya: Dance of the Whirling Dervishes

All these dates are liable to vary from year to year, so check first from the nearest Tourism Information Office.

Money

Turkish currency is the lira, which is counted in hundreds and thousands. At the beginning of 1988, the lira topped one thousand to the dollar. The pundits estimate that it will continue sliding at maybe 30% per year, depending on inflation. Theoretically one lira divides into a hundred kuruş, like splitting the atom.

Mostly it is paper currency, in denominations of 100, 500, 1000, 5000 and 10000 lire. Warning: be careful not to confuse the 10000 lire note for a 1000. It's very easy to mis-read the zeroes. Keep the 10000-lire notes separate, or swap them quickly for lower denominations.

Coins do exist - 5, 10, 50 and 100 liras - but always in short supply when needed, like tipping a lavatory attendant. Restaurant bills are normally rounded to the nearest hundred. Likewise, most shop prices end with at least two zeroes.

Currency Exchange

There is no limit on importing Turkish and foreign currency into Turkey.

Don't rely on plastic. Visa, American Express, Access and other international credit cards are established in Turkey, but are often accepted with reluctance. Even some of the prestigious hotels are very choosey. A credit card can come handy if you finally decide that you really must buy a carpet, but haven't brought enough funds. But it will narrow your scope for bargaining. There is a great preference for cash.

Take a starter kit of UK banknotes for immediate exchange into local currency at the arrival airport. Then continue with standard traveller cheques or Eurocheques. Banks are open 8.30 a.m. till noon; then 13.30 till 17.00; closed on Saturdays, Sundays and public holidays. Turkey is rich in banks - somewhere around 50 - and they all quote virtually identical daily exchange rates. Take passport when changing, and prepare yourself for ten or fifteen minutes to complete the deal. Much paperwork is involved,

going from clerk to clerk. Hotels give similar exchange rates, consuming less paper and time. But they often charge a commission.

All West European currencies and US dollars are freely convertible into Turkish lira. For many years a considerable black market bridged the gap between official and unofficial exchange rates. But current financial policy is to let the lira float freely, so there is little divergence between official and free market rates.

Hence the standard rule: have nothing to do with any street dealer who offers a much "better" rate than is posted outside banks and exchange bureaux. The currency black market has ended. A hustler can only make money through some other kind of swindle like switching of banknotes. However, shopkeepers sometimes offer a slightly better rate on foreign currency, just to close a sale. It's rather like a small discount to make you feel good, but it's probably covered by the initial mark-up.

Finish your lira supply before leaving Turkey, though it is now legal to take out a maximum of US $ 1000 equivalent of Turkish currency. A reasonable surplus can readily be changed back at the departure airport or border post. Keep some currency-exchange dockets, to support the conversion. If you are departing into Greece, Turkish lira will be scowled upon, and you'll lose on the exchange. Even your friendly UK bank will probably give you a lousy rate.

News

One can feel somewhat starved of English-language news in Turkey. Here are some lifelines to find what's going on outside - or even inside - Turkey.

The London newspapers normally reach Istanbul by late afternoon, and are available in the big hotels and on a few strategic news-stands from 6 pm. These papers are then distributed to Ankara, Izmir and the main beach resorts on the following day. Price is around £1.40 per copy for the heavyweights, even more for the Sundays. The tabloids cost about £1. Cheapest are the "Financial Times" and European Edition of "The Wall Street Journal" for 50p. In the expense-account hotels, businessmen get either of these two papers free, courtesy of the management.

Basic reports from the wire services are also published by the "Turkish Daily News", printed in Ankara, with coverage of the Turkish political and economic scene, international sport (and even an occasional paragraph on cricket), and heavily laden with smiling faces at Embassy cocktail parties. The combined Saturday-Sunday edition is printed Friday and updates you on Thursday's news.

It is worth travelling with a short-wave radio, to pick up the regular on-the-hour news bulletins of the BBC World Service. Reception varies according to time and location. You can usually find the BBC by fishing around these frequencies: 1323 kHz on Medium Wave, from their powerful transmitter on Cyprus; 9410 kHz on 31-metre band; 6180 kHz on the 49-metre band; or 3955 kHz on 75-meter band.

Despite the BBC's unnerving habit of signing off the bulletin with the statement ". . . that is the end-of-the-World News," you can normally look forward to a while longer before it happens.

Another news source is Turkish Radio's 3rd Programme, mainly devoted to music, but giving condensed three-minute bulletins - successively in Turkish, English, French and German - at 9.00, 12.00 noon, 17.00, 19.00 and 22.00 hours. The English bulletin comes on at three minutes past each of those hours. The bulletins focus much more on news of Turkish interest, with some international.

Finally, on Turkish TV Channel 2, the 21.30 hours' news bulletin is followed by news in English, finishing at 22.00.

Which WC Door?

To ask the way: "Tuvalet nerede?" - "Where is the toilet?"

Bay (men's room) or E = Erken
Bayan (ladies) or K = Kadın

In your daily tote-bag, *always* carry a sufficient supply of toilet paper for emergencies. Public toilets are often bare of such amenities. Practise the knees-bend squatting position, which you'll probably need some time unless your Turkish holiday is very sheltered.

A small tip for the custodian is expected at bus depots and suchlike havens for the desperate. The equivalent of 4p or 5p is adequate for the experience.

What to Pack

It depends what Turkish holiday you plan, where and when. In high summer: be prepared for extremely hot weather, into the 90's. Dress is casual in the main resorts. It's worth travelling extra light, to leave space for purchases of low-cost textiles - dresses, T-shirts, swimsuits, whatever. Take something a bit more formal if you plan to visit Istanbul's top restaurants, and don't want to look like a complete tourist.

For entry into mosques, "decent" clothing is required: a light head-scarf and a proper skirt or jeans for women; trousers, not shorts, for men. Pack good walking shoes or trainers for rough walking around classical sites. Rainwear is not needed for south coast resorts, but is occasionally required as you get closer to Istanbul. Along the Black Sea coast, a brolly is essential, whichever month you go.

On a winter-break to Istanbul, weather is little different from England. Pack accordingly. The further east you go, past Ankara, the colder it becomes, with deep snow. In contrast, along Turkey's Mediterranean coast, the winter weather is extremely mild, and a light overcoat is enough, plus umbrella.

Major brands of film are now available in Turkey, but pack a good supply to save spending holiday time in restocking. Likewise, take your full needs of sun-tan lotions, medicaments and toiletries. Why not binoculars, for the bird-life?

Tipping

Tipping is expected wherever you would tip in Britain, but on a more modest level. Ten percent is added to restaurant bills, but it's normal to leave something extra for good and friendly service. Standard porterage charges are posted at airports, around 12p per bag; but porters usually hope that foreigners will be somewhat more generous. For taxi drivers, just round up to the nearest hundred, whatever is on the meter. That's not really a tip: it's just to save the cabbie the bother of making a few pennies change.

Pollution

With so much of the Mediterranean now graded as a cess-pit, how does Turkey rate? In general, the Sea of Marmara is the worst affected, with effluent from Istanbul - city of seven million - slopping out around the shores. Fortunately for tourism, the beach resorts are far, far removed from that area. Near to Dalaman, in the south, the sea is polluted for a dozen miles with effluent from a paper mill. Otherwise, Turkey has a clean record. The sea water in virtually every resort, and in the neighbouring bays and coves, is of unbelievable clarity.

City pollution is something else. In some of Istanbul's busy main streets, exhaust fumes from an overworked bus fleet can be choking. Older industrial zones on the city outskirts cast their pall of factory smoke, though changeable winds disperse the nuisance before it reaches the tourist areas.

Ankara is infamous for winter smog, due mainly to central heating systems based on low-grade coal. In recent times the problem has abated somewhat, thanks to import of higher-quality fuel. Izmir has a smoke-belching industrial zone, but it is well removed from the city centre. Bursa, an important industrial city, is remarkably free from any sign of smoke-stacks. Petrochemicals are concentrated at Izmit (not to be confused with Izmir) - 90 kilometres east of Istanbul, at the tip of the Gulf of Izmit. Elsewhere, industrial plants and small factories are scattered: often an untidy ribbon development, but not obtrusive if you look the other way. Near to Muğla in the holiday south, a thermal power station is threatening forest areas with acid rain. But that problem has nowhere reached European proportions.

Mosquitoes

The mosquito count varies greatly from place to place. If mosquitoes normally have you for supper, "the machine" is recommended: a mosquito killer which plugs in to the mains, heating vapour-producing tablets. Sold in chemists' or luggage shops, the cost is £5 to £6 in Britain, or a similar price in Turkey.

Beach Equipment

You can buy a woven straw beach mat for £1 - a good investment for sun-worshippers.

If you plan to wade in the sea, perhaps exploring sunken cities, always wear plastic sandals. Sea urchins lurk amid the under-water remains. If you tread on a sea urchin and its painful spines, the local wisdom is to cover the affected area with olive oil so that the spines work their way out. The nearest restaurant will always help in this emergency. Also recommended is to use tooth-paste!

Telephones

In many parts of Turkey, the phone system is still in the Steam Age. Try to make a call across Istanbul, and you get all steamed up with frustration. Few businesses or hotels have anywhere near the number of lines they'd like. During peak business hours, everybody in Istanbul has the phone off the hook, busy dialling, so that all lines are permanently busy and nobody gets through. Everyone still persists, dialling and redialling until finally they get through to someone who has given up dialling through sore fingers. According to local legend, rainfall has a particularly dire effect on the system: when you get through, it's a wrong number.

Long distance calls are much easier outside the main business hours. International calls are expensive, and the cost usually doubles when routed through hotel switchboards. There are call boxes at Post Offices (PTT) and at many central tourist locations. Their operation requires a token (jeton) - small token for local calls, big jeton for long-distance. For something like a three-minute call to Britain, feed the hungry slots with at least £2 worth of tokens.

For inter-city numbers: dial 9; when you hear a continuous tone, dial the city code and the phone number.

For international calls: dial 9; wait for a new dial sound, and dial 9 again; then the country code; then the area code but dropping the initial zero; the phone number; and the best of luck. Country codes are: Britain 44; USA and Canada 1; Australia 61; New Zealand 64.

Shopping Hours

In the principal cities, shops open rather blearily around 9 o'clock. There are no Italian or Greek ideas of an afternoon siesta, nor any north-European ideas of closing at 5.30. Instead, shops do peak business in the early evening hours, with haphazard closing by about 7 or 8 p.m. Little corner shops - grocers, greengrocers and the nut and dried-fruit shops - often stay open even later. All shops work a full six-day week, firmly closed on Sunday.

In the main beach resorts, shops that sell the main items of heavy tourist expenditure - leather, textiles, carpets and variegated giftware - cheerfully stay open till midnight. Most sun-worshippers do not waste the daylight hours on shopping. Instead, they treat shop-gazing as part of the nightlife scene, a leisured activity before or after dinner.

Weddings

Saturdays and Sundays are favourite days for weddings. Flower-bedecked cars drive through the streets, horns honking, with a bride in European-style white wedding gown.

If you get the chance, peep inside the hotel or restaurant where the wedding reception is held. Normally there is wildly exciting Turkish dancing, though in modern dress, to the live music of a traditional band. It's a fascinating piece of local colour, whether it's an up-market reception at the Hilton Hotel, or a working-class knees-up in a modest restaurant along the Bosphorous.

Culture Shock

There are many misconceptions about Turkey. Be prepared for some degree of culture shock, depending how close you have previously been to the southern or Eastern Mediterranean. Among the more positive aspects of tourism is that visitors go home with a better impression of Turkey than they had before.

The greatest pleasure in Turkey comes from taking it slowly. Stop now and then and look around at new angles and sights to charm the eye. Sit in a tea garden for an hour, just contemplating nothing in particular. That is relaxation, Turkish style: a holiday in itself.

Chapter Eighteen
Basic Turkish for Travellers

So you can't speak Turkish? It doesn't matter! All you need for extra enjoyment is a basic holidaymaker's smattering. Straightforward words and very brief phrases are quite enough. Sentences and grammar are only a needless obstacle to the non-linguist.

The traveller who plunges in with pidgin-Turkish will get faster results and have more fun than the character who laboriously constructs a fine, grammatical sentence and then stumbles miserably over the pronunciation, and anyway cannot understand the reply.

First word to learn in any language is 'Please!' In Turkish, that's 'lütfen'. Then give a cheerful grin and look up the basic noun for whatever you want: an ice cream (dondurma), a beer (bira), a newspaper (gazete) – maybe toss in an appropriate adjective, like vanilla (vanilya), big (büyük) or English (İngiliz). How many? Hold up the appropriate number of fingers, or learn the simple numbers... bir, iki, üç. The word 'bir' meaning 'one' also serves as the indefinite article 'a' or 'an' in English. So 'bir sandviç' is 'a sandwich' or 'one sandwich'.

Tack them all together: your grin, your self-confidence, the few basic words, and Lütfen! Nine times out of ten, the message gets across. There's no need for years at night school.

But isn't the Turkish language 'difficult'? Yes! The grammar is fiendish. The Turkish language suffers from agglutination: bits and pieces are glued to the end of the basic stem-word, so that a final noun or verb becomes a nightmare. A simple noun has six cases, single and plural, making twelve different suffixes. Don't wreck your holiday by trying to learn the system. Just stay with your travellers' smattering.

The good news is firstly that Turkish is totally phonetic; secondly that a considerable number of words are 'international', quick and easy to learn.

Let's digress a moment into the history of the Turkish language. It originated, with its basic pronunciation and grammatical structure, in the steppes of Central Asia. The vocabulary of a thousand years ago served the simple needs of the nomadic tribes. Then, with conquest of Persia and the Arab countries, innumerable words of Persian and Arabic origin were adopted into Ottoman Turkish, using Arabic script.

The big reform came in 1928, when Kemal Atatürk decreed that Arabic writing should be replaced by a modified Latin alphabet, completely phonetic. The language was purged of most of the Persian and Arabic borrowings, greatly simplifying the structure. Into the vacuum, hundreds of international words have introduced themselves. The process continues. Virtually all words of 19th- and 20th-century origin have been adopted into Turkish, virtually unchanged from their English or French equivalent. Happily for the visitor, these are precisely the words of which he has most need: from otobüs to telefon and taksi.

Pronunciation

It's worth taking a few minutes to learn the exact pronunciation of the vowel sounds, and of the few consonants which are different from English.

The vowels total eight: the five vowels as in English, plus i without a dot (ı), and o and u with umlauts (ö and ü). These eight vowels split into two groups:

Front vowels – e, i, ö and ü – which are formed near the front of the mouth. Capital i is printed İ, with a dot on the top.

e as in egg	pronounced
i as in pin	with lips straight
ö as in French jeu	pronounced
ü as in German über	with rounded lips

Back vowels – a, ı, o and u – which are formed towards the back of the mouth. Capital ı is printed I.

a as u in hut, or a in bar	pronounced with lips straight
ı as in the second vowel of passion	lips straight
o as o in falsetto u as in bull	pronounced with rounded lips

As a general rule of 'vowel harmony', words of Turkish origin have vowels that are all front, or all back.

The consonants There is no Q, W or X. But there are three additional accented consonants – ç, ş and ğ. Pronounce all consonants as in English, with these exceptions:

c as j in jam
ç as ch in Charles
j as s in pleasure
ş as sh in shed
y as y in yacht

ğ is something special. When it immediately follows a back vowel – a, ı, o, u – it stretches that vowel but makes no sound itself. You meet it most often in Turkish surnames like Hasanoğlu (which means 'son of Hasan'). Make no attempt to pronounce the ğ, and that's near enough. When ğ follows a front vowel – e, i, ö, ü – then it is softly pronounced like y in yet. So long as you don't pronounce ğ like a regular hard g, don't let it worry you.

Stress

Even in a longish Turkish word, give each syllable equal stress. Place slightly heavier accent on the final syllable. This is sharply different from the English style of hitting one syllable hard, and swallowing the rest – like comfortably, which the English pronounce kum-f-t-bli; and which the French pronounce com-for-ta-ble-ment with totally even stress on each syllable. The nearer you get to the French style of full pronunciation of each syllable, the closer you'll get to pronunciation which will draw delighted compliments from the Turks. Try practising on all the instant and quick words in the vocabulary lists which follow.

Basic Turkish Vocabulary

Travel and Tourism

Instant astronot; bagaj; bikini; dans; diskotek; dok; ekspres; feribot; foto; fotoğraf; grup; helikopter; hippi; kamp; kamping; kaptan; kilometre; koridor; kupon; lokomotif; mesaj; minibüs; motel; motosiklet; otel; otobüs; ozon; paraşut; pasaport; piknik; pilot; platform; postrestant; prospektüs; resepsiyon; romantik; salon; seks; siklon; şoför; stop; stüdyo; taksi; taverna; telefon; teleks; telgraf; terminal; trafik; tramvay; transit; tren;

troleybüs; tünel; turing; turist; turistik; turizm; vize; zikzak.

Quick aquarium – akvaryum; asphalt motor-road – asfalt; baksheesh, tip – bahşiş; ball, dance – balo; bidet – bide; boat – bot; brochure – broşur; bus depot – otogar; cable car – teleferik; café, casino – gazino; caravan – kervan; caravansary – kervansaray; club – kulüp; comfort (in hotels etc) – konfor; compartment – kompartiment; conductor (on a train) – kondüktör; consul – konsolos; consulate – konsolosluk; couchette – kuşet; diesel

train – mototren; English – İngiliz; entrance hall – hol; hammock – hamak; hostess, waitress – hostes; hot spring – termal; houri, beautiful girl – huri; jeep – cip; manoeuvre – manevra; name – nam; phaeton, carriage – fayton; pose, exposure (camera) – poz; postal service – posta; postcard – kart; public park, parking place – park; rendezvous, appointment – randevu; spa cure – kür; station – istasyon; subway – metro; taxi meter – taksimetre; the police, policeman – polis; ticket pass – paso; toilet, WC – tuvalet; tour, promenade – tur.

French connection

bath	bagno (Ital)	banyo
beach	plage	plaj
bend of a road	virage	viraj
boarder	pensionnaire	pansiyoner
book of tickets	carnet	karne
boulevard	boulevard	bulvar
bus or railway platform	peron	peron
central heating	calorifère	kalorifer
cloakroom	vestiaire	vestiyer
club premises	locale	lokal
country fair	kermesse	kermes
courier	courier	kurye
covered vegetable market	halles	hal
exchange rate	cours	kur
full, occupied	complet	komple
gendarme, police soldier	gendarme	jandarma
glider	planeur	planör
highway	chaussée	şose
hitch-hiking	auto stop	otostop
ice skating; skidding	patinage	patinaj
lift; elevator	ascenseur	asansör
museum	musée	müze
pension, boarding-house	pension	pansiyon
police superintendent	commissaire	komiser
Post Office	P.T.T.	P.T.T.
postcard	carte postale	kartpostal
print (photo)	cliché	klişe
railway	chemin de fer	şimendifer
railway carriage	wagon	vagon
railway station	gare	gar
residence	logement	lojman
season	saison	sezon

ship's cabin	camara (It.)	kamara
shoulder of a road	banquette	banket
shower	douche	duş
skate, roller skate	patin	paten
steamer	vapeur	vapur
subscription; season	abonnement	abonman
suburb	banlieue	banliyö
suitcase	valise	valiz
telephone exchange	centrale	santral
ticket	billet	bilet
ticket window	guichet	gişe
token (coin)	jeton	jeton
wardrobe, cloakroom	garde-robe	gardırop
wash-basin	lavabo	lavabo

Easy Turkish bed – yatak; boat, caique – kayık; church – kilise; city – kent; covered bazaar – bedesten; direction – yön; ground floor – zemin; harbour – liman; highway – karayolu; holiday – tatil; hot spring – ılıca; left, left side – sol; right – sağ; narghile, hubble bubble – nargile; lane – sokak; road – yol; one-way street – tek yol; room (hotel etc) – oda; sand – kum; slow – yavaş; slowly, slowly – yavaş yavaş; summertime sea breeze – imbat; toilet paper – tuvalet kâğıdı; travel, journey – seyahat; Turkish bath – hamam.

The Basics
Yes – evet; no – hayır; thank you – teşekkür ederim (but 'mersi' as in French is much easier); OK – tamam; hello – merhaba; good morning – günaydın; good evening – iyi akşamlar; Welcome! – Hoş geldiniz!; how are you – nasılsınız; goodbye – allahaısmarladık (said by the person leaving) güle güle (said by the person who stays); excuse me – pardon; I'd like... – ...istiyorum; God willing, I hope so – inşallah; and – ve; Fire! – Yangın; Help! – Imdat!

Question Marks
Where is...? – ...nerede?; When? – Ne zaman?; How much? – Ne kadar?; How many? – Kaç tane?; Who? – Kim?

Handy Adjectives
big – büyük; little – küçük; easy – kolay; difficult – güç; early – erken; late – geç; good – iyi; bad – fena; worse – beter(!!); many, much, very – çok; few, a little – az; very few, or very little – çok az; new – yeni; old – eski; young – genç; old (person) – yaşlı; beautiful – güzel.

Pronouns
I – ben; you (familiar, singular) – sen; he, she, it – o; we – biz; you (plural, polite singular) – siz; they – onlar.

People
Father – baba; mother – ana; grandfather – büyükbaba; grandmother – büyükanne; gentleman – centilmen; man, human being – adam; lady, Miss or Mrs – hanın; man – erkek; woman – kadın; girl, maiden – kız; male cousin – kuzen; female cousin – kuzin; foreigner – yabancı.

Time
Year – yıl; month – ay; week – hafta; day – gün; night – gece; morning – sabah; evening – akşam; hour, time, watch or clock – saat; minute – dakika; now, at present – şimdi; tomorrow – yarın; future, next – gelecek.

Food and Drink

Instant aperatif; bar; bira; cin; dipfriz; glikoz; kalori; kantin; kafeterya; kokteyl; kotlet; limon; limonata; margarin; mayonez; menü; omlet; organik; restoran; sakarin; salata; sandviç; vanilya; viski; votka; yoğurt.

Obvious alcohol – alkol; alcoholic – alkolik; beef-steak – biftek; cake – kek; canapé – kanepe; caviar – havyar; champagne – şampanya; chocolate – çikolata; cocoa – kakao; coffee – kahve; cognac – konyak; coke – kok; cream – krema; cup, mug – kupa; grapefruit — greyfrut; liqueur – likör; liquid – likit; macaroni – makarna; marmalade – marmelat; pasteurized – pastörize; pepper – biber; portion (of food) – porsiyon; potato – patates; purée – püre; regime, diet – rejim; rum – rom; salámi – salam; samovar – semaver; sardine – sardalye; sauce – sos; sirloin steak – bonfile; soya bean – soya; spinach – ıspanak; spirits, alcohol – ispirto; sugar – şeker; table d'hôte – tabldot; tangerine – mandalina; tinned food – conserve; toasted sandwich – tost; tomato – domates.

French connection

bonbon, sweet	bonbon	bonbon
cake, pastry	pasta (Ital)	pasta
claret	Bordeaux	bordo
corkscrew	tire-bouchon	tirbuşon
delicatessen	charcuterie	şarküteri
entrecote	entrecôte	antrkot
garnish	garniture	garnitür
ham	jambon	jambon
hors d'oeuvre	hors d'oeuvre	ordövr
in Turkish style	à la turque	alaturka
pineapple	ananas	ananas
recipe	recette	reçete
sausage	saucisse	sosis
stewed fruit	compote	komposto
taste	tâter	tat
waiter	garçon	garson

Easy Turkish bon appétit! – afiyet olsun; cheers! – Şerefe!; bread – ekmek; breakfast – kahvaltı; carbonated water – gazoz; coffee-cup – fincan; cold – soğuk; hot – sıcak; egg – yumurta; food, meal – yemek; butter – tereyağı; fresh – taze; fruit – meyve; milk – süt; olive oil – zeytinyağı; olive – zeytin; salt – tuz; Turkish delight – lokum; vegetable – sebze; water – su; wine – şarap. (For a more detailed Guide to the Turkish Menu, see Chapter Nine.)

Numbers

1,000,000,000 milya;
1,000,000 milyon; 1,000 bin; 100 yüz.

10 on	1 bir
20 yirmi	2 iki
30 otuz	3 üç
40 kırk	4 dört
50 elli	5 beş
60 altmış	6 altı
70 yetmiş	7 yedi
80 seksen	8 sekiz
90 doksan	9 dokuz

There are no variations on the standard layout of complicated numbers. Thus: three thousand four hundred sixtytwo is üç bin dört yüz altmışiki. Numbers 1 to 5 are easy to pick up; 6 to 9 demand more concentration, particularly as number 8 sekiz is often confused with 6.

Half by itself is yarım. But 2½ is iki büçük (and a half).

Chapter Nineteen
A Guide to Price Levels

The message is that (a) Turkey is a cheaper country for the holidaymaker than anywhere in Europe; but (b) Turkey's rate of inflation is also higher than anywhere in Europe. So how does this affect the visitor?

Current financial policy is to let the Turkish lira float freely. In the Orwellian jargon of the financial world, 'float' means 'sink'. Daily movement of the exchange rate compensates for inflation. If Turkish lira prices have increased by 30% within a year, you can expect about 30% more liras for your pounds, D-marks or dollars. Thus, even over a period of several years, Turkish prices in foreign-currency terms have remained remarkably stable.

However, prices don't necessarily move smoothly in line with month-by-month inflation. Official bodies may change their prices only once a year. To give an idea on what to expect, here are some typical holiday-price figures.

Buses

Local city buses normally cost 10p or 12p any distance.

Medium-distance buses: Yalova to Bursa, 40 miles, 50p; Marmaris-Datça, 50 miles, 60p; Izmir-Çeşme, 52 miles, £1.35; Selçuk-Pamukkale, about 120 miles, £1.50 single, £2.60 return.

Long-distance: from Istanbul or Ankara to Datça (at the far tip of southwestern Turkey, past Marmaris) takes 16 hours and costs £5. A similar 6-hour journey from Izmir costs £2.50. Bursa-Izmir, 200 miles, £2.50. Izmir-Çanakkale, 210 miles, £2; Çanakkale-Istanbul, 210 miles, £2.30.

Dolmuş

Anywhere in Turkey, short dolmuş rides of two or three miles cost 10p; say 25p for 12 miles; Datça to Knidos, 24 miles, cost 60p.

Ferry Prices at Istanbul

Single journey across to Asia, 11p; Bosphorus round trip 75p; Princes Islands 65p round trip.

Turkish Maritime Lines, from Istanbul to Black Sea ports: 24-hour journey to Samsun, tariffs for various grades of cabin are £8, £7 and £6. Prices for two-day journey to Trabzon are £11, £8 and £7.50.

Taxis

In Istanbul, around 30p at flag-down; about 50p for a shortish journey of a mile or so; around £1 from Taksim to the Sultan Ahmet area; £4 from Istanbul airport to downtown hotels. Everything's on meter, and no tipping.

Travel-Agency Guided Coach Tours

Istanbul city sightseeings: half-day £10; whole-day £20 including lunch. Whole-

day tour to Bursa, £26 with lunch.
Coach tours from Çeşme: Ephesus or
Pergamum £17 including lunch; Izmir
£7.
Kusadasi to Pamukkale and
Aphrodisias, £18 including lunch; to
Priene, Miletus, Didyma and Altinkum,
£11 without food.

Museum Entrances

Aphrodisias classical site, 75p.
 Topkapi Palace £3, half-price at
weekends.

Boat Trips at Beach Resorts

Whole-day circuits (say, 10 a.m. till 6
p.m.) from £2 to £4, depending on the
boat and how badly the Kaptan needs
the business. A lunch aboard - freshly-
caught fish grilled, with rice, salad and
bread: £2.

Ferry Boat Bodrum-Datça

Price for the two-hour journey is £4.50
one way, or £7 return.

Ferry Boats to Greece

Bodrum to Kos, £8 one-way or £12
return.
Çeşme to Chios, £13 for one-day
excursion.
Kusadasi to Samos, with island coach
tour, £21 day trip but food not
included.

Holiday Villages

With their wealth of included facilities,
holiday villages restrict the entrance of
non-residents. Enquire at the gate, and
usually there's a charge for day
entrance. Typical prices: £2.60 for
entrance to the Marmaris Turban
beach - £3.70 for the disco. Club
Diana at Kusadasi, £3 for beads to
spend on food and drink.

Food and Drink Prices

At an average-grade restaurant in a
beach resort: soup 25p; ayran 11p;
beer 35p; substantial portion of
chicken for 60p; sis kebap 60p; a fish
sis for £1.50.

Another middle-range restaurant:
soup 45p; coban salad 45p; omlette
45p or 60p; biftek £1.50; beer 40p;
bottle wine £2; glass of tea 8p; ayran
16p and Turkish coffee 16p.

Reckon £2 to £3 for an average meal.

Self-Service Cafeterias

For lunch or evening meal, it's hard to
spend more than £1.50, however
much you pile the tray.

Buffet Prices

On Princes Islands, Istanbul, here are
some prices at a buffet overlooking a
small beach: Tea 11p, Coca-Cola 19p;
sandwich 22p, two-egg omlette 22p,
sausage and eggs 40p. That compares
with 7p for a glass of tea on the ferries;
or a sandwich for 15p from street
peddlers in Istanbul.

Fruit & Veg Prices

In Istanbul market, prices per kilo
were: citrus fruits 22p, apples 19p,
chestnuts 45p, bananas 60p, cherries
75p, peaches 30p.

At Üsküdar farmers' market,
enormous cauliflowers, probably
weighing four pounds each, sell for
around 15p each. Other prices, per
kilo: apples from 11p to 16p,
mandarins 9p, huge onions 7p;
oranges 8p; spinach 7p; grapefruit 7p;
bananas - which have to travel
hundreds of miles from southern
Turkey - 50p a kilo.

Hotel Prices

Upper-grade hotels normally quote their room rates in US dollars or German marks. In Istanbul, where there's a shortage of luxury-grade hotel rooms, tariffs are 'international' rather than Turkish. Travel agencies can negotiate special rates, so that a package deal of transport and hotel room normally comes much cheaper than dealing direct.

Tourist hotels, as opposed to expense-account hotels, are reasonable. Reckon £18 for a double room in a good motel. A typical small hotel at Bursa charges £5 for single without shower; £7 with shower; £8 for double without shower; £10 for double with shower. Breakfast is included.

Another Bursa hotel by the bus garage costs £5 for a single room with bath.

Turkish-type breakfast, 70p - a normal price at any unpretentious eating-place.

At pensions and ungraded hotels, reckon on a range from £2 to £6 per person, depending on facilities.

Night-Life

Entrance to Halikarnas disco, Bodrum, including first Turkish drink: £7.50. This could be the most expensive resort disco in Turkey. Halikarnas folk show with Turkish dinner: £11.

Turkish Night in Kusadasi £15 with no-limit drinks.

Istanbul by night - illuminations tour plus dinner and show at Kervansaray night club - £22.

TOP TRAVEL TITLES FROM SETTLE PRESS

The following books by Trevor Webster all feature in the highly popular series WHERE TO GO IN GREECE published in association with Thomson Holidays.

WHERE TO GO IN GREECE
by Trevor Webster
An up-to-date, easy-to-read, illustrated guide to the islands and mainland centres, containing a wide range of travellers' advice based on the author's recent personal impressions.

£5.99 paper 0907070264 ☐
3rd reprint 1986
(Revised Edition)

"If only I'd had Trevor Webster's Where To Go in Greece . . . ! Annette Brown *Daily Star*

"an exceptional title for both those seeking culture and the sun". *The Bookseller*

CORFU AND THE IONIAN ISLANDS
by Trevor Webster
Travellers are offered a modern Garden of Eden with Trevor Webster as their personal guide.

£9.99 hard 0907070329 ☐
£6.99 paper 0907070272 ☐
featuring 32 pages of full colour: publication November 1986

RHODES AND THE DODECANESE ISLANDS
by Trevor Webster
The appeal and atmosphere of Rhodes and the nearby islands, including tiny Kassos and Symi with its stunning harbour are brought to life by Trevor Webster

£9.99 hard 0907070353 ☐
£6.99 paper 0907070310 ☐
featuring 32 pages of full colour: publication April 1987

ATHENS, MAINLAND AND THE NORTH AEGEAN ISLANDS
by Trevor Webster

Athens within an hour or so of beach resorts is a perfect staging post for visiting the spectacular sites of Peloponnese, Delphi and Cape Sounion and for the ferries to the islands. Trevor Webster takes the reader on a magic tour of the mainland and over twenty islands.

£9.99 hard 0907070337 ☐
£6.99 paper 090707280 ☐
Featuring 32 pages of colour
Publication November 1986
Publication November 1986

CRETE AND THE CYCLADES ISLANDS
by Trevor Webster
Crete and the Cyclades are islands of great colour, character and contrast. The atmosphere of their stupendous mountains, beaches, harbours, folklore and history is relayed by Trevor Webster.

£9.99 hard 0907070388 ☐
£6.99 paper 090707396 ☐
Publication November 1987

WHERE TO GO IN SPAIN
A guide to the Iberian peninsula
by H. Dennis-Jones

£9.99 hard 0907070426 ☐
£5.99 paper 0907070434 ☐

Adding to the wide canvas of the Settle Press travel series, it contains rating guides for all the Spanish coastal regions and colourful descriptions of the interior.

A carpet seller waits patiently for customers.

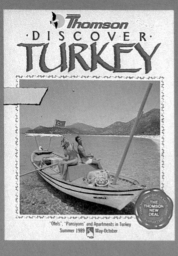

- ○ Discover the best of Turkey with the new Thomson "Discover Turkey" brochure.

- ○ A range of quality small hotels, pensions and apartments along the Aegean and Mediterranean coasts.

- ○ Including a unique gulet cruise between Bodrum and Fethiye.